Building Survivable Systems

ISBN 0-9770191-3-6

Library of Congress Control Number: 2006933619

Disclaimer: Since no system is immune from catastrophic failure, this book does not guarantee "unconditional" survivability. It focuses on informing the readers (system developers, researchers, and decision makers, etc.) on the how to explore possible sources of failures and develop countermeasures to ensure essential functioning of their systems to achieve mission objectives.

Printed in the United States of America.

SEGMA BOOKS
An imprint of ILORI Press Books LLC
13217 New Hampshire Avenue, #10332
Silver Spring, MD 20904

Cover design/layout © ILORI Press Books
Cover photo © bowie15/123rf

Building Survivable Systems

Principles and Applications for Complex Product, Process, and Organizational Change Models

Jidé B. Odubiyi, Ph.D.

SEGMA BOOKS
Silver Spring, Maryland

Building Survivable Systems

Acknowledgements

Part II of this book consists of ideas from my doctoral thesis and I would like to thank my dissertation committee—Dr. Lee Lee (chair), Dr. Duane Tway, and Dr. Clarence J. Schumaker—for their insightful and constructive comments, which significantly improved the quality of the research; and to Dr. Ruth Maurer for her informative tutorial on sample size estimation. Thanks to Dr. Marcus Thint of British Telecom (BTexacT) and Dr. Mark Klein of MIT's Center for Coordination Science for their suggestions on agent cloning strategies, and to Mr. George Meekins of British Telecom for reviewing the proposal for this research and providing critical comments on network polling issues. My sincere gratitude also goes to Mr. Peter Etten of BT North America, who compiled the network performance data used in this research. Also, I wish to express my appreciation to Mike Kelly and his team at the TeleManagement Forum (World) who granted me the permission to use the diagrams that describe the standard business process framework (i.e., the enhanced Telecom Operations Map) for the telecommunication industry. Finally, I am very thankful to my wife Marion, and my daughter Folasadé, for their selfless support, honest input, and review of the final manuscript.

Building Survivable Systems

CONTENTS

PREFACE 1

CHAPTER 1: INTRODUCTION 7

Definitions of Systems, System Concepts, and System Types 8

System Concepts 9

Types of Systems 11

Imperatives for System Survival 13

Three System Theories and their Proponents 14

General Systems Theory, or Ecology Theory—von Bertalanffy 14

The Contents 16
    Part I 16
    Part II 16
    Summary 17

CHAPTER 2: REQUIREMENTS 19

Elements of a Survivable System 20

Establishing a Metric for a Survivable System 21
    Fault Tree Modeling and Risk Management 22

Analysis of an Organizational System from the Perspective of Bertalanffy's
Theory of Living Systems 24

Analysis of a Natural System (Ant Colony) from the Perspective of Bertalanffy's
Theory 26

Origins of Conflicts in Social Insects 27

The Theory of Self-Organization 28

The Theory of Dissipative Structures—Prigogine 29

Nonlinear Dynamical Systems, or Theory of Complex Systems 32
  Mathematics of Patterns 33
  Two Reinforcing Perspectives on the Properties of Complex Systems 34
  Computers and Solutions of Complex Dynamical Systems 36
  Phase Space and Strange Attractors 37
  Using Attractors to Explain Behaviors of Complex Systems 38

Conclusion 40

CHAPTER 3: PRINCIPLES AND METHODS 43

Finite Element Modeling and Analysis for Product Modeling 43
  Six Steps of the Finite Element Modeling Procedure 45
  Limitations of the Finite Element Method 48
  Concluding remarks on the Finite Element Method and Analysis 49

Modeling and Simulation Science for Process Modeling 49
  Systems, Models, and Simulation Concepts 50
  Steps in a System Modeling and Simulation Study 52
  Limitations of Simulation Models 54

Complex and Nonlinear Systems Theory for Organizational Change Modeling .. 54
  Different perspectives for and against complexity theory for business process
  modeling 56
  Motivations for understanding complexity or chaos theory 56
  A Case against Using Complexity Theory 59
  Approaches for Managing Complex Systems 59
  Applications of Complexity Theory to Business Processes 62

Conclusion 64

**CHAPTER 4: PRODUCT MODELING AND APPLICATIONS
USING FINITE ELEMENT METHOD 65**

Front-Impact and Crashworthiness Modeling of a Car 65

Related Work of Others on Application of FEM 67

Conclusion 69

CHAPTER 5: PROCESS MODELING AND APPLICATIONS USING SIMULATION SCIENCE 71

Graphite Composite Manufacturing Process Simulation 73

The US Postal Service Mail Processing Automation and Delivery Process
Simulation 74

Earth-Mars Telecommunications and Information Management System Process
Modeling 75

Related Research Using Modeling and Simulation Science 76

Conclusion 77

CHAPTER 6: BUSINESS PROCESS MODELING AND APPLICATIONS BASED ON COMPLEX SYSTEMS THEORY. 79

BPM as a Management Discipline 81

BPM-Enabling Technologies 83
Executing the Process 84
BPM and Service-Oriented Architecture (SOA) for the Enterprise 85
Globus Service-Oriented Infrastructure and Open Source Grid Software 86

The Value of Business Process Modeling 87

Selected Criteria for Evaluating BPM Tools 90

Applications of BPM Technology 92

The Role of Leadership in Business Process Modeling 93
Services Science, Management and Engineering (SSME): An Emerging Discipline
.... 95

Conclusions and Some Predictions 96

CHAPTER 7: OVERVIEW OF SECURITY CONCEPTS FOR THE ENTERPRISE RESOURCES AND SERVICES 99

What is Security? 101

Information Security 101

Information Security Technologies and Strategies 102
  Security Perimeter 103
  Firewalls 103
  Demilitarized Zone (DMZ) 105
  Proxy Servers 105
  Intrusion Detection and Prevention Systems IDS/IPS 105
  Routers 106
  Virtual Private Network (VPN) devices 106
  Access Controls 110
  Honeypots/Honeynets 111

Vulnerabilities of Network and Information Assets and Defensive Measures 111

Security Policy Development Process 112
  Security Tools Applicable to IP Networks 113
  NIST Security Self-Assessment Guide for Information Technology System 114

Ten Principles of Computer and Network Security 115

Conclusion 116

PART II: A RESEARCH ON ENGINEERING EXCEPTION HANDLING STRATEGIES FOR SURVIVABILITY OF A DISTRIBUTED BUSINESS PROCESS 119

PREFACE TO PART II 121

CHAPTER 8: INTRODUCTION TO THE STUDY OF EXCEPTION HANDLING STRATEGIES USING AGENT TECHNOLOGY ... 123

Introduction to the Research 124

Definition of Terms on Telecommunications and Agent Technology 127

Problem Statement 134

Background 136

Communication Network Topology and PVC 144
Managing Complexity in Open Business Systems 147
Categories of Exceptions 148
Coordination, Exceptions, and Role Commitment Violation Analysis 149
Handling Exceptions in Multiagent Systems: Collaborative Survivalist vs. Citizen
Agents 149
Multiagent Architecture and the Citizen Approach 153

Purpose of Research 154

Theoretical Framework 155
Telecommunications Network Routing 155
Network Management and Design Functions 156
Collaboration among Agents 157

Quasi-Experimental Conditions and Assumptions 158

Scope and Delimitations 158

Hypotheses 159

Significance of this Research 160

Conclusion 161

CHAPTER 9: LITERATURE REVIEW ON EXCEPTION HANDLING STRATEGIES AND MULTI-AGENT SYSTEMS... 163

Literature Search Strategy 164

Rationale for Using Software Agent Technologies in Telecommunication Networks
.... 165

Agent-Oriented versus Object-Oriented Thinking 165

Distributed Computation and Cooperation among Processing Entities.............. 166

Agents' Distribution 167

Agent Communication 168

Agents' Persistence or Temporal Continuity.. 168

Agents in Open Systems... 169

Commitment Protocols in Multiagent Systems 169

Exception-Handling Strategies... 171

Research in Agent-Oriented Approaches to Exception Handling 173

Related Research on Applying MAS to Real-World Business Processes 174

Conclusion... 178

CHAPTER 10: RESEARCH METHODS FOR EXCEPTION HANDLING STRATEGIES TO ENSURE SYSTEM SURVIVABILITY 181

Research Process 184
    Internal Validity of the Multiagent Agent System................................ 186
    Architecture of a Victor Agent 189

Quasi-Experimental Design.. 194
    Cluster Sampling 194
    Sample Size Estimation... 194
    Quasi-Experimental Procedure.. 196
    Communications Network System-Related Variables 196
    Multiagent Testbed and the Survivalist Agent Architecture................. 199
    Customer Link Failure Identification and Restoration Process 201
    The Citizen Agent Approach and Exception-Handling Strategy............ 203

Measurement of Quasi-Experimental Variables 206

Conclusion... 209

CHAPTER 11: RESEARCH RESULTS AND SUMMARY OF FINDINGS 211

Summary and Integration of Results 211

Explanation for Findings 212

Integration of Findings with Literature 220
    Convergence of Findings 220
    Divergent Findings 220

Contributions of Findings to the Literature 221

CHAPTER 12: CONCLUSIONS 223

Limitations of Findings 224

Suggestions for Future Research 225

Research Conclusions and Recommendations 225
    Social Significance of this Study 226

Concluding Remarks on Building Survivable Systems 228

REFERENCES 229

ACRONYMS 251

APPENDIX A: COMMUNICATIVE ACTS AND AGENT COMMUNICATION LANGUAGE 253

The Grammar for ACL 256

Reinforcement Learning Paradigm 258
    Strategies for Reinforcement Learning Problems 259
    Rationale for Selecting Reinforcement Learning Paradigm 260

APPENDIX B: SAMPLE DATA 265

ATM_PVC_STATS_HR – CUSTOMER CONNECTION 266

ATM_TRUNK_STATS_HRLY 267

APPENDIX C: SCRIPTS FOR STARTING AND RUNNING THE EXPERIMENTS 273

APPENDIX D. ANNOTATED BIBLIOGRAPHY 293

Annotated Bibliography on Complexity Theory and its Application to Complex System Development 293

INDEX 321

ABOUT THE AUTHOR 353

TABLES

Table 8-1: Dimensions of organizational operational context 124

Table 10-1: Global communications network topology data 193

Table 11-1: Statistics on restoration times for failed customer connections
....213

Table 11-2: Sum of link restoration times 214

Table 11-3: Statistics on link restoration times 214

Table 11-4: Descriptive statistics on system recovery times 217

Table 11-5: Statistics on system recovery times 218

Building Survivable Systems

FIGURES

Figure 1-1: A Taxonomy of systems 9

Figure 2-1: Survivability requirements for a typical system.................. 19

Figure 2-2. A typical organization viewed as a living system 24

Figure 2-3: A taxonomy of performance for system development 25

Figure 3-1: A Finite Element Model 44

Figure 7-1: Information security architecture: Defense in Depth 100

Figure 7-2: A typical firewall architecture ....……..104

Figure 7-3: A Virtual Private Network from firewall to firewall .... .107

Figure 7-4: An IPSec tunnel with encryption and authentication 109

Figure 8-1: Relationships between a Link, a Path, and a Route 127

Figure 8-2: Components of an agent communication language 131

Figure 8-3: A global telecommunication network of Concert 138

Figure 8-4: Relationship among processes, functions, and data 139

Figure 8-5: Telecom operations map, business process framework......... 141

Figure 8-6: Network maintenance and restoration process 143

Figure 8-7: A conceptual model of a global communication network
          topology 144

Figure 8-8: Relationships among PVCs, trunks, and switches in a
         network 145

Figure 8-9: A conceptual model of a global communication network
         topology 146

Figure 8-10: Architecture for an MAS with exception-handling
         strategy.. ...151

Figure 8-11: Multiagent System (MAS) architecture using citizen
         approach   152

Figure 10-1: Victor System Implementation Architecture 187

Figure 10-2: Architectural Components of an agent in Victor   189

Figure 10-3: Multiagent system architecture using the survivalist agent
         strategy 201

Figure 10-4: Multiagent system architecture using the citizen agent
         strategy.. 204

Figure 10-5: Interactions among agents to restore downed customer
         connections 206

Figure 11-1: Sequence plots of restoration times 216

Figure 11-2: Sequence plots of system recovery times from agent
         death 219

PREFACE

A survivable system is one that will deliver essential services on time, even when significant elements of the system become disabled. Quality attributes of a survivable system include fault tolerance, performance, availability, reliability, security, and affordability. For example, an automobile with sound structural integrity is drivable after a crash. A business organization with an established business continuity policy will continue to provide essential services even after the integrity of its information systems has been compromised due to a denial of service attack. A survivable financial system must be able to provide secure, confidential, reliable, and timely services in the event of any failures in its communication components. One of the most effective means for building a survivable system is to employ tools that can aid in investigating a variety of design and operational scenarios that can aid in selecting the most viable option.

As stated above, *fault tolerance* is a quality attribute of a survivable system. A fault tolerant system does not always ensure survivability. Fault tolerance addresses the statistical probability of a fault or a combination of failed components in a system. A fault tolerant system establishes a threshold for the statistical probability of failure of system components, with the expectation that the probability of component failure, while possible, is very slim. A survivable system, on the other hand, would provide a contingency to ensure that the system continues to provide essential services, even when the components' performance falls below established threshold values. When a survivable system incorporates *redundant* components, it ensures that these components do not exhibit identical failure mode. That way, the redundant components can operate within the same environment and ensure the survival of one component, in the event of the failure of the other, thereby guaranteeing system survival.

A common failure of some organizations to meet their mission objectives could be due to the inability of their leaders to innovate critical change drivers successfully. Sawhney, Wolcott, and Arroniz (2006) have proposed 12 different ways for companies to innovate. The 12 dimensions are decomposable into three categories of *change drivers*: product, process, and business innovation. Product offerings, deployment platforms, network-centric offerings, and product branding fall under *product innovation*. The process of creating solutions for customer's problems; processes to improve efficiency and effectiveness; and value capture through redefinition of new revenue stream fall under *process innovation*. The last five of the 12 dimensions (i.e., identifying underserved customer segments, redesigning customer interactions, changing the form, function, and scope of activity of the organization; redesigning the supply chain, and creating new distribution channels) fall under the *business innovation* category.

The Boston Consulting Group and BusinessWeek conducted a joint global survey of 1,070 senior executives in 63 countries (46% from North America, 30% from Europe, and 16% from Asia) to identify the world's most innovative companies. They concluded that *product*, *process*, and *business model innovation* are the organizational change drivers of the top 25 most successful companies (Jena McGregor, 2006). To ensure organizational growth and survival, leaders of organizations need to understand and support the implementation of one or all of these three categories of organizational change drivers. Unless an organization innovates, it cannot adapt to the changes in its environment and consequently, it cannot survive.

This book describes approaches for using these change drivers to achieve an organization's mission objectives. It presents the principles and applications of finite element modeling for *product* innovation; modeling and simulation science for *process* innovation; and complex and nonlinear systems theory and organizational learning theory for *business model* innovation. Using my twenty-five plus years of industrial and academic experience, I present the principles and applications for building survivable systems.

Employing real life examples, this book will instruct the reader on the theory and strategies for building survivable systems for engineering structures (automobile and airplanes); telecommunication networks, computer and network security; and software engineering. The book also presents strategies for developing measures of system survivability. This book has two parts. Part I (Chapters 1 through 7) covers the basic thesis of the book. It includes system definitions, system theories, categories, survivability requirements, principles, applications, and overview of computer and network security concepts. Part II (Chapters 8 through 12) presents the methodology and findings, from an in depth research on intelligent agent-based exception-handling strategies, to support business model innovation and survivability of a global telecommunication network, plus the conclusion of the book. The term business (as used in this book) covers all forms of social and technical organizations. While some ideas, models, and theories presented in this book are complex, I have tried to define these concepts to aid the general reader. Where necessary, I have moved some detailed information about certain concepts to the Appendix so as not to detract the reader from the main points. The reader may also wish to skip detailed discussion of some of these concepts without missing key elements.

Building Survivable Systems

4

PART I:
GUIDELINES FOR
BUILDING
SURVIVABLE
SYSTEMS

CHAPTER 1:
INTRODUCTION

> *"If you don't know where you are going,*
> *you will probably end up somewhere else."*
> Dr. Laurence J. Peter, American Educator and Writer, 1919-1990.

This book presents the principles and applications for building survivable systems. Survivable systems are systems that will achieve their mission objectives on time, even when significant elements of the systems become disabled due to accidents or other disruptions. This book is based on the author's intellectual, academic and professional experiences of over twenty-five years working for several large organizations, research institutes, and academia (as a Product Design Engineer, Principal Engineer, Research and Development Manager, and University Professor). This book describes the principles and real life applications to identify some common criteria and strategies for building complex product, process, and organizational change models for survival. The real life examples include automobile and aircraft engineering design, aircraft manufacturing, global telecommunication networks, air traffic control operations, satellite ground and space control systems, US Postal Service mail processing and delivery operations, knowledge fusion from distributed sensor networks, and computer and network security of business enterprises.

A common failure of many organizations to meet their mission objectives could be due to the inability of their leaders to innovate critical change drivers successfully. To ensure organizational growth and survival, leaders of organizations need to understand and support the

7

implementation of one or all of these organizational change drivers. It is also imperative that the builders of these drivers understand the basic principles and have access to tools that would aid them in achieving their mission objectives. Since most real life systems are complex and nonlinear, this book describes approaches for understanding, predicting and managing complex systems for survival (Ormerod, 2006). As eloquently stated by Dr. Laurence Peter in the quote on the previous page, it is difficult for people to arrive at a specific destination if they do not know where they are going. This statement is true for system developers. It is therefore imperative that they base their product, process, or business innovation process on sound scientific principles and employ tools that help them to select a viable scenario from a list of candidate scenarios. This goal is achievable with modeling techniques and tools.

This book describes approaches for using organizational change drivers to achieve an organization's mission objectives. It presents the principles and applications of finite element modeling for *product* (re-engineering) innovation, discrete event modeling and simulation for *process* innovation, and complex and nonlinear systems theory and organizational learning theory for *business model* innovation. The book begins by defining what we mean by systems, categories of systems, system survivability, and requirements for survivability.

Definitions of Systems, System Concepts, and System Types

It is very difficult to comprehend what constitutes a system without identifying the context in which the system exists and some underlying assumptions of systems theory. There are a number of reasonable definitions. A system is a collection of interrelated objects or variables (Bertalanffy, 1956, p. 3). Another definition of a system is that of a set of related objects where the attributes of the objects are also related (Hall & Fagen, 1956, p. 18). The following paragraphs describe system concepts and types.

System Concepts

The concept of a system consists of the identification of its operational characteristics, some boundary conditions, the mechanisms used by the system elements to control its behavior, its openness or closeness, and preconditions for its survival.

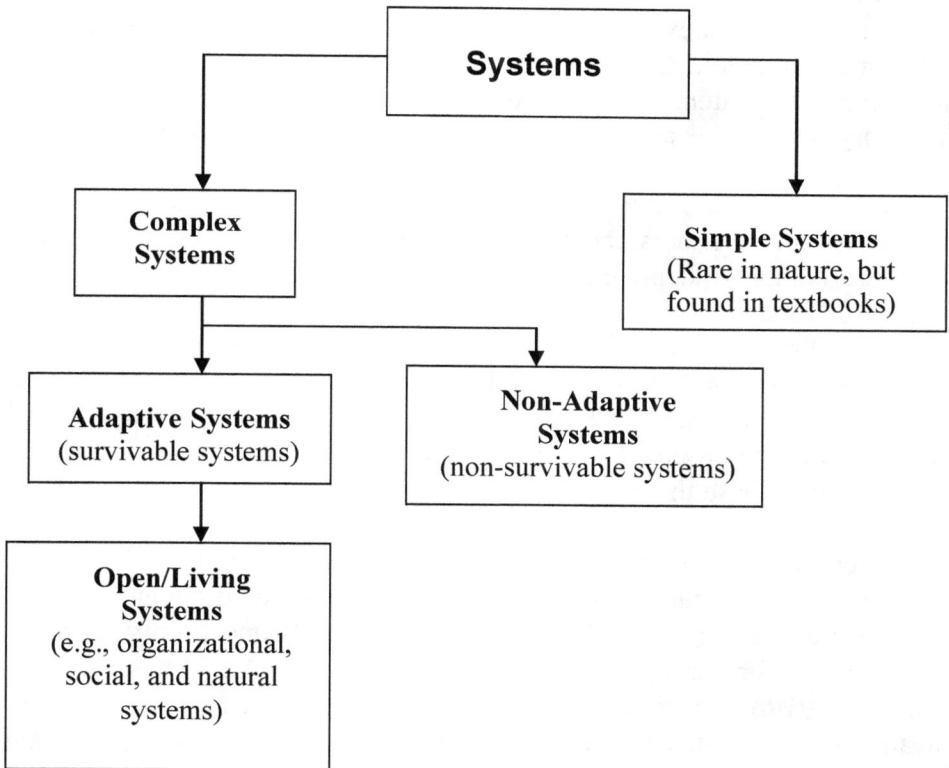

Figure 1-1 Taxonomy of Systems (*adapted from Casti, Kauffmann, et al, Colloquium on Complexity Science*)

The diagram illustrated in Figure 1-1 depicts the taxonomy of systems. Complex systems are easy to identify because they exhibit behaviors that are hard to understand, as there are intrinsic uncertainties in their parameters while simple systems possess intrinsic predictive properties. The diagram shows that complex systems are either adaptive or non-adaptive. Non-adaptive systems do not meet survival imperatives and consequently, they die. Complex, adaptive systems use feedback or self-organizing mechanisms as found in biological, social and behavioral disciplines, and they survive. The stock market, telecommunication networks, ant colonies, road traffic networks, business organizations, and the immune systems have feedback mechanisms and fall into the category of complex adaptive systems which are called living systems.

Since living systems are complex adaptive systems, in order to manage them, one must understand how the three theories are interconnected. Because complex adaptive systems are living systems, von Bertalanffy's theory of living systems (early 19th century) applies. Since they are also adaptive, Prigogine's (1960s) theory of dissipative structures applies. To deal with uncertainties and instabilities in complex systems, one must use the new mathematics of complexity from nonlinear dynamical systems theory or chaos theory. Chapter 2 provides a more detailed discussion of these theories.

A system's ability to survive is attributable to its measure of *entropy*. *Entropy* is a system's inherent characteristics to dissipate energy, becomes less effective, and die or a measure of its uncertainty. Entropy killed these former corporate giants including PanAm, SwissAir, and Enron. *Negative entropy* is a system's ability to self-regulate to avoid death. Negative entropy ensured the survival of Coca-Cola Company and Bayer. Coca-Cola Company management's immediate response to customer complaints after introducing Coke Classic demonstrates the management's ability to self regulate. Johnson and Johnson's immediate response to Extra Strength Tylenol tampering in 1982, which led to the death of seven people in Chicago area, demonstrates the benefits of negative entropy. Tylenol market share fell from 35% to 8% but rebounded in less than a year due to immediate nationwide withdrawal of the drug from all drugstores and super markets, distributed warnings to hospitals, and new tamper proof packaging.

Types of Systems

Before discussing different perspectives on the theory of systems, the following paragraphs define different system theories.

Frameworks are systems composed of interconnected static elements, such as the skeleton of an animal or the frame of a building.

Clockworks are systems with simple predictable dynamic behaviors, such as the cosmos.

Cybernetic systems are systems with self-regulating capabilities through feedback mechanisms. Two examples of cybernetic systems are the thermostat and the autopilot on an airplane. A thermostat working together with a control system can provide a feedback to the mechanism to control the temperature of the environment. An autopilot can sense the speed of the airplane and send guidance instructions to the speed or directional control units of the airplane.

Autonomic systems are systems with self-configuring, self-healing, self-optimizing, and self-protecting capabilities (Craig Fellenstein, 2005). In an organizational environment, a system that dynamically integrates and manages its business rules and policies to enable the organization to meet its business objectives is an example of an autonomic system. Such a system is built to perform like the human central nervous system.

Open systems are systems such as organizations that are open to their environments and rely on exchange of information not only between their internal structures (e.g., personnel and resources) but also with their environment.

Symbol-processing systems are systems with the ability to process logical constructs, language, and mathematics. Humans operate at this level.

Social systems are organizations (Scott, 1998, p. 17) with fully connected internal structures (i.e., a social structure; goals; technology; and participants, or actors), sharing social common laws, and operating in an open environment where economic, political, and cultural forces thrive.

Otopoietic or autopoietic systems are "a network of production processes common to all living systems" (Capra, 1996, p. 98). They are self-organizing systems in which the spontaneous appearance of structure or order may lead to a decrease in entropy and the evolution of new behaviors.

Complex systems are open systems characterized by corrupted data that are difficult to observe or measure because attempts to measure them will introduce value judgments (Flood & Carson, 1993, p. 120). Corrupted data in complex systems introduce built-in unpredictability, thus making it difficult to manage them (Battram, 1998, p. 11). While the details of a complex system are difficult to discern, the system as a whole (e.g., weather) can be understood because of human ability to recognize patterns (Battram, 1998, p. 20).

Chaotic systems are systems in which underlying patterns cannot be defined or understood. A pile of sand is an example of a chaotic system because "it has little or no internal structure [and] interactions between the components are local and unpredictable" (Battram, 1998, p. 32).

Complex (chaotic) systems are systems whose emergent behavior can be predicted in the short-term but not in the long-term.

Complex adaptive systems are complex systems that can adapt (i.e., self-organize) to their environment. The components of a complex adaptive system are constrained by links to other components. For example, the actions of individual traders are not coordinated in a market, but the emergent behavior of the whole market is the result of individual actions of the participants. Also, nonlinear interactions among the components can influence the behaviors of the components and the system as a whole. Other examples of complex adaptive systems are organizations, ant colonies, social systems, business processes, multiagent systems, and cultures.

At this point, it is important to define two additional concepts that affect systems thinking: *complexity* and *complexity theory. Complexity* is an interdisciplinary science including physics, biology, systems theory, and other areas. Complexity is not "a single technological innovation, but a shift in scientific approach" (Casti, Kauffman, Epstein, & Meyer, 1998, p. 8).

Complexity theory is a scientific approach aimed at understanding the principles that guide complex systems. It is also a theory of dynamic systems aimed at explaining systems in motion, such as the stock market and population growth (Devaney, 1998). The theory includes such concepts as *fitness landscape* (a search strategy to determine the knowledge required to improve system performance), self-organization, emergence, and *attractors* (discussed later in Chapter 2).

Imperatives for System Survival

To survive, social and technical systems must satisfy a minimum of four preconditions. They are a) a purposeful existence (i.e., goal driven), b) self-maintenance, c) adaptation to changing environments, and d) the ability to maximize their values (i.e., self-optimizing). A system can survive if it meets the requirements for an autonomic system. An autonomic system is designed to exhibit the self-managing capabilities of the central nervous system (i.e., Self-configuring, Self-healing, Self-protecting, and Self-optimizing (Fellenstein, 2005). I will provide a more detailed discussion of self-managing systems in Chapter 2.

Three System Theories and their Proponents

An operational definition of "theory" is necessary to make it relevant to organizational and social systems. A theory is defined as a "group of statements, taken as a related whole, that is used as our basis for design, judgment, and guidance of action" (McMaster, 1996, p. 19). Bacharach (1989) provided a more precise definition of theory as "a system of constructs and variables, in which the constructs are related to each other by propositions and the variables are related to each other by hypothesis" (p. 498). Theories equip the researcher with patterns, understanding, and order to deal with complex organizational and social systems. Theories are needed as guides to make explicit and to test one's mental models (be they verbal or visual), so that they can be challenged and modified. A theory is always on trial. It can be falsified when new paradigms are developed. According to Bacharach, theories are not ideal but merely operational to support current constructs. This point is relevant to practitioners. The development of a survivable system needs to be based on a theory. This premise drives the discussion and recommendations for using theory based approaches for building survivable product, process, and business models.

General Systems Theory, or Ecology Theory—von Bertalanffy

Ludwig von Bertalanffy (1998) was one of the biologists who started studying the new science of ecology in the early 19th century. His studies led to the formulation of the general systems theory, or the theory of living systems. According to him, three kinds of living systems exist—organisms, parts of organisms, and communities of organisms—all integrated into wholes of multi-creature organisms. In his view, ants and bees cannot survive in isolation because they need what he called "collective intelligence" (Resnick, 1997) and an adaptive ability to survive. To survive, they need to exist in a network fashion, through feeding relations or food webs.

Von Bertalanffy's general systems theory has three main propositions. The whole is more important than the sum of its parts. He believed in the holistic view of systems thinking. To understand a system, he thought, one should understand the emergent behaviors of the system as a whole and see that the relationships between the parts create values or utilities. It is the summation of the relationships across the parts that create values. When the relationships between two entities in a system are changed, the values they contribute will change as well. For example, changes in human or technical capital inside a socio-technical organization will affect the value of the organization. This is a departure from the Aristotelian view of the whole/part relationship of a system.

The most effective model for understanding open living systems is to view them as primarily organic. In biological systems, the properties of a part are not essential. Instead of seeing parts, one sees a network of relationships. Von Bertalanffy argued that biological phenomena required new ways of thinking that would transcend the traditional methods employed in the physical sciences. He saw systems thinking as process thinking. This contrasts with Descartes's and Newton's mechanistic view of systems thinking, which conjectured that forces and mechanisms interact to yield processes. The Cartesian paradigm assumes scientific objectivity, and scientific descriptions are seen as objective. In general systems theory, by contrast, all natural phenomena are interconnected, and the perception of systems is colored by one's method of observation, because all scientific concepts and theories are "limited and approximate" (Capra, 1996, p. 41).

Living systems do not seek equilibrium. For a living system, equilibrium corresponds to death. Von Bertalanffy held that living systems use tension, or instability, to adapt and improve organizational performance. This challenges the notion that living systems seek equilibrium. Success in an organization may lead to an organization's equilibrium, which may lead to failure, unless the organization has some supporting mechanisms to feed the success and push itself out of its state of equilibrium. This could be achieved through organizational learning from the environment and experiences and by using feedback to rejuvenate organizational processes.

The Contents

There are two parts to this book. Part I, (Chapters 1 through Chapter 7), describe the principles and applications for building complex product, process and business systems to ensure their survival. Part II, (Chapters 8 through Chapter 11), consists of my doctoral thesis, which describes an in-depth research on the use of collaborative and distributed agents to ensure the survival of the operations of a global telecommunication network.

Part I

Chapter 2 provides the requirements for survivable systems, followed a presentation of the principles and methods for building them in Chapter 3. Topics covered include finite element modeling, fault tree analysis, modeling and simulation, and complex and adaptive system concepts. Chapters 4, 5, and 6 cover applications of modeling concepts to ensure survivability of product, process, and business systems respectively. The variety of domain covered range from automotive engineering, air traffic control, telecommunications network management to space systems engineering. Chapter 7 concludes Part I of this book by introducing the reader to the concept of computer and network security guidelines for intra- and inter-enterprise resources and services.

Part II

Chapter 8 begins Part II of the book. It describes exception- handling strategies using software agent technology for building and managing a business process. A literature review on the application of intelligent agent technology and multi-agent systems to support survivable business processes is presented in Chapter 9. Chapter 10 presents some research methods for an in depth case study, using exception-handling strategies, to enhance operational effectiveness of distributed business processes (i.e., a global telecommunication network). Chapter 11 discusses the results from applying the research methods from chapter 10 and the contributions of the research.

Summary

This book concludes with a summary of its contents followed by some recommendations and conclusions in Chapter 12. Appendix A describes agent communicative acts and the Agent Communication Language (ACL). Appendix B lists sample data formats for the system variables of the network elements. Appendix C contains a list of software scripts for running the experiments for the research described in Part II of this book. Appendix D provides an annotated bibliography on complexity theory and its application to complex system development.

Building Survivable Systems

18

CHAPTER 2: REQUIREMENTS

"He who defends everything defends nothing"
Sun Tzu, The Art of War.

No matter how hard we try, it is impossible to build a system that can be fully protected from all attacks or without any vulnerable component. As stated earlier, the purpose of a survivable system is to ensure that the system will continue to operate and meet its mission objectives, in a timely manner, even when the functions of some of its components have been compromised.

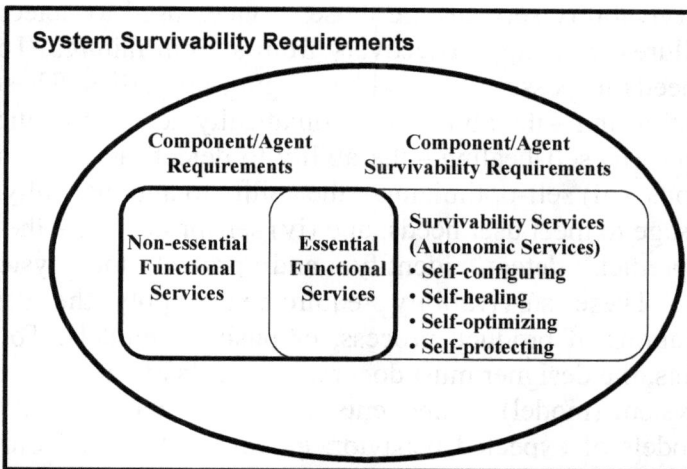

Figure 2-1: Survivability Requirements for a Typical System

19

Elements of a Survivable System

A typical system consists of components or agents whose interactions determine the emergent behavior of the system. The survivability of the system therefore depends on successful integration of a set of quality attributes such as performance, availability, reliability, security, fault tolerance, affordability, (autonomic services) of the components into system design as depicted in Figure 2-1 (Mead 2003, Fellenstein, 2005). Ellison, Fisher, Linger, Lipson, Longstaff and Mead (1999) and Mead (2003) have proposed five requirements for a survivable system in the telecommunications domain. The requirements are applicable to most domains. The requirements identified in Figure 2-1 are (i) component/agent requirements, (ii) survivability requirements for the component, (iii) non-essential functional services, (iv) essential functional services, and (v) survivability services.

The basic structural and operational requirements of the component need to be addressed followed by the components survivability attributes. The designer must enumerate what constitutes essential and non-essential functional services for the system. Finally, the designer must incorporate survivability services (i.e., autonomic services or strategies) into system design. Survivability services are those services used to detect, predict, prevent failures, and support recovery from system failures. To survive, a system needs to possess four self-managing properties. These include (i) self-configuring—the ability to automatically adapt to changes in the environment; (ii) self-healing—the ability to detect, diagnose, and react to disruptions; (iii) self-optimizing—the ability to automatically optimize resource usage to meet user needs; and (iv) self-protecting—the ability to anticipate/predict, detect, identify, and protect the system from disruptions. These survivability requirements apply the design and usage/operations of product, process, or business models. To meet the requirements, the designer must document models of causal relationships between system (model) components, models of actual behavior of the system, models of expected behavior, models of known failure modes, and policies for corrective actions (Robertson and Williams, 2006).

Policies and acceptable system performance tradeoffs usually drive a system survivability goal.

Establishing a Metric for a Survivable System

The determination of what constitutes essential services is usually based on an organization's policies and experience of the decision makers. Survivability is achievable if it can be measured. It is the proportion of essential services that must be met to the normal system performance level. While the example described below focuses on the telecommunication network modeling domain, the same approach is applicable to establishing survivability values for products and other business systems. Survivability can be represented in a formal form as follows (Moitra and Konda, 2000):

$$Survivability = (level\ of\ performance\ at\ the\ new\ state)/(Normal\ level\ of\ performance)$$

The value for survivability falls between 0 (total failure) and 1 for (normal) operation. The challenge is to determine a measure of performance. This is easy to explain with the approach used in the telecommunication industry. Telecommunications Service Providers (TSPs) use a customer's Committed Information Rate (CIR) to establish a service level agreement. CIR is the volume of traffic that the provider promises to transmit for the customer over a specified period. However, the TSPs classify the customers into two groups—premium and regular customers. In the event of any system failures, the TSPs's policy is to ensure that premium customers' connections are always operational even if a little degraded. This policy is built into the design and operations of the telecommunication network management system. Survivability of "essential" services is the degree to which the CIR has survived system failure for selected (premium) customers. A formal representation of survivability of a system after a failure can be described as follows:

Let $D(S_n, CIR)$ represent the degree to which CIR has been affected at the new state S_n (i.e., after an incident). The new state (S_n) could be normal operation, minor degradation, serious degradation, or non-functional. Each of these states could correspond to normal CIR traffic load, minor or major reduction in traffic load, or no traffic in network. Let w(CIR) represent the weight or priority assigned to each customer's CIR. Then a policy-based *survivability* of the system can be represented as the *product* of the *weighted sum* of customer priorities and the volume of traffic delivered at the new state, S_n:

$$\text{Survivability } (S_n) = \Sigma_{CIR} \, w(\, CIR \,) * D(S_n , CIR)$$

Instead of using weighted survivability as described by the equation above, Moitra and Konda (2000) have proposed the following representation for Survivability in a worst-case scenario:

$$\text{Survivability } (S_n) = \text{Min}_{CIR} (D(CIR, S_n \,))$$

This is the minimum level of essential services that can be provided to meet selected customer service level guarantees. When the probability of failure of a critical component and the degree to which the failure will occur are know, Moitra and Konda provide the equation for calculating *expected* survivability. Calculating expected survivability relies on a significant number of assumptions. For example, the value for the probability of failure of significant components may be unreliable resulting in an inaccurate expected survivability. My research reported in Part II of this book provides a multi-agent based approach to establishing system survivability.

Fault Tree Modeling and Risk Management

The concept of fault tree modeling has a long usage history in the engineering disciplines.   It has been used to understand machine reliability and the reliability of automated systems. The same concept (a.k.a. threat modeling) is now in use to identify software vulnerabilities (weaknesses) in software engineering. Also known as attack tree modeling, the designer builds the attack tree from the point of view of the ways the system can fail--attack scenarios (Odubiyi and O'Brien, 2006). Attack tree modeling can be used to generate and test solutions to problems. The system developer should think of possible scenarios that an attacker can use from the attacker's perspective, to exploit any vulnerabilities in the system. Whether in hardware engineering or software engineering, the goal is to determine the possibility of component failure and the severity of risk associated with such failure. Risk analysis is critical to the design of survivable systems. Risk is the product of probability of occurrence of an incident and its impact.

Risk = Incident Probability X Incident Impact

There are three phases of risk analysis: (i) building threat profiles of the assets, (ii) identifying system vulnerabilities, and (iii) developing strategies and plans to mitigate system vulnerabilities. Mead (2003) proposes eight steps for implementing the three phases of risk management and its contribution to survivability engineering.

This background information presented in the preceding paragraphs provides a framework for identifying survivability requirements for system design. The reader can gain a better appreciation for these requirements by understanding the theories of living systems, self-organization, and complex (chaotic) systems.

The remainder of this chapter examines the works of Ludwig von Bertalanffy (1998) on the theory of living systems and of Ilya Prigogine (1988) on the theory of self-organization and the theory of complexity, or dynamical/non-linear systems. The three theories were selected because they help in tracing the growth of systems thinking from mechanistic views of system—as theorized by Rene Descartes, Isaac Newton and others—to the current views of systems as non-continuous and chaotic. These three theories have played a major role in advancing systems thinking and systems research in organizational and social systems. Because social and organizational systems do not behave as linear and continuous systems do (Hallinan, 1997), they it is beneficial to view from a chaotic and catastrophic perspective and study them as complex, dynamic, and open systems.

Analysis of an Organizational System from the Perspective of Bertalanffy's Theory of Living Systems

An organizational system, as shown in Figure 2-2, can be used to explain how Bertalanffy's theory of living systems can be applied. An organizational system exists in an environment, where it interacts with the economic, political, and cultural forces. Its mission, vision, and strategy define the organization's goal.

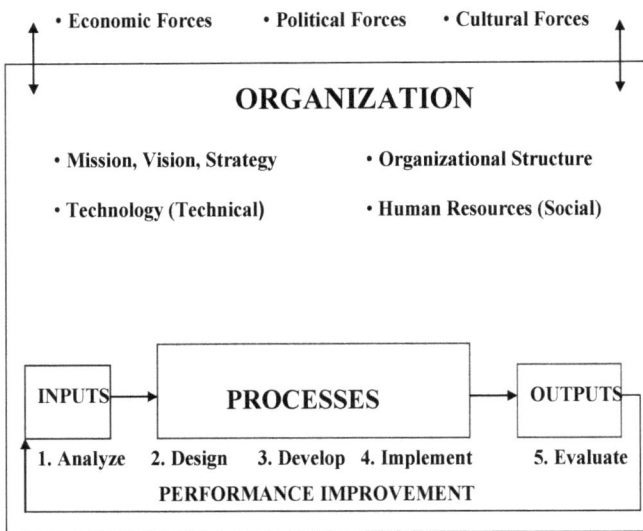

The organization has a structure and uses its technology and human resources to transform its inputs into outputs. After analyzing its inputs, it processes them in a three-stage process of designing, developing, and implementing to generate the outputs. It evaluates the outputs and applies

Figure 2-2: A Typical Organization Viewed as a Living System (Source: McGettigan, 1999 Summer Seminar: Theories of Organizational Systems, Walden University).

the knowledge garnered, through feedback to improve the system's performance. Regardless of the innovation process (product, process, or business model), this flow process, coupled with a feedback mechanism is critical to the success of the innovation and the survival of the organization. Natural systems employ the same strategy to survive.

Von Bertalanffy theorized that the performance improvement process can produce a crisis. A crisis can, then, lead to the invention of new methods and processes, which, will result in improved performance. His taxonomy of performance can be represented as a pyramid of activities, as depicted in Figure 2-3.

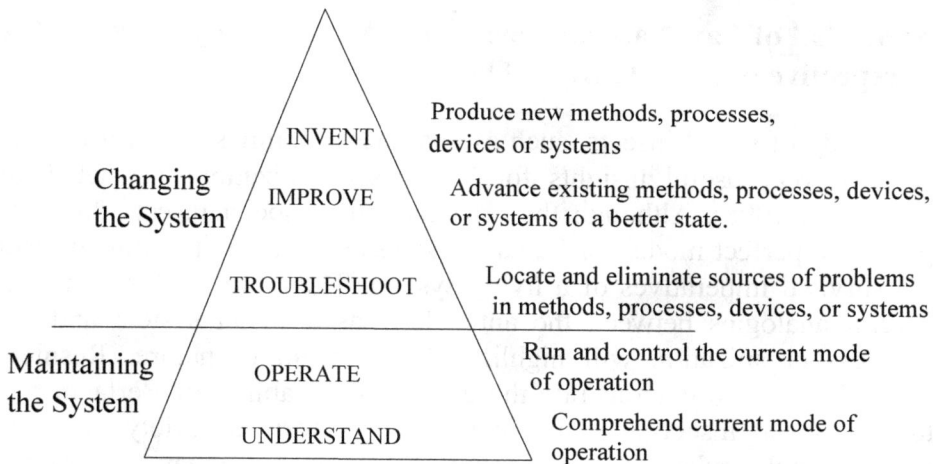

Figure 2-3: A Taxonomy of Performance for System Improvement.
(Source: McGettigan, 1999 Summer Seminar: Theories of Organizational Systems).

According to Bertalanffy's theory, every system is part of another system; it has characteristics that are similar to or derived from the characteristics of the other system. He sought to establish his general systems theory on a solid biological basis, emphasizing the difference between physical and biological systems. Von Bertalanffy's Living Systems Theory (LST) applies to cells, humans, organizations, and societies. He developed some postulates, backed by mathematical differential equations, on how living systems maintain some stability in spite of instabilities in their environments. Each living system aims at minimizing the instabilities created by differences between internal elements and with the environment (Vancouver, 1996). The relationships between the parts create the value of the system. Any changes in the internal elements of an organization will affect the utility of the whole system.

Analysis of a Natural System (Ant Colony) from the Perspective of Bertalanffy's Theory

The study of social insects, such as ants, bees, termites, and wasps, can produce very useful insights for business organizations (Donehey & Bonabeau, 1998). Although the organization of social insects does not provide a perfect model for human business processes, it seems to meet the survival imperatives of a living system. Therefore, a closer look at several analogies between the ant colony as a social system and the business organization will highlight the wisdom of nature (Resnick, 1997, 59-60) and demonstrate the general applicability of Bertalanffy's theory. Social insects use simple rules to perform a variety of tasks. Using simple rules, leaf-cutter ants have been known to perform agricultural functions. They cut leaves, transport them to their nest, and use them to grow fungi, which they eat. The tasks performed by social insects are not limited to only simple ones. In building their nests, termites build highly organized air-conditioning systems that provide complex interfaces between the atmosphere and the nest. Through collective behaviors and simple interactions between the social insects and their environment, emerge complex collective behaviors.

While we witness the wisdom of nature through these collective behaviors, these simple rules have also been known to result in some inconstancies. An example of an absurd behavior in ants is the way they may misuse simple rules of pheromone tracing to guide them to food sources. When an ant discovers a source of food, it leaves a trace of pheromones to guide other ants. The higher the concentration of pheromones, the faster the ants run and the more pheromones they lay on their tracks. If by chance it rains and all the chemicals in the pheromone is washed away, having lost their trail back to the nest, the ants continue to run faster in circles laying more pheromones until they all die. This can be identified as one of the non-adaptive features of a living system.

Origins of Conflicts in Social Insects

Much conflict is evident in the behavior of social insects (Donahey & Bonabeau, 1998). They spend much of their time waging wars against other colonies and within their own colonies. One major source of conflict is reproduction. Since the desire to reproduce is assumed to be universal and inborn in social insects, assigning reproduction duties to insects in the colony must be achieved through some incentives from the most dominant insects. Without adequate incentives, dissatisfied insects may leave. The size of the colony impacts the labor force; in addition, a small colony exposes itself to being overtaken by a larger colony. As a result, social insects use conflict for efficient reorganization. The dominant ants become the reproducers, the middle class turns into soldier ants that protect the colony, and the worker ants, at the bottom of the brood, are responsible for foraging for food. Through such division of labor, ant colonies operate efficiently just as do business organizations.

The assumptions underlying Bertalanffy's theory of living systems are critical to the efficient operation of both organizational and social systems (e.g., business entities and ant colonies, respectively). The theory of self-organization and the theory of complex systems discussed in the following pages support Bertalanffy's theory to provide a robust foundation for systems thinking.

The Theory of Self-Organization

Several theorists have contributed to the theory of self-organization. The concept originated among scientists (cyberneticists) modeling neural methods in the early 1940s. In their paper, entitled "A Logical Calculus of the Ideas Immanent in Nervous Activity," neuroscientist Warren McCulloch and mathematician Walter Pitts described a model of the nervous system as a network of binary (on/off) switching neurons (Capra, 1996). The paper described the neural system as a set of interconnected networks of neurons, in which previous activities of neighboring nodes control the behavior of each node with switching rules. The theory states that a node will switch "on" at the next time step only if a group of surrounding nodes is in the "on" state at the current time. The authors postulated that such a simple model can represent the operations of the nervous system. This motivated several scientists in the 1950s to experiment with binary models of neurons of the nervous system using a set of light bulbs, which turned on or off. In the experiment, each light bulb represented a neuron switched on and off. After running the experiment for a while, the scientists found to their surprise that after some initial irregular flickering, the node flickering developed into an ordered pattern of networks. The emerging pattern formed different geometric shapes (circles, waves, etc.). Even though the first turned-on light bulb was selected at random, it was observed that the randomly initiated starting conditions had no effect on the spontaneous emergence of the developing patterns. The term "spontaneous emergence of order" gave rise to the term self-organization (Capra, 1996).

Heinz von Foerster, in late 1950s, developed a qualitative model of self-organization in living systems. He described the process a system can employ to obtain order from "noise." He postulated that a system could import order from its environment by absorbing the energy from its environment to increase internal order. Researchers in several countries refined Foerster's model of self-organization in the 1970s and 1980s. They applied the theory to both small and large systems. Among these researchers were Ilya Prigogine in Belgium with his dissipative systems theory, Hermann Haken in Germany with his laser theory, James Lovelock in England and Lynn Margolis in the United States with their theory of the earth as a living system, and Humberto Maturana and Francisco Verala in Chile with Autopoiesis (Waldrop, 1992; Capra, 1996). Their combined activities resulted in a unified model of self-organizing systems. The model has three important characteristics:

1. It exhibits spontaneous emergence of new patterns and new forms of behavior.

2. A spontaneous emergence of new forms of behavior and patterns develop only in open systems, and when the system is far from equilibrium.

3. It has the internal elements interconnected in a nonlinear manner, which gives rise to internal feedback loops. This nonlinear pattern of behavior can be described only with nonlinear equations.

The Theory of Dissipative Structures—Prigogine

The Russian-born chemist, physicist, and Nobel laureate Ilya Prigogine, who was a physical chemistry professor at the Free University of Brussels, contributed the most informed explanation of self-organizing systems with his theory of dissipative structures, in the early 1960s and 1970s. The theory explains that the instabilities at the point where a system moves out of equilibrium (i.e., the bifurcation point) are not typically the cause of chaotic behavior but provide the chance for a new dynamic order. The new dynamic state allows the system to handle emerging unpredictable and complex behaviors. Prigogine was fascinated by the fact that living systems (organisms) are able to maintain their life forms (active life) under disequilibrium conditions. Prigogine and his research partner Liu reported that two types of behaviors are characteristic of systems: under certain conditions there is a tendency to move towards a state of disorder and under certain other conditions, there is a tendency to move towards a state of equilibrium (Liu, 1996). Disorder emerges when the system is in a thermodynamic equilibrium. The scientists concluded that the sources of order in the system are to be sought in the distance from equilibrium and the nonlinear behavior of the system. They researched and explained the exact conditions under which systems that are far from thermal equilibrium, are stable. They used the theory to explain why systems far from equilibrium can be described only with nonlinear equations.

To explain a system's stability, when it is far from equilibrium—instead of studying living systems— Prigogine studied thermal diffusion, that is, heat convection, also known as Bénard instability. His experiment demonstrated that heating a jar of liquid uniformly from the bottom does not initially affect the movement of the liquid. Heat is merely conducted from the bottom to the top while the liquid is in a state of equilibrium. However, when the difference in temperature between top and bottom attains a critical value, heat flux (i.e., conduction) ceases and the heat is transferred through convection and a large number of molecules moves around in a set of ordered hexagonal cells, like a honeycomb. The phenomenon was attributed to the fact that hot liquid rises through the middle of the cell (known as Bénard cell), while cold liquid descends along the sides. Prigogine performed detailed analyses of Bernard cells and concluded that there comes a critical point of instability, while a system is moving away from equilibrium, when spontaneous patterns of hexagonal cells appear, and it is at this point that the self-organization phenomenon develops. Prigogine also explained the cause of circular imprints on sand dunes and on arctic snow: It is attributable to hot air from the earth escaping into the atmosphere, a process similar to that of Bernard cells.

Prigogine's most notable explanation of self-organization of systems came from his experiments with chemical reactions, known as chemical clocks. He demonstrated how, when two types of molecules (some red, some blue) react at a critical point, all the molecules will be blue at one point in time and red at another. This cycle continues over time. The experiment was replicated under different experimental conditions with identical results. This led Prigogine and his fellow scientists to conclude that for the whole liquid to change color spontaneously, all the billions of molecules had to coordinate their activities. The scientists believed that such coordination and emergent behavior of the liquid happen at a critical and unstable point, when the system is far from equilibrium. Prigogine also concluded that the excess production of entropy is the cause of a system's instability. In the 1960s, he developed a new mathematics of nonlinear thermodynamics to explain the phenomenon of self-organization of open systems when they are far from equilibrium.

Prigogine dismissed the view held by classical thermodynamicists of the time that claimed that structures, such as crystals, were always in equilibrium. He explained that Bénard cells are structures that are far from equilibrium. While the theory of classical thermodynamics claims that dissipation of energy and the like through heat transfer is wasted energy, Prigogine explained that dissipated energy in open systems provides a form of order, and dissipative structures can evolve to maintain a stable state far from equilibrium. Such evolution leads to the emergence of more complex structures. Prigogine's theory of dissipative structures helped to establish the importance of nonlinearity for self-organizing systems.

Hermann Haken identified a weakness in Prigogine's theory: While the theory identifies the source of instability at the bifurcation point, it does not explain how to determine and classify newly emerging phenomena. Haken explained that instabilities in the system at bifurcation points are due to the influence of external factors, that is, the environment. He enhanced Prigogine's theory of self-organizing systems by explaining that coordinated light emission from individual laser atoms that yield the coherence observed in laser light cannot be described with a linear theory. Haken's laser theory is based on the application of energy from a heat source to an object, causing its atoms to become excited into another state and in the process emitting laser light. The new state is unstable, and with continuous application of energy, the atoms' transition to new states will again emit laser light in the process. Haken concluded that the transition from normal light to laser light is an example of a self-organizing system, operating in a region far from equilibrium. Manfred Eigen used hypercycles—a self-organizing and self-producing process—to explain the origin of the universe. Maturana's research and theory of autopoieses explain that self-organization is common to all living systems.

Nonlinear Dynamical Systems, or Theory of Complex Systems

The need to better understand and solve problems related to complex systems became critical to industrial enterprises in the 1950s and 1960s because of the emergence of chemical, electronic, and communication technologies. Managers and engineers had to deal with large numbers of individual components and the effects of interaction among the components in both physical and organizational systems. This motivated engineers and managers to formulate explicit strategies and methodologies that explicitly use systems concepts. Given the complexity of these new systems, it was critical for organizational leaders to think strategically. Systems analysis became the most popular technology. Rand Corporation, a Federally Funded Research and Development corporation pioneered systems analysis in the late 1940s. The Rand Corporation became a model for many so-called think tanks for policy making and the brokerage of technology. Systems analysis grew out of operations research, that is, the analysis and planning of military operations during WWII. After the war, managers used the approach to solve similar problems in business. This gave rise to the term "systems-oriented management."

Dynamical systems have engendered a branch of mathematics aimed at explaining systems in motion, such as the stock market, the weather, population changes, and so forth. Some dynamical systems are predictable, others are not (Devaney, 1992). The most popular explanation for the difficulty in understanding complex systems has been the large number of variables. According to Devaney, this is just part of the reasons why systems with only a single variable have been found to behave unpredictably in complex systems. Examples include the stock market and hurricanes. The cause of unpredictable behavior in complex systems is called "chaos" (Devaney, 1992). With the understanding that the simplest systems can exhibit chaotic behaviors, scientists now have the opportunity to study chaos in its most primitive state. It is expected that understanding chaos in its most simple form will help provide the answers to chaotic behaviors in complex systems with many variables.

Mathematics of Patterns

The theories of self-organizing systems, as discussed earlier, dealt with very complex systems with thousands of interconnected networks and interdependent chemical reactions. The new mathematics that describes the nonlinear theory of complexity is called dynamical systems theory— a mathematics of patterns. It is qualitative rather than quantitative. This triggered a paradigm shift among mathematicians and scientists on how to think about systems. The theory of complexity is not a theory of physical phenomena; it is a mathematical theory applied to several phenomena, such as cloud formation and population growth (Capra, 1996, p. 113). Chaos theory, fractal theory (or fractal geometry), and complexity theory are branches of dynamical systems theory.

The development of high-performance computers has played a major role in mastering the new mathematics or science of complexity. Computers with their ability to solve massively complex equations and discover new qualitative patterns of behavior have contributed to a new understanding of complexity. Until the development of tools that could handle nonlinear equations, linear approximations were used to linearize complex nonlinear equations that describe complex phenomena. Now, complex equations, previously considered too difficult to solve, can be solved. Qualitative patterns of behavior of complex networks can be explained and exploited. This is very important for understanding and managing organizational and social systems. The new tools can help managers explain underlying interrelationships of interrelated elements and emerging chaos. Since business organizations are living systems, their pattern of organization should be viewed from a living systems perspective.

The pattern of organization has been a central theme in systems thinking. The early systems thinkers defined pattern as a system of relationships. Ecologists recognized the network as the general pattern of life. The Cyberneticists identified feedback as a circular pattern of causal links. The new mathematics of complexity is focused on solving the mathematics of visual patterns. Complexity scientists insist that an understanding of how a pattern and structure approach is to be integrated is a precondition for understanding living systems. The pattern of organization of any system, living or nonliving, is the configuration of relationships among the system's components.

Two Reinforcing Perspectives on the Properties of Complex Systems

Richard Pascale (1999, 2000) and Fritjof Capra (1996) provide reinforcing views on the properties of complex systems. Pascale considers the following four properties as characteristic of complex systems:

1. must operate in a state far from equilibrium. Equilibrium is considered a precursor to the death of a complex system. (This characteristic is inherent in von Bertalanffy's theory of living systems and Prigogine's theory of self-organization)

2. must be able to self-organize with complex emergent behaviors

3. complex systems tend to move towards a chaotic state when presented with a complex task, (A complex system in bounded instability is more prone to evolution than it is in a stable equilibrium)

4. a living system that cannot be directed; it can only be disturbed. (Weak cause-and-effect linkages are characteristic of complex systems).

Capra (1996) identified the following three properties of complex systems, similar to the four characteristics described by Pascale:

1. Nonlinear systems are characterized by complex and apparently chaotic behavior, which can yield ordered structures with patterns. The mathematics of nonlinear systems helps explain the patterns.
2. It is often impossible to predict emergent behavior of a nonlinear system, even when the equation may be deterministic.

3. There is a correspondence between the magnitude of changes and the source of the change. Unlike linear systems, where the sum of the changes corresponds to the magnitude of the changes, in nonlinear systems a very small change may result in dramatic effects and new patterns of behavior due to self-reinforcing feedback.

Both Pascale and Capra conclude that organizations provide useful insights into their behavior and strategic management when viewed as complex systems.

Computers and Solutions of Complex Dynamical Systems

At the turn of the 20th century, Henri Poincaré (1890) the French mathematician laid the foundation for the mathematics of complex dynamical systems. He developed the theory from his study of differential equations. Rather than rely on analytical methods to explain the global properties of solutions of nonlinear dynamical systems, he applied qualitative methods of geometric and topological maps. For Poincaré, the behavior of a system, observable from a combination of all solutions of the system's components, was more important than the behavior of individual elements, obtained from analytic solutions of individual elements (Devaney, 1989). Using topological concepts, he analyzed the qualitative characteristics of complex dynamical physical phenomena. He challenged the principles of Newtonian mechanics by showing that simple and deterministic equations of motion can produce complex patterns that are very difficult or almost impossible to predict. He solved the three-body problem, in which he was able to determine their trajectories under their independent gravitational attraction (Capra, 1996, p. 127). Two events pushed Poincaré's idea into the background for about 60 years: The first was Planck's discovery of energy quanta; the second was Einstein's publication of his special theory of relativity. Yet, the need to solve complex problems in quantum mechanics and chaotic systems forced scientists to revisit the mathematics of complex dynamical problems in the 1960s. Birkoff built on the works of Poincaré by using discrete dynamics to explain the complex dynamics generated by differential equations (Devaney, 1989).

Before the advent of computing tools, linear equations were solved analytically, while nonlinear equations were solved numerically, that is, by trial and error. For a nonlinear equation, various combinations of numbers were tried for the variables until a set was identified that matched the equation. The process was and still is typically cumbersome, time consuming, and yielded only approximate solutions. With computers, however, one can generate reasonable solutions to very complex equations faster. The solution obtained for nonlinear equations is not a formula but rather a large set of values for the variables of the equation. The computer can then be programmed to connect the values. The connections can emerge as a curve or a group of curves in a graph. This has helped scientists and business organizations solve complex nonlinear equations, which yield chaotic behaviors, and discover the order within the apparent chaos. Several problems in operations research (e.g., dynamic programming) and fractal geometry are solved in like fashion.

Phase Space and Strange Attractors

Equipped with a new tool for solving very complex equations, scientists are now able to delve into the realm of qualitative mathematics to explain patterns in physical and natural phenomena. The variables of a complex phenomenon can now be displayed in an abstract mathematical space—called phase space—to reveal the ordered pattern. The phase space technique, in which every variable in the system is linked with a different coordinate in an abstract space, is based on Poincaré's topological approach, developed early in the 20th century. This technique allows data analysts to visualize complex phenomena and explain their behavior. Unlike classical mechanics—in which even the oscillation of a pendulum is assumed to be deterministic, since the effect of air friction is always ignored—in nonlinear dynamics, a trace of the motion of a pendulum generates a curve in two-dimensional space with decreasing radius in a spiral that moves towards the center. The termination point is called an *attractor*, because that is where the pendulum motion ends, owing to air friction. It is the state which attracts other different states of the system. Scientists have identified three types of attractors to explain the behaviors of complex phenomena. The three basic types of attractors are:

1. *Point attractors*, correspond to an equilibrium state where all other states within the system converge, such as a pendulum. A group of workers working on a task would tend to speed up to catch up with the fastest worker or slow down to accommodate the slowest performer to converge at a common pace;

2. *Periodic attractors* are generated by periodic oscillation of a closed system; and

3. *Strange attractors*, also known as *chaotic attractors*, correspond to patterns generated by chaotic systems. The most popular example is an electronic chaotic pendulum, studied by the Japanese mathematician Yoshisuke Ueda in the late 1970s.

Solutions of complex problems can now be modeled as trajectories in phase space, and with a limited number of attractors, the behavior of complex phenomena can be classified topologically. This permits the problem solver to understand the dynamics of a system by the shape of its attractor. This is a significant discovery. In 1963, Lorenz employed Minkowski's space-time interval, whereby trajectories of moving objects were plotted in a complex space (from x, y, z, t to x', y', z', t'). This marked the start of chaos theory. (Prigogine, 1988, p. 167).

Using Attractors to Explain Behaviors of Complex Systems

Lorenz attractors are used to explain the behavior of certain classes of complex systems. This would help one define what is known as a phase portrait, or a dynamical picture of the whole system. Bifurcation points—critical points of instability, where the system takes on a new form—mark the changes in the system's phase portrait. To analyze a dynamic system qualitatively, one can employ the following three steps:

1. Identify the system's attractors;

2. Identify the basins of attraction of the system's attractor (i.e., a region of phase space where all trajectories that originate eventually terminate). The concept of basins is analogous to river basins where rivers flow into different basins. Bifurcation points determine the basin to which the river will flow. In an organization, this is synonymous with groups of employees attracted by common interests. Each group constitutes a basin of attractor.

3. Classify the basins of attraction according to their topologies. The key is to identify the bifurcation points that forces one employee to be attracted to one group over another. This knowledge of group dynamics (i.e., topologies of the basins of attraction) should be used to enhance the performance of the organization as a whole.

Today, mathematicians have identified about 27 bifurcation types. The bifurcation events can be classified topologically. This demonstrates and confirms Prigogine's theory, which says that, in a self-organizing system, points far from equilibrium take on new forms. The French mathematician René Thom was able to classify several basic bifurcation events topologically in the 1970. He used the term *catastrophes* in place of bifurcation. The French mathematician Benoit Mandelbrot developed fractal geometry, or the geometry of irregular phenomena, (independent of chaos theory) to explain the structure of chaotic attractors (Wheatley 1992). These days strange attractors are commonly described as trajectories in phase space that exhibit fractal geometry.

Conclusion

The three theories on systems thinking described earlier carry a common thread: An open system is a living system, which must satisfy system survival imperatives. These systems must be adaptive, be able to maintain themselves, and interact with the environment in which they exist. They must also exist for a reason (i.e., they must be goal-driven). Several scientists have tested the three theories and none has been falsified. This demonstrates their strength. Von Bertalanffy's theory of living systems (or theory of deep ecology) demonstrates the wisdom of nature. In building new organizational systems, one does not need to reinvent the wheel: There are abundant examples in nature.

Prigogine's theory of self-organization reinforced von Bertalanffy's theory. A system without a feedback mechanism will not survive. This notion is emphasized in the theory of nonlinear dynamical systems (in chaos theory or catastrophe theory). New computing tools have aided the generation of more accurate solutions, providing better insights into the behavior of complex phenomena.

The contributions of Pascale, Capra, Poincaré, and others have demonstrated the utility of complexity theory and useful insights into behavior of complex systems such as organizations.

The three theories have established fundamental principles for managing organizational and social systems. The inadequacies inherent in the mechanistic, or simplistic, view of systems thinking and analysis are clearly described in each of the three theories. Each explained how living systems cannot survive in a closed environment, and they cannot be fully understood with the assumptions made about them through Newtonian solutions. The theories push for a change in mental models held by system thinkers. The push for a change in mental models fits the title of Tentenbaum's (1998) article "Shifting Paradigms: From Newton to Chaos." In her address, Professor Maureen Hallinan (1997) of Notre Dame University, encouraged researchers of social change to switch from the simplistic way of conducting research, whereby changes are assumed to be linear and continuous, to an approach where the systems are viewed as complex and nonlinear. Since changes in our organizations and social systems are never linear or continuous, but complex and fraught with uncertainties, she argued that simple measurement techniques could not yield intelligent solutions. She encouraged researchers to employ appropriate tools (provided by chaos, or catastrophe, theory) to solve complex problems of organizational and social systems. We should change from working in the realm of what she called "simple science" to "extraordinary science."

Following the line of thinking that scientific knowledge is limited and incomplete, scientist and economist Brian Arthur emphasized the fact that humans cannot predict anything. Arthur advised that "predictions are nice if you can make them. But the essence of science lies in *explanation*, laying bare the fundamental mechanisms of nature" (Arthur, quoted by Waldrop, 1992, p. 39). In essence, we should use these new theories to understand emergent properties of organizational and social systems.

Chapter 3 will provide a more in depth rationale for recommending the nonlinear dynamical systems theory or complexity theory as necessary for building survivable systems in open systems domain. This theory builds on the theory of self-organizing and self-regulating systems; it can help explain complex behaviors of complex operations support systems.

Building Survivable Systems

CHAPTER 3: PRINCIPLES AND METHODS

Effectiveness, even survival does not depend solely on how much effort we expend, but on whether the effort we expend is in the right jungle.

Stephen R. Covey, *7 Habits of Highly Effective People.*

While there are a variety of methods for building survivable systems, this book focuses on those methods that are applicable to different disciplines and domains. These methods include Finite Element Modeling (FEM) and Failure Mode and Effect Analysis (FMEA) for structural engineering and engineering system design; discrete and continuous system modeling and simulation for process design and management; and complex and nonlinear systems theory for business process modeling and organizational change management. This chapter presents the inherent characteristics of these approaches that make them most suitable for building survivable systems. A common feature of these approaches is their ability to provide the designers with a variety of system behaviors under different operational scenarios. The resulting design can predict what is likely to happen, and the feasibility of the design, before investing time and efforts. Combining these methods with prototype development enhances the chances of building survivable systems.

Finite Element Modeling and Analysis for Product Modeling

If you have been searching for a very versatile modeling tool you will find it with a sound knowledge of Finite Element Modeling and Analysis (FEMA) technique. You can use FEMA to predict automobile crashworthiness, to recognize faces of the participants in a video conference, to predict the consequences of a fractured human skull, and to estimate potential failures of heat shields of the US Space Shuttle. Developed originally for analysis of engineering structures, the Finite Element Modeling (FEM) method, is now commonly used in the areas of structural soil, and rock mechanics, fluid mechanics, heat transfer problems, and many non-engineering applications.

FEM is a process in which a body or a structure is represented by a combination of its components, known as finite elements. These elements with geometric shapes (i.e., lines, triangles, rectangles, trapezoids, etc.) are interconnected at points called nodes or nodal points as shown in Figure 3-1. FEM can accommodate complex and difficult problems encountered in determining the non-linear stress and strain behavior (i.e., deformation) of non-homogeneous materials, and complicated boundary conditions of a variety of structures (e.g., soil, rock, steel, etc.).

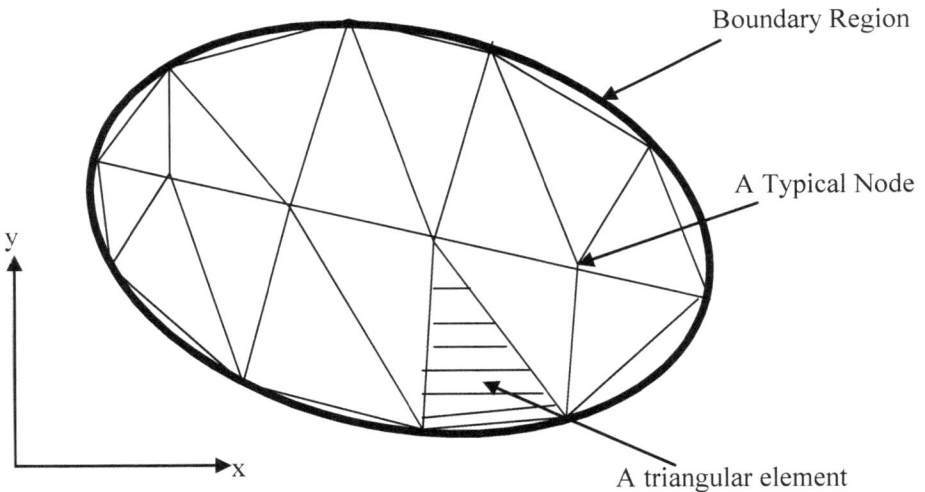

Figure 3-1: A two-dimensional region of an object represented as a combination of triangular finite elements.

The finite element modeler typically develops the model in two phases. The first phase covers the division of the complete body into individual geometric elements and the study of the elements. The second phase consists of the assembly of the elements for the whole body, to predict the behavior of the structure. The two phases consist of six solution steps to generate a final solution. To be able to apply these solution steps (i.e., understand the theory and application of FEM), the potential user must have a working knowledge in at least four fundamental areas. These areas include *matrix algebra, solid mechanics, variational methods* (mathematics), and *computing skills*. Matrix algebraic technique is the most efficient and logical method to handle and store a large number of equations required in the finite element method. Matrix techniques are very suitable for solutions of equations for equilibrium, eigenvalue (i.e., vibration), and propagation problems discussed later in this section. Since most applications of FEM are in structural and soil mechanics, the interested reader needs to acquire an understanding of solid mechanics to benefit from published research in the field. The interested reader also needs to understand the principles of calculus of variations, a mathematical procedure used for selecting the correct solution from a number of speculative solutions. Wolfram (2006) provides a brief treatment of calculus of variation with a list of reference materials.

Six Steps of the Finite Element Modeling Procedure

Modeling and analyzing a structure using the FEMA process consists of six steps regardless of the structure (metals, graphite composite, plastics, or ceramics, etc.). The details may vary in each step depending on the sophistication of the model or the modeler. The following six steps provide a summary of the process:

1. Discretize the physical body or a conceptual sketch of the body or structure.

   The first step demands the discretization of the structure being analyzed into an equivalent system of finite elements. These elements may be triangles or quadlaterals for a two-dimensional structure. Figure 3-1 shows a two-dimensional object broken down into a system of triangular finite elements. For a three-dimensional structure, the finite elements may be tetrahedral, rectangular, prisms, or hexahedra. While there have been several attempts to automate the process of dividing a structure into its elements, this process still depends on the judgment of the analysts or engineer.

2. Select the displacement models

   The basic philosophy of the finite element method is to obtain an approximate solution to a complicated problem by subdividing the object into a series of finite elements and employing a relatively simple function to obtain the solution for each element. For a displacement model, the simple function constitutes the displacement model that approximates the actual distribution of the displacements. A linear polynomial is commonly employed as a displacement model. The displacement functions that approximate the displacement of each element are called displacement models, displacement fields, or displacement patterns.

   Three factors influence the selection of the displacement model. First, the designer needs to select the type and degree of the displacement model. Secondly, the magnitudes of the displacements (i.e., the displacement of the nodal points) need to be determined. The third factor demands that the model should meet some requirements that ensure that the results approach the correct solution. In addition, the displacement models must be continuous within the finite elements while the adjacent element must deform without causing any openings or discontinuities between the elements. The model should ensure a rigid body displacement rule, whereby the assumption is that all points on the element experience the same displacement.

3. Derive the element stiffness matrix using a principle of variational calculus.

One of the variational principles of solid mechanics is used to calculate the element stiffness matrix and load vector (ref Desai and Abel, p. 113). The stiffness relates the nodal displacements to the forces applied at the nodal points. The concentrated forces applied at the nodes are derived from the distributed forces applied to the structure.

The following simultaneous linear algebraic equation can be used to express the equilibrium relation between the stiffness matrix [K], the nodal force vector {Q}, and nodal displacement {q}:

$$[K] \{q\} = \{Q\}.$$

4. Assemble the algebraic equations for the overall discritized structure

This process consists of assembling the global stiffness matrix from the element matrices and the global force (i.e., load vector) from the element nodal force vectors. The analyst can use the following set of simultaneous equation to represent the overall equilibrium relations between the total stiffness matrix [K], the total load vector {R}, the nodal displacement vector {r} for the entire structure.

$$[K] \{r\} = \{R\}$$

5. Generate solutions for the unknown displacement

    The designer can use matrix algebra techniques to solve the algebraic equations to obtain unknown displacements for linear equilibrium problems. To obtain solutions for nonlinear problems requires a series of steps that modify the stiffness matrix or load vector.

6. Compute the element strains and stresses from the nodal displacements

    In some simple cases, the nodal displacements provide all that is required to obtain a solution. Computation of other variables such as stresses and strains, may be obtained as proportions of derivatives of the displacements. The derivatives of the displacement provide the average value of the stress or strain at the center of each element.

Limitations of the Finite Element Method

One of the major problems in applying FEM is the representation of a non-homogeneous structure. The FEM must account for non-homogeneity by assigning different properties to different elements in the structure (i.e., the continuum). In addition, the method must be able to accommodate certain phenomena, such as cracking and fracture behavior in solid mechanics, and failures of composite materials. Modeling of non-linearity in solid mechanics requires the understanding of behavior of materials and material science.

The most tedious aspect of the method is the process of subdividing a structure into finite elements and generating error-free input into the computer program. While some aspects of this process have been automated, some engineering judgment is still required in dividing the structure into appropriate geometric elements.

Concluding remarks on the Finite Element Method and Analysis

The finite element method is a technique that has been generalized and it is a powerful and versatile tool for application to a wide range of problems. Several software packages are available in the public domain. Over 75 of these packages are available with free source code are available from the URL: http://www.engr.usask.ca/~macphed/finite/fe_resources/node137.html. An additional 30 are available without the source code. The most popular packages include ASAP, NASTRAN, STRUDL, and SAFE.

The following URL: http://www.engr.usask.ca/~macphed/finite/fe_resources/fe_resources.html provides additional software resources including automated mesh generators.

Modeling and Simulation Science for Process Modeling

The second principle described in this book for building survivable systems is system simulation. Modeling and simulation is the process of using the computer to simulate the operations of various kinds of real world facilities or processes. In order to simulate the system, we must first make certain assumptions. The assumptions are in the form of mathematical or logical relationships in order to understand how the correspondence system behaves. If the model of the system and the relationships between the entities, which compose the model, are simple enough to permit the use of mathematical methods such as algebra, calculus, or probability theory, then an analytic solution is all that is needed. Since most real life problems are too complex to obtain realistic solutions with analytic models, we must resort to computer simulation to evaluate a model numerically over a period of interest. We can then use the data obtained to estimate the true behavior of the model.

The power of simulation rests in the fact that it can be used to estimate cost reduction or cost avoidance during a system design process. The modeler can evaluate a variety of system operational scenarios before embarking on the development of a physical facility (e.g., a manufacturing process or a telecommunication network). Discrete event modeling and simulation is one of the most widely used techniques in Information Technology (IT) to understand and predict the behavior of business processes. However, its wider acceptance has been limited, due to the limited knowledge of some developers.

First, modeling a large and complex system is very tedious and analyzing the results to make valid predictions about the system is very critical to its usefulness. A simulation modeler needs to have a strong knowledge of the domain of interest, basic mathematics including discrete mathematics, and discrete structures. In addition, a sound understanding of probability and statistics, and a programming language are required to be able to develop and execute the model, and effectively analyze simulation output and make intelligent prediction about the system behavior with some degree of confidence.

Systems, Models, and Simulation Concepts

As discussed in Chapter 1, a system is a collection of interacting entities (e.g., people and machines) aimed at achieving a specific goal. Scoping the boundaries of a system depends on the study. One complex system could be a subsystem within a larger system. For example, modeling the traffic flow around the beltway in Washington DC, USA is still a subsystem of the traffic flow in Metropolitan Washington, DC. A system modeler needs to have a full understanding of the following concepts:

System State is a collection of variables required to describe the system at a particular time with respect to the objectives of the study.

Discrete System is a system for which, the entities or state variables change only at finite number of points in time. For example, the state of a road traffic model changes when a vehicle leaves or enters the system.

A Continuous System is a system for which the state variables change continuously as time changes. For example, a flying aircraft is a continuous system because its position changes continuous with respect to time. Defining a system as discrete or continuous depends on the rate at which the attributes of the entities, within the system change. Modeling a system as a discrete, continuous, or hybrid depends on the judgment of the system designer.

A Model is an abstract representation of a system developed to help to study the system. Logical or mathematical relationships used to represent a model describe the system in terms of state entities and their characteristics, processes, events, and delays. Types of models include static, dynamic, deterministic, and stochastic (i.e., contains one or more *random* variables).

Entity is any object in the system such as a message packet, a router, a switch, or a server in a communication network that must be modeled explicitly.

Attributes are the properties of a particular entity.

Event is an instantaneous occurrence that changes the state of a system, such as a new vehicle joining a row of waiting vehicles at a railroad crossing.

Delay is a time duration whose length is undefined or not known until it ends, such as the time spent in a queue.

Clock is a variable that represents simulated time.

51

Activity Duration can be specified as deterministic (a new customer arriving at a bank every 15 minutes), stochastic (time to load a truck is function of truck size) or statistical (a random draw from among a set of processing times with equal probabilities).

Steps in a System Modeling and Simulation Study

A typical simulation study should follow the scientific problem solving process (i.e., observe, hypothesize or predict, test, accept provissionally, report on findings). It is not mandatory to follow all the steps listed below for each simulation study, but the researcher should attempt to incorporate most of the steps. As with any scientific research process, the researcher should plan to go back to a prior step, when a better understanding of the system at a step, calls for such a move:

1. *Formulate the problem and plan the study.* The designer should start with a clear formulation of the problem with the objectives of the study, criteria for success, the amount of resource required in terms of people, cost and time required for each phase of the study.

2. *Collect data and define the model.* Since the objective of a simulation study is to improve the performance of an existing system, if one exists or to evaluate the behavior of a non-existing system, the modeler needs to collect baseline data to estimate input data and statistical distributions of input data. Data collected on an existing (baseline) system typically serve as a validation tool for the simulation model.

3. *Validate both input and output data with domain experts.* The model's intended users and decision makers should be involved in the model development and analysis process. Just as with most

software development processes, unless potential users and decision makers are involved, the chance of accepting the final product is very low.

4. *Design and build the model in selected programming language or simulation package.* There are several simulation packages to choose from. In May of each year the Institute of Industrial Engineers publishes IIE Solutions, a guide which presents a "Simulation Software Buyer's Guide". Every two years, Operations Research/Management Science (OR/MS) Today also publishes a simulation software survey including simulation support packages such as data analyzers (Banks, pg. 100). In evaluating simulation language, the user should consider ease of use, speed of execution, and ensure that the simulation model can link to user code or software packages written in external programming languages such as Java, C, C++, etc.

5. *Make pilot runs and validate output.* Make pilot runs to test the response of the system to different input parameters. If a similar system exists, then that system can be used to validate the output from the pilot runs.

6. *Design experiments for the study.* Since there are many possible alternative systems to simulate, the modeler must decide which system scenarios to simulate. For each system design to be simulated, the modeler must resolve such issues as initial conditions for each run of the simulation, the length of each run of the simulation, and the number of replications (i.e., number of independent simulation runs).

7. *Make production runs and analyze output data.* Construct a confidence interval to determine which simulation model meets some specified performance measure for the proposed system, based on outputs from production runs.

8. *Document simulation results.* In the simulation results, the modeler must state all assumptions that went into the simulation modeling process and those used in developing the simulation software program.

Limitations of Simulation Models

While simulation has several benefits, the modeler needs to be aware of the following drawbacks:

1. Developing simulation models can be very expensive and time-consuming.

2. Since each run of a stochastic model produces only estimates of the true behavior for a given set of input parameters, therefore, it is imperative that the modeler make several independent runs for each set of input parameters and use statistical means to average the results. Because an analytic model can produce the actual true behavior of a model for a variety of input parameters, the modeler is advised to select an analytic model when suitable.

3. Sometimes, decision makers and modelers tend to place more confidence in simulation results because of the large volume of data generated. This can lead to erroneous conclusions about the value of the simulation model.

Complex and Nonlinear Systems Theory for Organizational Change Modeling

The third principle for building survivable systems (discussed in this book) is the use of complexity theory (i.e., complex and nonlinear systems theory) for complex, business process modeling. Casti (1998) defines organizational change as an "emergent" process, a system behavior that results from the interactions of many actors internal and external to the system. It is not feasible to predict the emergent behavior of the system from an understanding of the behavior of each actor in isolation. In an organizational setting, these actors could be people on loading docks, or software response personnel at call centers. Even with proper instructions, people on loading docks do not check the integrity of the pallets in the same manner, neither do call center personnel handle each customer's complain with the same courtesy. For decades, Psychologists, and Experimental Economists have concluded repeatedly, that individuals within the organization do not always act as *consistent rational actors*. If one cannot assume a uniform behavior from the members of the organization, it is impossible to predict any organization emergent behavior (Lissack, 2005; as cited in Staw, 1991; and Hogarth and Reder, 1987).

While social pressures tend to move members of an organization to comply with uniform norms, values, and perceptions, "there are still very powerful forces remaining that steer people towards peculiar behavior" (Homan, 1950; cited in Lissack, 2003). These peculiar differences among the members of the organization make up the elements that must be understood before one can predict the behavior of the organization.

The application of complexity (chaos) theory to explain the behavior of an organization aims to help managers understand the complex interactions between the actors within the organization and the implications of the emergent whole (Levy, 1994). It is also helpful to know that complex (chaotic) systems exhibit some degree of order in the short term, thereby providing the possibility to understand the patterns of interactions of the actors. Complexity science can help explain how peculiar differences of the actors interact to predict the emergent behavior of the organization in the short term. Since it is impossible to make long-term predictions for complex (chaotic) systems, due to uncertainties in the behaviors of the actors, "an organization must be flexible enough to adapt, creative enough to innovate, and responsive enough to learn" (Crossan, White, Lane, and Klus, 1996; cited in

Lissack, 2005)

Different perspectives for and against complexity theory for business process modeling

To develop a basis for recommending the application of complexity theory to build survivable system, the following paragraphs present a review of fifteen articles grouped into four categories:

1. Motivations for understanding complexity or chaos theory

2. A case against using complexity theory

3. Some approaches for analyzing complex systems

4. Application of complexity theory to business processes.

The following paragraphs group the articles according to their respective category and describe the main contributions of each article. I have provided a more in-depth and critical review of each article in Appendix D for interested readers.

Motivations for understanding complexity or chaos theory

Five of the articles make very convincing cases for a need to understand complexity theory. (1) Beyerchen (1998)-How the Language of Complexity Reveals Hidden Habits of Mind. (2) Pascale (1999)-Surfing the Edge of Chaos. (3) Tetenbaum (1998)-Shifting Paradigms: From Newton to Chaos. (4) Warren and Franklin (1998)-New Directions in Systems Theory: Chaos and Complexity. (5) Hallinan (1997)-The Sociological Study of Social Change.

A common strand that runs through the five articles is the need for people to change their mental models in order to understand and appreciate the power of complexity theory. Beyerchen (1998) attributes the cause of a slow acceptance of the science of complexity to people's habits rooted in language, attitudes and organizations. The current style of observing the environment is rooted in linear cause and effects. To understand complexity, one needs to modify one's language to include the language of complexity, such as chaos, fractals, self-organizing systems, complex adaptive system, nonlinearity, metaphors and so on. Beyerchen's advice that people should start thinking in nonlinear ways and embrace the use of metaphors (a network of suggested relationships) as powerful cognitive filters to shape our habits and actions is fundamental to any social change. Thinking linearly limits people's learning and growth both in organizations and in politics.

Pascale's article *Surfing the Edge of Chaos* (1999) presents peoples' linear ways of thinking from a historical perspective by tracing application of complexity theory to strategic management process. In tracing the history of strategic management theories from the 1940s through the 1980s, several limitations of the old theories reveal people's linear ways of thinking. The old theories rely on the Newtonian laws of dynamic equilibrium. It is important to understand that organizational systems do not follow the laws of dynamic equilibrium and the theory of complexity is more suitable to manage complex adaptive systems. Pascale's suggestion of the need to embrace complexity theory is believable from a report on how the theory was applied successfully in Royal Dutch/Shell to evolve a new organization.

The title of Tetenbaum's article *Shifting Paradigms: From Newton to Chaos* (1998) repeats the need for a change in linear way of thinking to nonlinear ways. The leaders of organizations would benefit from a shift in management thinking from mechanistic linear and continuous view of the Newtonian model to the complex and unpredictable phenomenon of chaos theory. Since organizational systems do not exhibit linear and predictive behaviors, managers or leaders that hold the belief that organizational systems behave in a linear and continuous form are bound to fail.

Viewing chaos and complexity as *new directions* in systems theory, Warren and Franklin (1998) advise social work professionals to consider the theory in their research. Many social scientists shy away from using complexity theory to study complex systems due to their poor skills in mathematics. It is never too late to develop the necessary skills to improve the quality of research. Social scientists who wish to overcome any concerns about the mathematics of the theory, should read the authors' presentation of the basic concepts underlying the discipline of nonlinear dynamics and their application to social work.

Hallinan's report on sociological study of social change is the most insightful piece of scholarly report because as a sociologist, she recognizes the limitations of the assumptions of linearity underlying current theories in social and behavioral science research. Also, she has a sound understanding of chaos theory and she is able to make a good case for its adoption by social change researchers.

The assumption that social change phenomena exhibit linear and continuous change has created a mindset in which the goal is to predict social changes, rather than explain them. Using the failure of traditional social change theories to predict several catastrophic social changes such as the collapse of communism in the former Soviet Union, the author invites readers to investigate and apply the merits of nonlinear dynamical theory. She explains that since chaos is inherent in social systems, the goal is to find the critical point when the system changes from being stable to being unstable. Her advice that the mathematics of chaos and catastrophe theories holds the promise to help explain nonlinear and discontinuous phenomena found in social systems, is the strongest motivation to exploit possible application in organizational change research.

In summary, the five articles ask for a paradigm shift in people's way of thinking about complex systems and call out to researchers and practitioners to embrace and understand the merits of the new science of complexity.

A Case against Using Complexity Theory

While most of the articles referenced earlier recommend the need for a paradigm shift in the way people observe social change phenomena and apply the theory of nonlinear dynamics, Khalil (1995) holds the opinion that the theory is being misapplied. He is in favor of applying nonlinear dynamics theory to systems that he defines as non-purposeful (i.e., systems such as mob behavior, the stock market, storms and fad cycles as non-purposeful because of the length of their existence).

While he recognizes the value of applying such a technique from the physical sciences to social systems, he is not convinced that using thermodynamic feedback is the right approach for understanding living systems (i.e., purposeful systems). The author endorses only those theories from the study of genes and biology that reflect evolutionary system dynamics. While considering the use of nonlinear dynamical theory to model social change as a fad, he did not provide any ideas on how to model what he calls non-purposeful systems even though those systems behave just as living systems. His point is worth investigating to determine the effect of temporal variables in modeling social systems.

Approaches for Managing Complex Systems

Six articles recommend specific methods for managing different aspects of complex systems. (1) Lloyd (1995) describes techniques for controlling complex systems. (2) Vladimir (1999) explains the use of fuzzy logic to address problems in social complexity. (3) Nakamura and Kunimatani (1998) demonstrate how a model of the foraging pattern of ants can be used to explain behavior of complex systems. (4) Talukdar (1999) proposes modeling complex systems in the form of collaboration rules among software agents could improve the performance efficiency of such systems. (5) Epstein (1999) recommends the use of agent-based computational models to conduct research in social science. (6) Liu (1996) describes the implications of self-organizing theory (i.e., dissipative structure theory) in managing information systems. Each of the following paragraphs presents a brief description of the approach proposed by each author or group of authors respectively.

Lloyd based his research on developing a general framework for the systematic development of algorithms for the control of complex, nonlinear systems in the face of incomplete system description and dynamic noise. The research, performed at Santa Fe Institute and the Massachusetts Institute of Technology (MIT), had a lofty research goal given the challenges in understanding the behaviors of complex system. The author is cognizant of the fact that controlling a nonlinear system requires insight and intuition, without which algorithms could not be developed. The author bases the research and development efforts on the premise that all complex systems exhibit two sets of features: (1) predictable and deterministic features that follow some simple rules and 2) random features that the rules cannot predict. The research relies on applying Shannon's information theory and adaptive control theory but the most formidable challenge lies in obtaining probabilistic information to help the author develop appropriate algorithms.

Vladimir describes the process of working with social complexity and claims that fuzzy logic can help in understanding chaotic behavior of social systems. He presents the results of a research on consensus seeking social system exercise based on fuzzy logic. The author identifies three opportunities in social systems which fuzzy logic theory can help understand: (1) Fuzzy logic can explain contradictions and inconsistencies in social systems, (2) It can also explain those issues that have been restrained due to traumatic social conditions, and (3) It can explain hidden or unobservable social phenomena. The author also emphasizes the most beneficial feature of fuzzy logic as its ability to deal with vague, ambiguous and uncertain qualitative concepts. This view is fundamental to the application of fuzzy logic in other disciplines.

The authors (Nakamura and Kunimatani, 1998) report research results that model the foraging behavior of ant colony. They describe the collective emergent behavior of the ants resulting from individual interactions among the ants. Lacking an approach to model how ants use the strength of pheromones to perform their foraging tasks, the authors developed a simplified model that employs the quantity of food available. While such a simplified model seems to balance the simulated performance of the social system, the authors do not explain how the ants, relying only on the strength of pheromone trails, are able to control their foraging pattern. The research methodology is promising but further research is needed to gain acceptance.

Talukdar (1999) explores the feasibility of employing software agents distributed over computer networks to collaborate efficiently. The author conjectures that an addition of software agents will improve the quality of the solution to a problem, and an addition of computers will improve solution speed is basic commonsense. On the assertion that there are simple rules for designing a multi-agent model of an organization to solve complex problems, the paper claims that collaboration among the agents obeying such simple rules is automatic and the system should be scalable. It would be more helpful if the author had mentioned the challenges inherent in developing the simple rules as reported by Sipress (1999).

Epstein (1999) argues that an agent-based computational modeling approach (e.g., modeling artificial societies) provides some unique strategies for conducting research in social science and defines a generative system as a system that grows (e.g., a living system). The author questions the traditional use of the term "emergence" (defined as stable macroscopic patterns that arise from interactions among local agents in a social system). The author disagrees with emergent theory (or classical emergentism) which states that the knowledge of the whole cannot be deduced from a complete knowledge of individual parts. The author also claims that agent-based modeling is incompatible with

61

classical *emergentism* because in the author's view agent-based modeling is *reductionistic*. The author believes that an accurate description of the rules of individual agents is possible because agent-based modeling is based on bottom-up observation as opposed to equation-based research used in classical *emergentism*. The view expressed in the paper shows a lack of knowledge of chaotic dynamical systems, because all the experiments described define the goal of social science as that of attaining stable equilibrium. Chaos theory and the theory of self-organization have demonstrated that a system in stable equilibrium is a dead system and it cannot adapt. However, he recognizes some of the limitations of agent-based modeling.

The author (Liu, 1996) examines the impact of the theory of dissipative structures and synergetics on the management of information systems. After presenting a brief summary of the theory, the author explains how entropy (the degree of disorder in a system) could be applied to information system management. The author's line of reasoning was easy to follow due to the author's definition of five types of entropy commonly found in systems: component, structural, functional, timeliness and situational. The author presents the relationship between dissipative structure theory and traditional management theory along with an explanation of the use of order to explain information systems. With an ample set of examples, the author presents how one could identify internal components and different types of entropy in different information subsystems. The use of the library as a complex information where order is paramount, followed by the use self-organizing theory, to explain how order in a complex system can be maintained helps in explaining the utility of the methodology.

Applications of Complexity Theory to Business Processes

Three additional papers by way of examples demonstrate the feasibility of applying complexity or chaos theory to three different domains (traffic management, network management and electronic commerce). This demonstrates a broad appeal of the methodology. The author (Sipress, 1999) reports ongoing research on application of complexity theory at Los Alamos Laboratory to understand highway rush hour traffic patterns in the Washington Post. The research applies traffic chaos theory with the goal of identifying "phase changes" in traffic. The phase changes could be considered bifurcation points when traffic pattern changes from free flowing to stop-and-go. The research compares phase changes to transition points when water changes to steam or ice. The primary goal of the researchers is to understand the exact timing of the bifurcation points. Since chaos is governed by simple rules (Tetenbaum, 1998) used by the agents within the system, the researchers need to understand the simple rules used by the commuters. This is not trivial, but a solution will help control traffic flow and reduce the frustration of commuters and commuting time.

The authors (Schoonderwoerd, Holland and Bruten, 1997) present an approach in which a model of mobile software agents, exhibiting ant-like behaviors, perform message traffic load-balancing tasks, in a telecommunication network. Load balancing is the process of distributing call traffic to avoid congestion in a telecommunication network. The authors compare three techniques: (1) conventional shortest path message traffic routing, (2) algorithmic and heuristic-based mobile agent technique and (3) a social systems approach that exploits the behavior of ants. The authors conclude that a method that employs the pheromone-laying behavior of ants exhibits the most efficient load balancing process. The method is interesting but further research is needed to gain a wider support in the research community.

The authors (Kelly, Maes, Sims and Morley, 1998) describe how complexity theory is being applied in the virtual marketplace-specifically, in the application of intelligent software agents to electronic commerce and business organizations. They identify three ways that organizations can use complexity in the marketplace. First, complexity is used as a metaphor to investigate other ways of doing business. Secondly, complexity as a metaphor used in simulations to observe new patterns that emerge and thirdly, complexity as a metaphor for embedding complex systems in business and using them to run the business. The authors then present the pros and cons of applying distributed agents that serve a virtual marketplace with some theoretical insights from professionals in the industry and academia to deserve a review. Answers from a panel of experts help identify the strengths and limitations of applying complexity theory to the market place.

Conclusion

This chapter has presented the principles and methods of finite element modeling for product modeling; modeling and simulation science for process modeling; and complex and nonlinear systems theory for organizational change modeling. The chapter also presents the benefits and limitations of each approach.

A review of the views of proponents and opponents of the theory of complexity, presents a balanced view of the approach. Five of the articles on complexity theory describe some motivations for mastering the approach and one paper presents an opposing viewpoint. Six papers present different approaches for researching complex systems while three papers present application of complexity to three different domains to demonstrate the general applicability of the methodology. The most important advice that all the papers have in common is the call to view social phenomena as nonlinear and unpredictive. Therefore, researchers in social and behavioral systems should adopt a paradigm shift in the way they view such systems. The next three chapters present the applications of the principles and methods described in this chapter.

CHAPTER 4: PRODUCT MODELING AND APPLICATIONS USING FINITE ELEMENT METHOD

Finite Element Modeling/Analysis (FEM/FEA) is a technique used to determine the structural integrity of a physical object by mathematically simulating and loading it to determine how it will behave under stress. It is a cost-effective approach to design a prototype and perform "what if" analysis on the system. Researchers and designers have used this technique to model systems/products as big as building structures, bridges, automobiles, and as small as small electronic components successfully. This chapter documents some of my work and related work of other researchers who have employed FEM for product modeling. The Chapter also describes research activities at the Stanford Research Institute, and examples of developed models and computation code available from their archive.

Front-Impact and Crashworthiness Modeling of a Car

The body deformation profile of a motor vehicle is critical to the survival of the occupants of the vehicle. Consumer Reports Magazine has reported comparisons of crash repair costs if identical vehicles are tested at 5 miles per hour speed, ranging from $100 to $1200.

As a product design engineer in the Body Engineering Division of Ford Motor Company in Dearborn, Michigan, I was involved in applying FEM to establish the crashworthiness of a mid-size car for compliance with the Federal Highway Traffic Safety Administration (FHTSA) safety standards. The focus of the research was to protect occupant survival by preventing deadly gyrations in the event of an accident. The goal was to use the structural integrity of the front bumper and deformation of the front section of the car to absorb most of the energy from the crash to protect the gyrations of the dummies inside the car. The amount of energy transferred to the crash dummies can be reduced significantly if the shock absorber responds as expected with the front bumper, and the metallic front fenders fold like an accordion. Using a car prototype, we developed a finite element model of the whole car and applied different loads to the front end to study deformation characteristics of the front end. Then, we subjected the car to frontal and angular impacts against a rigid barrier at speeds of 5, 10, 15, and 35 miles per hour. The instruments and cameras, at the crash site, provided us with the amount of force applied to the car, speed, and image of the deformation, and other parameters for further studies. Using the information on the failed components, we were able to identify the causes of the failures. We use this information to redesign the components. We then had the components fabricated and installed in the car, then subjected the car to a new crash test. We repeated this process of modeling failed components, fabrication of a new component, and crash tests until we obtained reasonable sheet metal deformation characteristics and energy transfer values that met the FHTSA crashworthiness standards. The FEM helped us reduce the number of times the car components was re-fabricated and the number of crash tests. We were able to predict how the car would respond in a real life crash.

We also employed FEM to determine a car's front bumper deep and rear bumper rise when brakes are applied, just before a rear end collision with a truck. There are many crash incidents where a car's (especially, the smaller types) front bumper is lower than the rear bumper on a truck, causing the car to go under the truck resulting in serious or fatal injuries to the occupant(s) of the car. This situation could be exacerbated if another vehicle collides with the rear of the car, thereby pushing the car further under the truck. The focus of our research was to determine the optimum design for truck rear bumpers, and cars' front and rear bumpers' configurations (heights) to meet FHTSA standards.

In addition, as a product design engineer at the Boeing Company in Seattle, I found the use of FEM very helpful in modeling the effect of heat and the effects that collision with external objects could cause on the nacelle (aircraft body) or the wing of an aircraft. The MCS/NASTRAN finite element modeling software was used for this research.

Related Work of Others on Application of FEM

A 1998 Audi A8 Crash Analysis: Aramayo and Bobrek (2001) have published the results from their research where they used a FEM of a 1998 Audi A8 for crash analysis. Funded by the U.S. Department of Energy, their FEM design was used to analyze frontal impact against a rigid material to assess the passenger vehicle's crashworthiness against the FHTSA standards. The researchers published their research strategy, the software tools used to generate the finite element mesh, the properties of the materials of all segments of the vehicle, the software used to generate the finite element mesh (TrueGrid^{TM}), plus the software and platform for simulating 35 mph frontal impacts, computation and analysis of results. The research, which modeled all the components of the vehicle, provided some detailed statistics of the product model. The model consists of 295,466 node points, 2,411 solid hexahedra, 290,048 shells, 797 beam elements, 198 component materials with an equivalent weight of 1.718 Metric tones (about 3,436 pounds). The research report includes images of the car's top and side view of front impacts and and references to additional research results.

Three Dimensional Model of the Human Skull and Brain: While I would not characterize this research as a product model, I think the research is worth describing to inform the reader about the power of FEM for modeling and analyzing any object, regardless of its complexity. Gerald Krabbel at the Institute of Automotive Engineering, Berlin University of Technology and Ralph Mailler at the Orthopedic Biomechanics Laboratory, Harvard Medical School reported their research on the development of a 3-dimensional FEM. The purpose of the research was to study human head impact tolerance to understand severe injury resulting from traffic accidents. Statistics on accidents has shown that head injury is the most frequent and serious type of injury experienced by car occupants involved in road accidents. Using a representative finite element human head model generated from CAT Scan and MRI digital data, allowed them to assess the effects of injury from different impact conditions. They were able to document injury mechanisms and formulate tolerances the brain can sustain in the event of an accident, which aided them to develop and recommend head injury protection criteria for the automotive industry.

The 3-D skull model consists of 13,962 solids with 20,876 nodes. The brain consists of 9,273 solids with 11,152 nodes. The research used linear elastic properties for the skull and visco-elastic properties for the brain.

FEM Examples and Computational Code at the Stanford Research Institute (SRI) Archive: The Center for Fracture Physics at SRI has conducted a variety of research on how structures respond under extreme loading conditions. These loading conditions include impact, blast, thermal, corrosion, fatigue, and large deformation static loads. Some of the examples available from SRI include fracture of welded steel structures, crashworthiness of high-speed trains, analysis of structures subjected to earthquakes, and analysis of biologic materials for medical applications.

Examples of computational code include *DYNA3D*—a nonlinear, explicit, 3-D finite element code for the large deflection dynamic analysis of solids and structures. *NIKE3D*—a nonlinear implicit, 3-D finite element code for solid and structural mechanics. *TOPAZ3D*—a nonlinear 3-D finite element heat transfer code for analyzing static and heat transfer in complex structures. *TAURUS*—an interactive 3-D postprocessor for analyzing data generated from DYNA3D, NIKE3D and TOPAZ3D. Interested readers should visit SRI website at http://www.sri.com/psd/fracture/fe_program.html.

Conclusion

This chapter has presented the applications of Finite Element Modeling to support the principles described in the previous chapter. The purpose of this chapter is to give the reader an appreciation of the variety of applications suitable for FEM. These application areas cover structures engineering (e.g., automobile, bridges, and aircrafts) and biomechanics (e.g., modeling the human skull and the brain). Just as modeling and simulation science supports the development of survivable solutions for complex processes, the use of FEM (where applicable) for product modeling will promote development of a survivable product. The next chapter presents the applications of modeling and simulation science.

CHAPTER 5: PROCESS MODELING AND APPLICATIONS USING SIMULATION SCIENCE

Over the years, modeling and simulation science has been a very powerful tool to assess different process design and operational scenarios. Used in compressed time mode, it provides the opportunity for a quick review of the consequences of selected courses of action. It is very common to use it in war games, to determine the amount of force to apply for a variety of battle campaigns. Only the creativity of the user limits its application. The concept of modeling and simulation is not complicated. Given any system, the modeler needs to identify the entity of interest whose system transit time is the focus of investigation. Each entity needs to consume some amount of resources as it passes through the system. It may need to wait in queue for some time before it can gain access to the resource. It must also spend some time consuming the resource (calculated as resource utilization). The length of time spent in queue and consuming the resource depends on the entity's priority and other characteristics, such as the amount of resource required and its position in the queue. The total amount of time the entity spends in the system (i.e. entry to exit) depends on the number and types of resource that it needs. What the modeler selects as the entity depends on the domain under investigation. In a telecommunication network, the entities are typically the messages or packets flowing through the network components (i.e. connections, switches, routers, concentrators, etc.). These components are the resources.

When modeling the road traffic system within a city, the entities are the vehicles, while the resources are the roadways, traffic lights, etc. Statistics of such values as the time spent in queue of each resource and resource utilization (the amount of time the resource expends servicing each entity) characterize the performance of the system. Since predicting the future behavior of a process system performance is the goal of modeling and simulation science, it is critical to use a sound statistical approach to defend any resultant recommendation. Prediction of the performance of specific scenarios should include a confidence level grounded in statistics. The rest of this chapter describes four simulation applications that I have been involved in developing over the years. I expect these applications to give those readers who are not familiar with modeling and simulation science, some appreciation of the benefits of the technique. The examples are: a) Modeling the manufacturing process of graphite composite at the Boeing Company. (ii) Modeling the national US mail processing and delivery system for the US Postal Service. (iii) developing a simulation model of the Earth-Mars Telecommunications and Information Management System including antenna-pointing determination for NASA Glen Research Center. Following the descriptions of these applications, I discuss other researchers' projects that employ modeling and simulation science. These research projects include:

- A simulation model for managing survivability of networked information system
- Airspace concepts evaluation system (ACES)
- The Federal Aviation Administration (FAA) Air Traffic Management for the National Airspace System, and the Department of Defense's net-centric operations for the Global Information Grid for battle management.

Graphite Composite Manufacturing Process Simulation

To meet production schedules for a new aircraft with graphite composite parts, the Boeing Company needed a simulation model of the new manufacturing process to produce the composites. A manufacturing process is required for cutting the sheets of graphite composites into acceptable geometric shapes with minimal waste, due to the high cost of the material. The left over pieces of the composites are not reusable. After cutting, the next process involved optimally loading the composites into autoclaves for a curing operation. Optimal loading of the autoclave was critical because each curing process could cost about $50,000. Optimum loading of the autoclave involved optimum configuration of the geometrically shaped materials to fit into the oven to reduce the number of times to fire the ovens, thus resulting in cost savings. After the curing process, each pieced went through an inspection process in the "through transmission ultrasonic" inspection unit to determine their porosity by running water over the surfaces. The manufacturing manager needed to know the size and quantity of the inspection unit to purchase to meet the new aircraft production schedule of 20 aircrafts per month. Large inspection unit costs over $100,000 while small unit costs about $74,000. The initial plan was to purchase one large and two small inspection units. We simulated the graphite composite as the entity that flows through the manufacturing process and consumed human resources at every stage of the process—cutting—visual inspection—autoclave—ultrasonic inspection. The simulation model produced a set of graphite composite that met production targets. We were able to recommend the purchase of only one large and one small inspection unit resulting in a cost avoidance of $74,000.

The US Postal Service Mail Processing Automation and Delivery Process Simulation

In response to customer complaints regarding delays in mail delivery, the US Postal Service decided to automate the mail processing operations at their mail processing centers. They were also interested in improving delivery schedules by trucks to the post offices and the mail sorting process at each post office. To aid the pedestrian mail carrier, the Postal Service was interested in finding ways to find the optimum route to deliver the mail and save time.

The USPS instructed us (as contractors) to work with four mail processing equipment manufacturers and USPS personnel to select one of four designs. After selecting one mail processing equipment, we then developed an end-to-end simulation model of mail flow from the processing plant to delivery to the customer. This process involved a hybrid simulation model. The mail processing at the processing center followed a continuous system simulation model since we had to consider hundreds of pieces per minute. We modeled the rest of the processes as discrete events. Just as with the previous application, we identified the entities and the resources. The pieces or bundles of mail constitute the entities and the resources include mail-processing machines, personnel, transport trucks and drivers, the Post Offices and mail sorting areas, mail carriers, and delivery routes. Using SIMSCRIPT, a simulation programming language with discrete and continuous event processing, and some graphics and statistical packages we simulated several scenarios and presented several options to the decision makers at the USPS. The decision makers had the tools to conduct several "what if" analysis and corresponding cost benefits or penalties for each option.

Earth-Mars Telecommunications and Information Management System Process Modeling

I was the Principal Investigator for the research on Earth-Mars Telecommunications and Information Management System (TIMS) network modeling and unattended network operations. NASA Glenn Research Center funded this research and a complete report is available from NASA's Center for Aerospace Information at http://sti.nasa.gov. The primary focus of the research is to investigate the feasibility of TIMS architecture which links the Earth-based Mars Operations Control Center, Science Data Processing Facility, Mars Network Management Center and Deep Space Network of antennae to the relay satellites and other communication network elements based in the Mars region. Two design requirements for this model are: 1) the model should be capable of guaranteeing message deliveries, and 2) it should support real-time and near-real-time, management operations with minimal human intervention. This was important because it takes about 20 minutes for a message to travel between the two planets. We used packets as the entities for the system.

To guarantee message delivery, we employed a message-flooding algorithm, such that every node receiving a packet forwards the packet to the nearest node, and sends duplicates to other forwarding nodes in its proximity. We used the Block Oriented Network Simulator (BONeS) to develop a TIMS network modeling and simulation model to support our investigation. We collected throughput statistics for each node in the network including statistics on the volume of messages/packets entering and/or leaving each node. We documented the results of several "what-if" scenarios along with reports on upgraded antenna visibility-determination software and unattended network management prototype.

Related Research Using Modeling and Simulation Science

A Simulation Model for Managing Survivability of Networked Information System: Moitra and Konda (2000) developed a survivability simulation model to test the effectiveness of defensive measures in the face of attacks on a networked information system. By introducing simulated random attacks on the network, (i.e., virus injection, denial of service, etc.), they were able to cause failures of network components. This provided an environment for assessing the impact on system survivability as measured by the type of services that can survive. The research follows the classic system modeling and simulation methodology and stochastic modeling strategy presented in Chapter 3 of this book. Using a typical network modeling strategy, message traffic (generated stochastically) flows through the system. The network is then subjected to random attacks (incidents) and network performance data are collected and analyzed. The research investigated different defense mechanisms to mitigate the impact of the attacks and rate of recovery of the network. Using this model, the research was able to investigate different scenarios that can lead to catastrophic failures. The researchers used different attack scenarios on the network, to develop a measure of system survivability as the ratio of system performance level at a new state to normal performance level. They also developed formal methods for establishing system survivability metric for worst-case scenarios. The simulation model provides an excellent environment for designing survivable networks and for training network managers. The same strategy is used to develop aircraft simulators and to investigate possible design flaws in aircraft avionics.

Airspace Concepts Evaluation System (ACES). Funded by NASA Ames Research Center, a consortium of companies have developed ACES to provide fast-time simulation and modeling capability to support design and trade-off investigation of the operations of the National Airspace System (NAS). The High Level Architecture (HLA) employs an agent-based modeling paradigm to assess the impact of new NAS tools and concepts on the overall system. A typical ACES simulation run involves about 38,000 agents, 150,000 activities, approximately 3 million messages pushed through 300,000 communication channels (Aronson, Manikonda, Peng, Levy, and Roth, 2002; Mario Perez, 2003).

The Federal Aviation Administration (FAA) has several modeling and simulation models to support Air Traffic Management and reduce the cost of congestions and delays in the National Airspace System. To investigate the performance of their Network-centric operations of the Global Information Grid (GIG), the Department of Defense and their contractors routinely use modeling and simulation science to create battles and simulate aircraft, tanks, and battalions of infantry to conduct network-centric warfare. As stated earlier, the use of modeling and simulation science is limitless.

Conclusion

Since the purpose of modeling and simulation science is to predict the future behavior (i.e., performance) of a process, it is critical that the analyst or researcher possess a sound knowledge of statistics to ensure a reliable prediction. The analysts should not underestimate the value that system managers place on the results from a simulation study. However, if later, they find the results to be unreliable, it will very difficult to convince the management to fund future efforts.

This chapter has presented a brief description of the applications of modeling and simulation science developed by this author and other researchers. A review of those reports should give some insights into the values of simulation science in building survivable processes. The next chapter describes the applications of complex systems theory to modeling business systems.

Building Survivable Systems

CHAPTER 6: BUSINESS PROCESS MODELING AND APPLICATIONS BASED ON COMPLEX SYSTEMS THEORY

As depicted in Figure 2-2 in Chapter 2, a business process consists of interactions of tasks, people, departments, divisions: internal and external economic, political; and cultural forces. The interactions of these organizational components make the organization a complex system. Therefore, selected business process modeling (BPM) software tools need to be able to support these complex interactions, plus the social and technical needs of the system. Each BPM tool consists of several software modules. Each module may represent a component of the business system. The models of the components must interact and conform to the theory of complex systems to produce a viable emergent behavior for the business system.

BPM is a management discipline that requires organizations to shift to process-centric thinking, and to reduce their reliance on traditional territorial and functional structures. BPM has evolved from past management theories and practices, such as total quality management (TQM) and business process re-engineering (BPR). BPM requires and enables organizations to manage the complete cycle of their processes, from process design to monitoring and optimization. In addition, BPM can accommodate frequent changes of processes to adjust to changing circumstances. Such rapid changes are impractical while processes are embedded in conventional applications. The development of BPM technologies is enabling business managers to conceptualize process flows and rules from the underlying applications and infrastructure, and to change them directly.

BPM is not a technology and it is also not an updated version of BPR, but an IT enabled management discipline. It represents a fundamental change in how businesses manage and run their operational processes. Businesses today face increasing competition, especially on cost and quality. They also face stricter regulations that require tighter business operations. On the other hand, uncertainty and volatility in business and politics continue to demand greater flexibility. To meet these challenges, organizations must find ways to improve the management of their business processes, that is, the ways in which they operate (Keen, 2004).

Only excellent processes can enable organizations to meet competitive challenges in organizational change management and demonstrate compliance with regulations. Only excellent and responsive process management can provide the flexibility needed to respond to changing conditions. Moreover, making processes visible will provide new information about business operations, enabling business managers to make better and timely business decisions, and possibly leading to innovations. In practice, these changes require a management discipline that treats processes as distinct assets and that is what BPM does.

BPM requires changes in governance to emphasize processes and shared performance goals, rather than functions and territories; and shared, rather than local, performance goals, new skills and supporting technologies. Purposefully deployed, BPM will make organizations more efficient and agile, and enable them to make better process outsourcing decisions. However, implementing BPM is difficult and human barriers of inertia and vested interests, can be a big problem to any significant change. The inflexibility of IT application systems and the immaturity of the necessary methods and tools are also impediments.

Although processes are increasingly being recognized as important, the approach to BPM implementation has been an ad hoc collection of applications, middleware, workflow, manual procedures and user knowledge. The key to BPM success is to represent the whole of each process in a single model and provide a comprehensive set of model-based tools that support all stages of the process life cycle. The tools that may be assembled into a Business Process Management Suite (BPMS) can then enable business managers to change processes more easily. The adoption of BPM will strengthen competitive advantage for companies. The companies will enjoy increased efficiency, less-intrusive compliance, increased alignment between operations and strategy, and greater agility. They will also get to play stronger roles in inter-organizational processes and may contribute to reshaping the industries in which they participate (Keen, 2003).

BPM as a Management Discipline

BPM is a management discipline that treats business processes as assets to be valued, designed and exploited in their own right. It is a structured approach employing methods, policies, metrics, management practices and software tools to manage and continuously optimize an organization's activities and processes. It aims to improve agility and operational performance. It treats processes as organizational building blocks with as much, if not more, significance as functional areas and geographic territories. The BPM discipline has implications for four aspects of business:

1. *Strategy* In their book titled *IT Doesn't Matter, Business Process Do*, Smith and Fingar (2003) restate Andrew Spanyi's view on Business Process Management as a Team Sport as follows:

> The ability to execute on strategy is the litmus
> test of great strategy ideas, and that test comes
> from tightly linking enterprise business
> processes to strategy formulation. Great ideas
> are one thing, the ability to execute them means
> technology-enabled business process management

The organization's business processes must execute the organization's strategy. Processes provide a shorter link between strategy and operations by overcoming the vested interests of territorial and functional managers. Although operational changes within a functional unit are relatively easy to make, conflicts of interest between functions often inhibit any shared understanding of the need for broader process change to reach strategic objectives.

2. *Governance* There should be explicit responsibility for business processes and policies at the highest levels of the organization, and for sub-processes at the departmental level. Business objectives drive process performance objectives, which motivate staff and business partners. There must be clear accountability for the approval, implementation and audit of process and business rule changes.

3. *Organization* The organizational structure must recognize the interdependencies and relationships that foster value creation across the enterprise. BPM de-emphasizes hierarchical reporting relationships and empowers employees to seek improvements across organizational boundaries.

4. *Culture* The methods, procedures and skills that support all stages of the process life cycle must be conducive to rapid change.

There is a culture of constant change to stay in step with fluctuating business conditions.

BPM-Enabling Technologies

BPM requires software tools that business managers can use to control and modify their processes. Specifically, it requires technologies that make processes explicit, that is, clearly expressed and readily changed. These tools provide graphical models that enable managers to control various aspects of business operations and invoke the relevant resources. BPM-enabling technologies have existed for many years as point products supporting explicit control of particular aspects of a process, such as human workflow, document and image routing, and system-to-system interaction patterns. However, since 2000 these products have been converging into suites to support business managers' desire for greater ability to control work, including manual and automated tasks. The greatest benefits will be obtained from the synergies between these technologies, especially from their capability to enable business managers to make rapid process improvements. The appearance of integrated BPM-enabling technologies is part of the disaggregation of application software and is an example of the trend toward building software systems from small "chunks." Currently, BPM-enabling technologies are available as separate specialty tools, as integrated BPM Suites (BPMSs), and are being added to some major application packages.

Process models are needed to help business and IT managers understand actual processes and enable them, by visualization and simulation, to propose improvements. Modeling tools also help produce the documentation required by various standards such as ISO 9000. Explicit process models are easily changed because non-technical managers understand them easily and they are independent of the underlying resources. Models provide a basis for cross-organizational collaboration between managers responsible for the separate parts of a process, as well as with IT professionals on the implementation of the resulting design. The key elements of a process model are the events that trigger actions, the sequences of steps, and the business rules used in and between those steps to support decision making and execution flow. To support simulation, the models must also embrace characteristics such as skills, availability and costs of the people, and other resources that perform the process. Business process modeling tools, also known as business process analysis (BPA) tools, provide a shared environment for the capture, design and simulation of business processes by business analysts, managers, architects and other IT professionals. Models are generally shown in graphical form. BPA tools are modeling-only environments, not execution environments.

Executing the Process

To support the entire process life cycle, from modeling through execution to monitoring, the process model must become the core of the actual business process. Making a model executable requires other BPM-enabling software, such as integration technology, a runtime environment and rule engines. Many of the enabling technologies continue to be available separately. When provided together, the system is known as BPMS.

A BPMS contains core BPM-enabling tools that include the following:

1. *Orchestration* engines coordinate the sequencing of the activities and steps (system and manual) according to the flows and rules in the process model.

2. *Business intelligence and analysis* tools support analysis of data produced during process execution. Capabilities can range from reporting to online analytical processing analysis to graphical

user dashboards. Business Activity Monitoring (BAM) systems do this in real time with proactive alerting.

3. *Rule engines* execute rules that abstract business policies and decision tables from the underlying applications, and make available more-flexible process changes.

4. *Repositories* contain process definitions, process components, process models, business rules and other process data to enable reuse across multiple processes.

5. *Simulation and optimization* tools enable business managers to compare new process designs with current operational performance. Scenarios are executed, altering resource constraints and business goals, to assess risk and display the financial and operational (that is, timeliness and quality) impacts on the organization.

6. *Integration* tools link the model to other system assets (data and logic) that support work steps.

As the market for BPMS matures, additional technologies, such as document management and collaboration support, will be integrated into BPMSs.

BPM and Service-Oriented Architecture (SOA) for the Enterprise

Most business processes require hardware and software resources to perform functions such as complex processing, storage and retrieval of information, and connections to trading partners. Many of these functions are available in application systems and software tools, and are designed to be used directly by people and/or to include hard-coded process flows. BPM requires functions that can be called from a BPM suite (BPMS) independently of their flow control since that will now be provided via the BPMS itself. Hence, technically, the best architectural style to achieve this is a service-oriented architecture for the enterprise.

Attempts in the late 1990s to interconnect heterogeneous business processes of partner organizations led to the development of Enterprise Application Integration (EAI) architecture. Unfortunately, EAI has been rather costly to implement and maintain due to the significant level of effort required to master the EAI tools. A SAP AG White Paper reports that companies that have deployed EAI expend five times more resources working with the tools than on the EAI system. (http://sdn.sap.com). SOA addresses the limitations of EAI by packaging discrete functions into modular, encapsulated, shareable elements ("services") that local or remote "consumer" parts of the system can invoke in a loosely coupled manner. In addition, a best practice recommends Web-based services that use the XML-based Simple Object Access Protocol (SOAP), an XML language and protocol, for message exchange between the client and the server. SOAP uses common web transport protocols including HTTP, SMTP, and FTP. A major limitation of current commercial offerings of SOA-based systems using web services is the issue of security. The availability of the open source Globus Toolkit as a Service-Oriented Infrastructure technology from the Globus Alliance (http://Globus.org) will resolve the security and other limitations of current vendor offerings of SOA-based systems. Government contractors and those with access to the Department of Defense (DoD) portals can benefit from the knowledge of the Information Assurance specification for the DoD Global Information Grid (GIG).

Globus Service-Oriented Infrastructure and Open Source Grid Software

Globus Toolkit from the Globus Alliance is a service-oriented infrastructure technology with the following features:

- Software for service-oriented infrastructure that supports new and existing resources
- Tools to build applications that exploit service-oriented infrastructure, such as registries, security, data management, execution management, and common run runtime (Java, C, Python, etc)
- Open source and open standards

The Globus Toolkit provides the following open source grid software:

- Core web services as infrastructure for building new services
- Security that applies uniform policy across heterogeneous systems (i.e., credential management, web service authentication and authorization, community authorization service, and delegation service)
- Execution management for provisioning, deploying, and managing the services
- Data management for discovering, transferring and accessing large data sets
- Monitoring for discovering and monitoring dynamic services

The Value of Business Process Modeling

The process management discipline of the industrial age focused on efficiency and was impersonal. Managers concentrated on things that could be measured, especially time and cost, and notions such as TQM and continuous improvement became ordinary management tools. However, more recently, management has recognized the importance of the human contribution to work, especially as computers have taken over routine industrial age work. As value networks are becoming increasingly interdependent, the ability to lead and collaborate has become important. Technology has matured to the point, where it is an integral part of work, even, of work that is largely interpersonal. Good management now requires a balance of skills in process, staff management and use of IT. BPM embraces an approach where people and system interactions are equally important and closely integrated. A key value of the BPM discipline is reducing the time needed to make changes to processes. This discipline is acquired by adopting two important concepts:

- First, every business process requires a continuous and unending revision cycle. Today, implementing the application is often seen as the end of the revision process.
- Second, the engagement of process stakeholders is vital at every step of the process revision cycle. Traditionally, business stakeholders are generally involved at the start of the process, but often drop out subsequently.

There are nine steps of the process revision cycle and each one of them creates value in its own right. The steps include discovery, modeling, simulation, deployment execution, monitoring, analysis, optimization, and refining.

1. *Discovery* identifies the intricacies of how a process executes. The value of the discovery methodology comes from how quickly and accurately an organization can establish consensus among process stakeholders as to how work is accomplished and how to measure success.

2. *Modeling* is valuable because it shows easy improvement opportunities, or at least the scale of the problem. Modeling helps business leaders collaborate regarding how the process improvements will help achieve corporate goals, irrespective of organizational boundaries.

3. *Simulation* reveals bottlenecks that are not obvious during static modeling. Adjusting the workflows or decision points provides

fine-tuning in the process model before moving to the next phase of real-time process execution.

4. *Deployment* then creates detailed process execution scripts and makes the required changes in systems. Training and facility changes that are needed for the new process to work must be coordinated. The system changes include integration with applications and databases, and may include the conversion of application systems into sets of reusable Web services components.

5. *Execution* is where the main value of BPM is realized, because it's where the actual improvement in the process is first seen.

6. *Monitoring* collects information from the executing process in real time. Because the BPMS supports manual and automated activities, monitoring is more complete than what was available previously. Because it is collected in real time, it allows immediate corrections to take place.

7. *Analysis* creates further value when key performance indicators based on process execution are linked directly to business objectives.

8. *Optimization* is a fact-based approach to process scenario optimization, which greatly reduces risk and delivers value by eliminating the guesswork and intuition that typically have taken place around process optimization.

9. *Refinement* establishes the way the stakeholders want work to be accomplished.

Selected Criteria for Evaluating BPM Tools

As of this writing, there are over forty BPM vendors offering BPM product suites. The buyer should be aware of some evaluation criteria before selecting any of these products. David Essex (2006) has compiled a list of evaluation criteria and features of selected product suites. The following recommendations are worth of note:

1. If possible, avoid selecting tools with too many third party software tools. Tools with too many third party software may indicate that the product was not developed from the ground up which may lead to integration problems

2. Select tools that are based on industry standards in terms of security, networking protocols, messaging protocols, service oriented architecture, etc.

3. Consider ease of use. Non-technical business analysts and executives should be able to change the configuration of the BPM to support any changes to the business system.

4. The tool should be scalable so that it can grow to support multiple organizations.

5. The system should be able to support a socio-technical system such that it is human/technology-centric (i.e., it combines interaction rules for people and systems). Look for tools that support exception-handling strategies.

BPM vendors and their products:

Listed below are some of the vendors, their product offerings, and selected features:

- Appian Corporation, Vienna, VA (www.appian.com): Appian Enterprise 5. (*Human-centric, tools for collaboration, process/rules engines, simulation support, and business activity monitoring, etc.*)
- BEA Systems Inc., Plano, Texas (www.bea.com): FuegoBPM. (*Human-centric, Public Key Infrastructure (PKI), rules engine, and exception management, etc.*)
- SAP America Inc., Newton Square, PA (www.sap.com): ARIS for SAP NetWeaver. (*Human-centric, workflow management, process monitoring and alerting, System Integration-Centric, etc.*)
- Tibco Software Inc., Palo Alto, CA (www.tibco.com): Tibco Software Process Suite. (*Human-centric, PKI, high-volume transactions, exception handling, rules engine, process forecasting, etc.*).
- webMethods Inc., Fairfax, VA (www.webmethods.com): webMethods BPM. (*System integration-centric, predictive monitoring, exception handling, workflow management, etc.*)

The list of vendors is not exhaustive. Other players in the BPM product market include:

- Adobe Systems Inc: Adobe LiveCycle Workflow 7.0
- Agentis Software: Adaptive Enterprise Solution Suite
- Chordiant Software Inc: Chordiant Enterprise Platform
- IBM Corporation: Websphere
- Fujitsu Software Corporation: Fujitsu Interstate Business Process Manager 7.0
- Verity Inc: Liquid Office 4.0

- Gensym Corporation: G2 ReThink 4.0
- newScale Inc: newScale RequestCenter 2005

Applications of BPM Technology

US Marine Corps: The US Marine Corps has reported a $9 million cost savings from the application of the Appian Enterprise 5 suite to replace their heritage paper-intensive operations by a web based systems that connects administrators, internal customers, and contractors. Appian Corporation of Vienna, VA provided the solution, which runs on top of the Marine Corps' legacy systems (Essex, 2006).

Access Grid: The Access Grid® (http://www.accessgrid.com) is an application of a BPM system, the Globus Toolkit. The system holds a set of resources including multimedia large-format displays, presentation and interactive environments, and interfaces to Grid middleware and to visualization environments. The system supports group-to-group interactions such as large-scale distributed meetings, collaborative work sessions, seminars, lectures, tutorials, and training.

The infrastructure supports the issuing of user and host security certificates using Public Key Infrastructure (PKI). The system has issued over 3,400 certificates to users across 47 countries. The client nodes have access to the high-end audio and visual technology needed to provide a rich research environment for developing distributed data and visualization corridors. It also provides an environment for the study of issues that relate to collaborative work in distributed environments.

Other BPM-based applications of the Globus Toolkit: The Globus Alliance website (http://www.globus.org/alliance/projects.php) holds a repository of several solutions based on the Globus toolkit from a large variety of domains. These domains include Astronomy, Civil Engineering, Climate Studies, Medicine, Physics, Oceanography, Geology, and Ecology.

The Role of Leadership in Business Process Modeling

BPM is another form of organizational change modeling. Organizational change requires commitment of the leaders or decision makers within the enterprise. I find it necessary to devote a few paragraphs to inform the reader on the critical roles of the leaders in successful implementation of BPM and survival of the organization. Since organizations are open systems that are exposed to the influences of their environments, the structure of leadership needs to be dynamic to accommodate the changes within the organization. Unfortunately, for the leader, not everyone within the organization would embrace changing from what they know (i.e., their comfort zone), to what they do not know. Dent and Goldberg (1999) propose strategies for challenging resistance to change. Rather than define change as it relates to individuals within an organization, the authors contend that organizations define change as systemic (i.e., administrative, technological, or structural changes). In essence, they recommend that all aspects of an organization should be considered an integral part of the organization and understand that any change made to a part of the system affects the whole system.

Harari (1999) defines the role of a leader as one of helping the followers stop fixing new problems with old solutions but that of identifying new solutions necessary to handle new problems. This observation is in line with Albert Einstein's belief as described in Covey (1991) which states that the problem we face cannot be solved with the current way of thinking (i.e., current problem cannot be solved with current paradigms). This issue is considered to be the most important task a leader will face. Harari provides the following reasons as to why it is difficult for leaders to change:

1. The belief that business lives need to be stable and predictable because humans believe that stability and predictability are the natural ways of things. He then cautions that due to changing factors our traditional focus on control and certainty of events would not work today due to technological advances, removal of global barriers, customer demands, and unorthodox competitors. He asserts that "perpetual change is both a given and a necessity in today's business environment" (p. 37). This assertion makes good sense when one views the organization and leadership as a living system.

2. His claim as to why change is difficult for managers because it frustrates and disappoints them relates to the previous point about why people resist change because it moves them out of their comfort zones. He asserts that management involves creating plans, setting goals, and making commitments to employees, customers, and stakeholders. The manager's inability to meet commitments typically leads to a loss of trust, which is very important in interpersonal relationships. Therefore, change should not be instituted without considering other factors that might affect the outcome of the task at hand.

3. Harari's third point relates to the second point above—change also makes our knowledge obsolete, making our goals in doubt, current plans irrelevant, and commitments in trouble, leading to personal discouragement and frustrations. Harari holds the reasonable view that as long as people believe that knowledge is power, and change invalidates the knowledge, which robs people of power, resulting in a sense of losing control over their affairs, people will always have the tendency to resist change. It is therefore the leader's duty to prevent the situation where people feel they are powerless. This can be avoided by sharing the decision making process with the participants and educating them about the change and why it is necessary.

4. Harari also views change as a demanding process, which makes people do a lot of work that they did not expect they have to do leading to high levels of emotional stress, increasing conflict, and valuing old patterns of behavior (i.e., the good old days syndrome). This is a major challenge for leaders who are responsible for changing people's behaviors, which is not an easy task.

Carroll and Hatakenaka (2001) recommend the following approaches to senior managers that face problems with managing changes within the organization:

- Solve problems together with people to gain their trusts and commitment
- Communicate frequently to all stakeholders
- Develop inquiry skills and be willing to change your mind
- Encourage employee participation through multiple forums
- Be patient because the seeds of change may take years to materialize.

Those readers interested in learning more about leadership and organizational change management can find a more extensive coverage in my book *Blueprint for a Crooked House* (Odubiyi, 2005).

Services Science, Management and Engineering (SSME): An Emerging Discipline

A new academic discipline of SSME is being offered at some universities. This discipline, called Services System "combines social sciences, business management, and technology engineering to solve complex real-world problems" (Maglio, Srinivasan, Kreulen, and Spohrer, 2006). The focus of this new discipline is service (business) innovation or enterprise transformation (Rouse and Baba, 2006). BPM promotes and includes all the elements proposed for SSME. Universities that offer SSME as a program or as a center include: UC Berkeley, MIT, Arizona State University, Georgia Institute of Technology, North Carolina State University, and the University of Maryland (Center for Excellent in Service).

Conclusions and Some Predictions

In many organizations, the adoption of BPM will begin as tactical initiatives for automating workflow, growing over time into an enterprise-wide cross-functional transformation. The BPMS will increasingly be recognized as essential for the management of business processes and will be integrated into application packages, transforming the application market. The work of IT departments will shift progressively from defining processes to enabling business managers to evolve and adapt their processes.

The knowledge of SSME will help enterprise leaders to see themselves and their industries as collections of processes, rather than collections of functions, territorial units and companies. This trend will continue and, indeed, accelerate so that by 2009 it will be the normal view in major enterprises and public bodies.

Through 2012, managers and consultants will develop process-centric methods and disciplines analogous to those used in traditional territorial and functional organizations. The new methods and disciplines will include:

- Methods for identifying a small set of major processes that constitutes a complete enterprise
- A governance discipline for organizations that must reconcile local, functional and enterprise process management requirements

- Activity-based costing aligned by process steps to improve product costing, pricing and profit planning.
- An iterative process evolution discipline that enables all aspects of a process to evolve in parallel in rapid response to changing business demands. This discipline will integrate elements from the HR, IT and facilities areas, as well as from line and change management.

These approaches will become part of all leading business schools' curricula by 2010. The skills needed to use these methods and disciplines will be scarce until at least 2010. Beginning in 2008, managers with these skills will command higher salaries. To maximize the advantage, companies will organize people with process skills into centralized centers of excellence. Adoption of BPMS and SOA technologies will enable managers to make an increasing proportion of necessary changes with little to no involvement of technical personnel.

Chapter 7 covers some guidelines for computer and network security for intra- and inter-enterprise resources and services to identify the significant importance of security in BPM.

CHAPTER 7: OVERVIEW OF SECURITY CONCEPTS FOR THE ENTERPRISE RESOURCES AND SERVICES

Effective information security architecture treats system security like an onion otherwise known as defense in depth as depicted in Figure 7-1. A defense in depth architecture provides layers of security such that the system will still survive even if one of the security layers is penetrated, another layer can still protect the system. The whole purpose of security is to protect the information in the kernel of the architecture. The information resides in the computer system (host) which consists of the hardware, the software and communication elements. The network system connects the host to other computers within the Intranet or the Extranet/Internet.

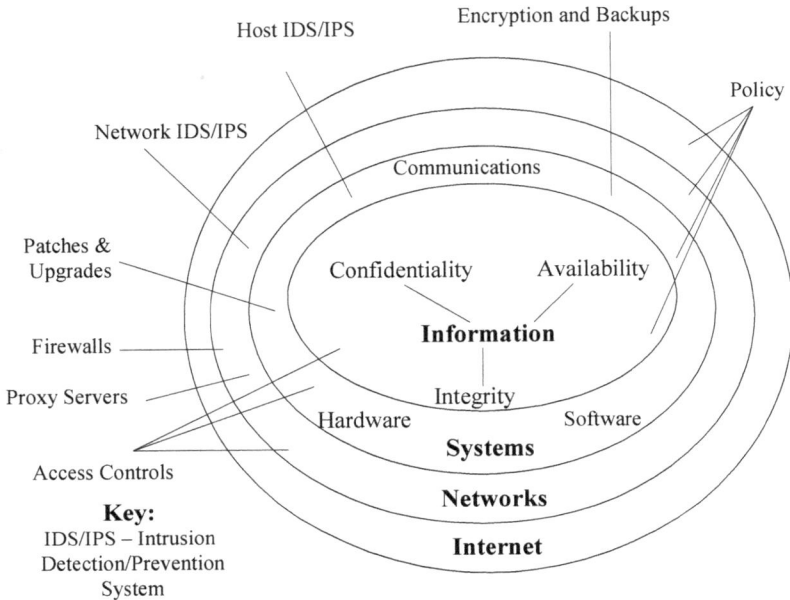

Figure 7-1: Information Security Architecture: Defense in depth

Figure 7-1 identifies respective technologies used to protect each layer from attacks. Viega and McGraw (2002) have proposed ten principles for protecting computer and networks. They claim that the ten principles including defense in depth can protect 90% of potential computer and network problems. These principles will be presented at the end of this chapter. The rest of this chapter will present an overview of these technologies. The overview is to aid decision makers to work with security professionals and policy makers to formulate a security deployment strategy for the organization's product, process, or business systems.

What is Security?

Security is the state of being protected from adversaries. It is the responsibility of every organization to institute layers of security to protect its operations. These layers include:

- *Physical security* which handles the process of protecting physical assets or areas of the company from unauthorized access
- *Personal security* is the process of protecting individuals or group with authorization to access and use organization's resources
- *Operations security* focuses on protecting all information about specific operations or tasks
- *Communication security* is the process of protecting an organization's communications assets including its media, technology, and content
- *Network security* is the process of protecting network components, connections, and content
- *Host security* is the process of protecting the computers from malicious attack of its physical (disks, hard drives, chips, CPUs, etc) and software (operating system, web servers, database management system, etc.) components
- *Information security* is the process of protecting information and the hardware that use, store, and transmit the information.

Information Security

Information security is the process of guarding digital information, which is typically processed by a computer (such as a personal computer), stored on a magnetic or optical storage device (such as a hard drive or DVD), and transmitted over a communication network. The primary goal of all the efforts devoted to computer and network security is to protect the information so that it can be delivered with all its characteristics intact. An information security strategy should balance information protection with productivity in a cost efficient manner. The elements of information protection include *availability*, *accuracy*, *authenticity*, *confidentiality*, *integrity*, and *utility*.

- *Availability* demands that information must be available in the right format to authorized users when required
- *Accuracy* demands that information is free from errors and it has value to users
- *Authenticity* demands that the quality of information is genuine and that it has not been tampered with
- *Confidentiality* demands that the information is disclosed only to those individuals with the rights and privileges
- *Integrity* demands that the information be uncorrupted, complete, undamaged, and it has not changed from its original state
- *Utility* demands that the quality of information has value to the end user.

Information Security Technologies and Strategies

This section describes the strategies and technologies for protecting information. The technologies are: access controls (information/computer systems/network); encryption strategies/cryptography (to protect the information); intrusion detection systems (host/network); firewalls (networks); proxy servers (networks); and patches and upgrades (computer systems). Corporate policy will guide applications of these technologies. A brief self-assessment guide based on NIST SP 800-26 Security Self-Assessment Guide for information technology system is provided.

Security Perimeter

A security perimeter is the protected boundary of the network, which might include the following elements:

- Firewalls
- Demilitarized zones (DMZs)
- Proxy servers
- Intrusion Detection Systems and Intrusion Prevention Systems (IDS/IPS)
- Border routers
- Virtual Private Network (VPN) devices
- Software architecture

A brief description of each of these elements is provided in the following paragraphs.

Firewalls

Firewalls are typically used to filter packets to prevent malicious attacks from networks and computers. Located at the network perimeter as the first line of defense, they can be configured as software or hardware devices.

Firewall Architecture

The *Outside Router* also known as the *border router* links the firewall system to the distrusted network. The border router is responsible for routing or exchanging packets, between trusted and distrusted networks. The distrusted network may be the extranet or the Internet. It may also perform rudimentary packet filtering and network address translation functions for the host.

DMZ

Web Server

Domain Name
Server (DNS)

Proxy Servers (e.g., FTP, Telnet)

Authentication Servers
(e.g., RADIUS, TACAS)

External
IP Links

Trusted
Network

Internal
IP
Link

Inside Router

Firewall Host

Outside Router

Distrusted
Network

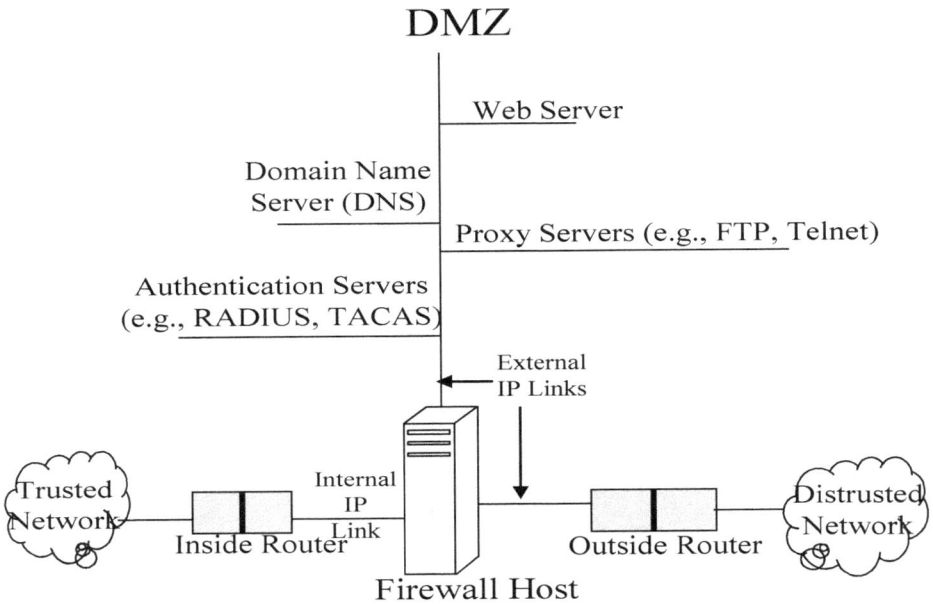

Figure 7-2: A typical firewall architecture, depicting the DMZ plus public IP addresses and public/private servers.

Functions of Firewalls

Firewalls restrict and control access to a trusted environment from a distrusted environment. Firewalls are typically used as access control devices to the Internet. To protect against Denial of Service (DoS) attacks that relate to authentication flooding, the firewall host should be able to control resource usage by authentication requests. Functions of firewalls include:

- Enhanced packet filtering
- Enabling creation of VPN

- Authentication by validating the identity of the host that send traffic through it
- Network Address Translation (NAT) –permits the hosts behind the firewall to be hidden from outside domain (i.e., the Internet).
- Logging: A Syslog server where a log of the firewall host is kept must be maintained
- Alarm Generation and Notification are mandated whenever firewall security rule is violated. For example, whenever a packet is blocked by any of the filters, a notification must be sent to the network management system host. It would be at this point that a response plan would be invoked and executed.

Demilitarized Zone (DMZ)

The DMZ is called the *dead zone* that bridges the gap between the trusted and distrusted networks. The firewall host is located in the dead zone. All servers such as mail servers, the web, and authentication servers accessed from distrusted networks must reside in the dead zone.

Proxy Servers

Proxy Services—A proxy server serves as a secure medium between a trusted and an distrusted network. The proxy server shown in Figure 2 is located in a part of the firewall known as the *Demilitarized Zone* (DMZ). It is situated between the inside and outside network. FTP proxy and Telnet proxy are examples of proxy services. They are responsible for deciding if certain packets meet established security standards.

Intrusion Detection and Prevention Systems IDS/IPS

A secure network should be able to prevent malicious attacks/intrusions and detect intrusion attempts. IDSs/IPSs can be implemented in two versions (host-based or network-based) or a hybrid. Host-based IDS resides on the computer system to monitor the status of files stored on the system. It learns the configuration of the files and alerts the system administrator of any suspicious activity. The network-based IDS (NIDS) monitors the patterns of network traffic to and from the intranet to detect anomalous patterns based on stored patterns. Some NIDS can perform host-based intrusion detection function. The two commonly used intrusion attack and recognition techniques are *Pattern Recognition* and *Effect Recognition*. *Pattern recognition* technique uses intrusion detection software to recognize a specific bit pattern, packet type, byte sequence or known keyword associated with a particular type of attack. *Effect recognition* technique identifies the attack by examining the effect of the attack.

Routers

A router is a network device that interconnects two or more networks. It serves as a gateway between networks, it becomes a critical device to protect from malicious attacks. Routers are used to forward packets between different network elements.

Virtual Private Network (VPN) devices

A Virtual Private Network (VPN) depicted in Figure 7-3, is an encrypted connection between two devices (e.g., host to host, gateway to gateway, or host to gateway) that enables secure communication between two trusted networks separated by a distrusted network.

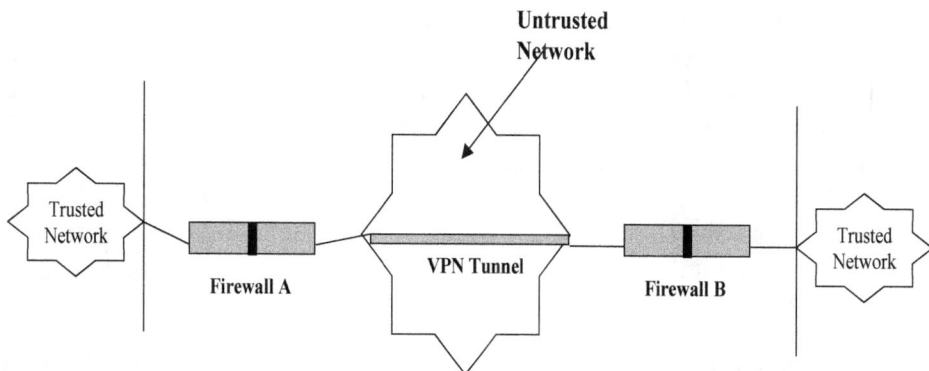

Figure 7-3: A Virtual Private Network from Firewall to Firewall

Encryption

There are two fundamental encryption technologies: (a) Single Key Encryption (SKE) and Dual Key Encryption (DKE). SKE performs a coding algorithm on the data before they are transmitted between two nodes in a communication network. The most commonly used SKE is the Data Encryption Standard (DES) which is based on 56-bit key to encode files in 64-bit blocks. This provides 2^{56} possible keys. The advent of supercomputing systems and high speed processing computers make it easy to crack the code within a couple of hours.

Triple DES uses 112-bit keys in a three-step process to encrypt data. One of the latest SKE methods is the Data Encryption Algorithm (DEA) which employs 128-bit key with a very complex eight-stage encryption algorithm. The demand that both parties must share the key constitutes a drawback for SKE. It is useful when both parties of each encryption tunnel belong to the same trusted network. It works well for a Virtual Private Network (VPN).

107

DKE: Dual Key Encryption requires the users at both ends of the encrypted connection each to have two keys, one for encrypting the data, the second for decrypting the data. It is mandatory that both keys be used but either one can be used for encryption or decryption. To ensure that that data actually come from a source they claim to have come from, the integrity of the source of information can be verified with DKE. This is achieved by decrypting any information encrypted by the sender's private key with the sender's public key. This is the technique commonly used in secure digital signature.

DKE algorithm produces the keys by multiplying two very large prime numbers. Generated keys are typically very large to the order of 1,024 bits. In order to crack the keys, the original prime numbers used to generate them must be determined (decoded) which is a daunting task.

Security Servers

Certain servers can be used to provide *authentication, authorization,* and *accounting* services to a network. Authentication is the approach used to validate the identity of the host at the end of the connection. Authorization is the process of determining the services that host can use. Accounting is the process for determining who used what services and for how long. These three techniques are commonly used to implement a **Remote Access Dial-In User Service** (RADIUS) or a **Terminal Access Controller Access Control System** (TACACS) server. It is recommended that access to any client or server is authenticated.

IPv6 and IPSec

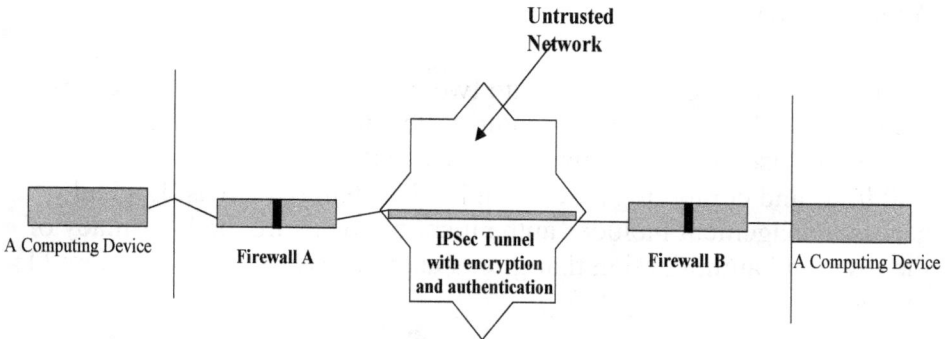

Figure 7-4: An IPSec tunnel with encryption and authentication

IP version 4 (IPv4) was developed to support security across networks presumed to be secure. Since security was not an integral part of its initial implementation, therefore to support security, a security patch protocol was added. One such protocol is IPSec (i.e., IP Security protocol). IPSec is optional with IPv4, each end of the connection must verify with its peer if it supports IPSec. IPv6 mandates IPSec and ensures that whenever IPSec is in use, communication can be secure. IPv6 uses 128-bit addressing structure. This is a strong rationale for switching to IPv6 to accomodate the growth of IP addresses. IPv4 with 32-bit addressing has forward compatibility with IPv6. IPSec negotiates secure tunnels between two peers similar to the implementation of a VPN.

Required security services provided by IPSec include:

- Data authentication: Data integrity and Origin authentication
- Data Confidentiality: Encrypting all traffic between IPSec peers
- Anti-replay: A service that allows a recipient to reject old or duplicate messages.

Access Controls

User-access management falls into two categories: (a) physical access control, and (b) logical access control. Physical access management consists of user access to any of the physical subsystems such as buildings and computing assets that hold system resources. Logical access management includes authentication to ensure the legitimacy of the user, and authorization that grants user-access to specific system IT resources.

Physical access controls must aim at controlling physical access to computing and network assets to prevent theft or damage to computing resources, unauthorized disclosure or destruction of sensitive information, interruption of business processes. This demands that controlled areas must be established with levels of security requirements depending on the sensitivity of the assets being protected.

Logical Access Controls include the following actions:

- Identifying and Authenticating users to ensure that the user is who he/she claims to be
- Defining and Protecting Resources to ensure only authorized access to the resources and protection of the resources
- Administration of Systems and Security: Keep an audit record to ensure the identity of authorized users and that only authorized users can modify, or disable security functions

- Logging Access Attempts to enable development of audit records for successful and unsuccessful attempts at access
- Reporting Access Violations and complying with response plans contained in the organization's security policy documents.

The most effective approach to implement logical access control is *Role Based Access* matched against *Data and Level of Sensitivity.*

Honeypots/Honeynets

A honeypot is a computer placed on the perimeter of a network with information intended to attract and trap hackers. The honeypot metaphor is analogous to placing a bowl of honey in the open to attract bees. A honeypot is designed with vulnerabilities such as web servers with poorly configured scripts, unprotected financial files, or outdated operating systems. The goal is to keep hackers connected long enough so their behavior or interests can be captured. A Honeynet is a connected set of honeypots.

Typically, organizations deploy two types of honeypot, a research honeypot to capture hackers' interests and the operations honeypot to test implement countermeasures based on knowledge gained from the research honeypot. Both commercial and open-source (e.g., honeyd) versions of honeypots are available.

Vulnerabilities of Network and Information Assets and Defensive Measures

Are the sets of information that must be protected clearly identified? What are the consequences if information is compromised? Has the analysis of all threats (internal and external) that could potentially compromise critical information been performed?

Internal threats:
- Physical security—control physical access to systems, data, and networks
- Incompetent employees
- Disgruntled employees
- Business competitors that attack from the inside by using employees
- Poor administration of security system
- Hot desks or laptop PCs in a distributed system. Advanced authentication methods should be employed to provide access from a laptop PC or PDA.
- Complacency: The company or managers have a written and well publicized security policy
- Limit access to network devices and analyzers to the appropriate personnel.

External Threats:
- Physical security
- Attacks on confidentiality, integrity or availability from malicious competitors
- Former employees or business partners
- Corporate vandalism or hackers
- The Internet
- Vulnerable corporate network such as Integrated Services Digital Network (ISDN) or Public Switched Telephone Network (PSTN)
- Social engineering—attacker socializes with an employee through office visits or telephone calls to gather sensitive information
- On-site third parties

Security Policy Development Process

The main goal of a security policy is to protect the confidentiality, integrity, and availability of company information assets with a tradeoff on productivity and cost-effectiveness. The following issues must be addressed by a security policy:

- Management should make information protection a priority
- Information assets along with potential threats and vulnerability should be identified
- Controls should be in place to prevent potential losses
- Periodically audit and monitor the effectiveness of an implemented security plan.
- Response plan(s) should be well understood by all participants.

Note: Security is a work in progress. It is never complete.
The latest security patches should be applied to the latest threats while ensuring that the latest patches are trustworthy.

Security Tools Applicable to IP Networks

Packet Filtering is the most popular technique used to filter inbound packets on routers. The following criteria may be used to filter inbound packets:

- Source IP address or a range of addresses
- Destination IP addresses or a range of destinations
- Source and destination port numbers used by the Transmission Control Protocol (TCP) and the User Datagram Protocol (UDP)
- Random port numbers greater than 1,023 assigned by applications
- IP protocols that do not use TCP or UDP transports such as the Open Shortest Path First (OSPF), a sophisticated and standardized link state IP routing protocol or Internet Control Message Protocol (ICMP).
- Allowing Domain Name System (DNS) requests from a distrusted LAN provided that the destination IP address is a DNS server within a trusted LAN

Password Management

The greatest network security threat to most organizations is likely to be a compromise of passwords. Suggested approaches for preventing password violations include:

- Make passwords difficult to guess or break
- Change passwords at regular intervals
- Use one-time password such as SecureID™ from Security Dynamics.
- Do not place passwords in areas or locations where they can be found
- Protect access to laptop computers.

NIST Security Self-Assessment Guide for Information Technology System

The National Institute of Standards and Technology (NIST) has published NIST SP 800-26—*Security Self-Assessment Guide for Information Technology Systems* (Whitman and Mattoro, 2003). The guide advocates implementation of three types of controls: Five management controls, nine operational controls, and three technical controls. The following seventeen controls can guide decision makers in assessing their security policy:

Management controls involve:

- Risk management
- Review of Security Controls
- Life Cycle Maintenance
- Authorization of how certification and accreditation is processed
- System Security Plan

Operational Controls involve:

- Personal Security
- Physical Security
- Production, Input/Output Controls
- Contingency Planning
- Hardware and Systems Software
- Data Integrity
- Documentation
- Security Awareness, Training, and Education
- Incident Response Capability

Technical Controls involve:

- Identification and Authentication
- Logical Access Control
- Audit Trials.

Ten Principles of Computer and Network Security

As stated earlier in this chapter, Viega and McGraw (2002) have proposed the following ten principles that could prevent 90% of potential problems in computer and network systems. In their view, defense in depth is one of the ten principles, but in the opinion of this author, it is the most critical. The ten principles are:

1. Implement a defense in depth approach as discussed in the opening section of this chapter

2. Ensure that the weakest link is secure

3. Let the system fail gracefully (i.e., securely)

4. Implement the principle of least privilege one grants just enough access to users only for specific tasks

5. Compartmentalize—modularize the system components such that any damage done to a component will be restricted to that component

6. Use the Keep It Simple Stupid (KISS) tune such that any problems in the software or hardware system is easy to diagnose and fix

7. Have a privacy policy

8. Know that it is difficult to hide secrets

9. Be very wary about trust. Know that hackers can gain access to the system from a server or the client software

10. Use community resources instead of using unproven software. Do not try to develop your own encryption software. For example, use encryption algorithm that has passed public scrutiny. The same is true for operating systems.

Conclusion

The network and computer administrator should be certified and be willing to learn new skills and be up to date on new system vulnerabilities and countermeasures. S/he should be aware of the Top 20 Computer and Network Vulnerabilities published periodically by the SANS Institute (http://www.sans.org/top20/). There are excellent reference materials that cover computer and network vulnerabilities and countermeasures to protect the web, email, instant messaging, Domain Name Servers (DNSs) servers, and software and operating system security (Simpson, 2006). Organization leaders should not underestimate the critical importance of maintaining a secure business system. It takes only one mishap to lose millions or billions of dollars of infrastructure assets. The potential for lawsuits, which could cause the collapse of the organization when certain customer data are compromised, is always present.

This chapter concludes Part I of this book. Part II begins with Chapter 8, which introduces an in-depth research on a strategy for building a survivable business process (i.e., a global telecommunication network) using multi-agent technology and exception-handling strategies.

PART II: A RESEARCH ON ENGINEERING EXCEPTION HANDLING STRATEGIES FOR SURVIVABILITY OF A DISTRIBUTED BUSINESS PROCESS

PREFACE TO PART II

The open business process model of the global communication network described here in Part II, was modeled with software agents (Odubiyi, 2003). The challenge for the research was to demonstrate the feasibility of employing vulnerable software agents to manage a complex model of a global communication network. The research presented here was conducted using two categories of software agents and exception-handling strategies. Agents in the first category employed the survivalist strategy for handling exceptions such as unreliable network infrastructure, and unpredictable operating environment. Each agent had the capability to handle anticipated exceptions. The second strategy employs the citizen agent approach in which another agent provided exception-handling services. The collective behaviors of the agents in each model determine the emergent behavior of the entire system. The agents in each model collaborate to ensure delivery of essential services, but with different policies. The focus was to identify the more effective strategy (i.e., survivalist or citizen) within system survivability framework.

The research expanded the works of Mark Klein (2001, 2003), on the application of survivalist and citizen agent strategy or policy to improve system performance using agent death exception. Part II provides some details on convergent and divergent findings of this research from previous research. It demonstrates the superiority of the citizen agent approach over the traditional survivalist agent strategy, in ensuring delivery of essential services in a global communication networks.

Automated management of complex business processes—such as telecommunication networks and air traffic control systems—requires embedded computer software programs that coordinate individual functions to achieve the goal of the whole system. Automated software systems that rely on design-time assumptions, to manage open business processes (characterized by nonroutine tasks in unpredictable environments) are bound to fail when design-time assumptions fail during business operations.

This research tested a multiagent system approach to managing complex business processes and developing strategies to handle exceptions (i.e., role commitment violations) among software agents that manage a global telecommunication network model. It employed a quasi-experimental research method to test the hypothesis that collaborative agents that outsource exception-handling services will improve operational effectiveness of a global telecommunication network model. Results led to a rejection of the null hypothesis, which predicted that the citizen agent strategy would not reduce the time to restore a customer network connection compared to the survivalist strategy.

The demonstrated methodology is generalizable to resolve unforeseen operational problems in a variety of complex business processes such as network management, flight path rescheduling, and end-to-end web services.

CHAPTER 8: INTRODUCTION TO THE STUDY OF EXCEPTION HANDLING STRATEGIES USING AGENT TECHNOLOGY

This study employed a quasi-experimental design to study conflict management among collaborative software agents that manage a model of a global telecommunication network. Throughout this study, the term agent(s) refers to software agent(s). The introduction to this dissertation provides an overall perspective for the research and is followed by a statement of the problem. The background section explains why this research was worth doing. The purpose statement explains how the research will benefit society. A section describing assumptions and limitations of the research follows the purpose statement. The generalizability of research results is explained in the research scope, which is followed by definitions of terms used in the study. Next, the study's null hypothesis and alternative hypothesis are described, followed by a section outlining the significance of the research.

This chapter presents a brief introduction to the study of exception handling strategies using agent-based technology. Chapter 9 presents a review of the literature on complex adaptive systems, multiagent systems, business process reengineering, and exception-handling strategies in automated systems. A description of research methods is presented in Chapter 10; these are sufficiently explicit to enable other researchers to replicate the study. The methods section also describes the data-gathering process, data-sampling approach, and data-analysis strategy. The dependent and independent variables are identified, followed by a discussion of approaches for internal and external validity. Chapter 11 presents a summary of the results, implications and limitations of the findings, and directions for future research. This book concludes with a summary of strategies for building survivable systems from approaches described in Parts I and II of this book, conclusions, and recommendations in Chapter 12.

Introduction to the Research

Business processes operate in one of four organizational contexts by performing (a) routine tasks in a predictable environment, (b) nonroutine tasks in a predictable environment, (c) routine tasks in an unpredictable environment, or (d) nonroutine tasks in an unpredictable environment (Birnberg, 1998).

Table 8-1: *Dimensions of Organizational Operational Context*

Nature of Environment	Nature of Task	
	Routine	Nonroutine
Stable/Predictable	Cell 1: Routine task in a stable environment (a)	Cell 2: Nonroutine task in a stable environment (b)
Unpredictable	Cell 3: Routine task in an unpredictable environment (c)	Cell 4: Nonroutine task in an unpredictable environment (d)

Adapted from "Some Reflections on the Evolution of Organizational Control," by J. G., Birnberg, 1998, *Behavioral Research in Accounting, 1998 Supplement, 10,* 43-44.

Table 8-1 describes the four categories of organizational operational context. Cell 1 in the Table can be used to describe a shop that makes products to customer order in very low volumes, where one or a few workers perform all the tasks. Examples include custom-made furniture and hand-made tools. Such business processes require highly skilled workers, and automation is not needed due to limited output.

Cell 2 represents business operations where production volumes are larger than those in cell 1 and produced items are replicated, leading to batch manufacturing. The machines may produce long runs but are reset for a new product. Examples are printing and clothing industries. As the volume of the product increases and the range of items narrows, a production-line operation may be instituted where workstations are sequenced, each repeating the same tasks in a short cycle.

Business processes representative of cell 3 include consumer electronics and automobile assembly operations. Environmental uncertainties include institutional regulations, unpredictable customer demands, competition, and market trends. When a product must be generated in large quantities, a continuous-flow process is required.

Processes represented in cell 4 require significant capital investment but have low labor needs. To meet the large production scale, automation of the processes is required (Westbrook, 2000). Examples of such business processes are paper mills, oil refineries, air traffic control systems, ground transportation management systems, and telecommunication network management systems.

In actual practice, organizations employ a mix of these four types of business processes. Technology plays a key role in automation because it links information technology to processing functions. The processing functions can be automated with distributed software programs such as software agents or other distributed object-oriented software programs. Once the processes are automated, substantial effort and resources are devoted to problem management to maintain acceptable performance levels.

Open distributed business processes are characterized by nonroutine tasks in unpredictable environments. Such business processes are known as complex systems (Coveney & Highfield, 1995; Pascale, 1999). "Because complex systems have built-in unpredictability, the certainties of the command-and-control approach to management no longer hold true" (Battram, 1998, p. 11). Therefore, for open business processes to survive, they must be managed as complex, adaptive systems (Battram, 1998).

Telecommunications service providers confront many challenges in meeting service requirements of their customers due to increased competition, demand for rapid and high-quality service, and network growth. To meet customer demands, telecommunications service providers need embedded and collaborating computer software tools that are responsive to solving customer problems, proactive in anticipating new problems, and adaptive to handling unexpected operational environments (Prouskas, Patel, Pitt, & Barria, 2000).

However, the most common mode of operation among telecommunication service providers is for engineers to project customer network traffic profiles and to service customers' networks on the basis of these projections. Since a telecommunication network is an open system with uncertainties in the environment and in the nature of the tasks, it may not perform as expected in operational modes, resulting in broken promises made to customers, loss of trust, and costly litigation. Problems faced by telecommunication service providers can be addressed by automating the management process with collaborative software agents that can anticipate possible problems with the aid of exception-handling strategies. This research employed agent death exception to develop strategies that can improve the operational effectiveness of telecommunication networks and similar business processes.

Definition of Terms on Telecommunications and Agent Technology

A *link* connects two nodes or switches A to B as shown in Figure 8-1.

A *path* (see Figure 8-1) is a series of links or connections that links an origin A—a node or a switch—to a destination C—another node or switch.
A *route* is a set of possible paths that a telephone call can use to connect an origin to a destination, as depicted in Figure 8-1.

A *permanent virtual connection* (PVC) is a specific route or a path in a communication network.

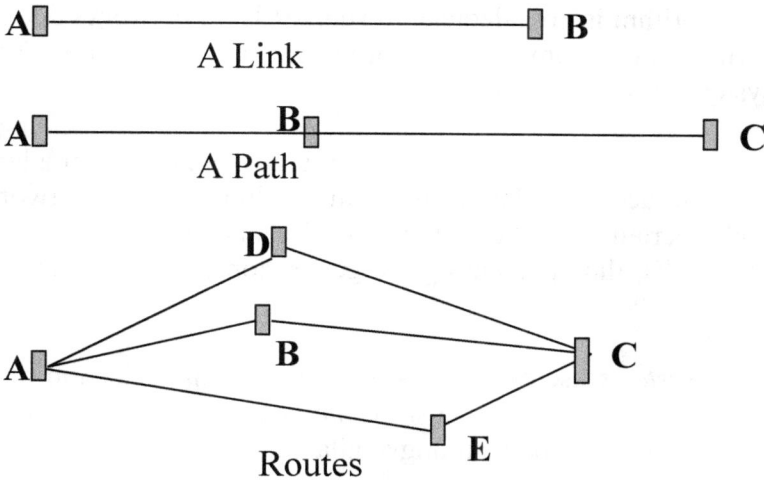

Figure 8-1: Relationships among a link, a path, and a route in a communication network.

A *routing table* is a data set of information that enables each switch to determine the next path to select before routing the next packet towards a destination.

A *network routing process* includes the following three core functions: (a) acquisition, organization, and distribution of information about user generated traffic and network states; (b) use of this information to generate feasible routes maximizing the performance objectives; and (c) forwarding of user traffic along selected routes. (Caro & Dorigo, 1998, p. 315).

A routing algorithm is a technique that employs routing tables to make message-forwarding decisions. The two categories of routing algorithms or systems are (a) centralized versus distributed and (b) static versus adaptive.

Centralized routing systems assign centralized software for updating the routing tables for every network node and determining routing decisions. This technique is useful only for small networks with a limited number of nodes. The algorithm is not adequate to support large networks due to the need to process a large amount of information, route network traffic, and update system information in real time.

Adaptive routing systems (routers) use routing algorithms that can adapt routing decisions to accommodate changes in conditions of the network over time. Under certain conditions, the algorithms have been known to lead to circular paths, thus preventing the generation of a new route in the network.

Minimal routing systems use algorithms that promote the selection of a path that would yield the minimum cost. *Nonminimal routing algorithms* promote the selection of any path among available paths.

Optimal routing systems use routing algorithms that take a global network perspective to select the routes that yield the best time to transmit data packets. On the other hand, *shortest-path routing systems* only consider the source and the destination of a packet to make routing decisions.

Shortest-path routing systems rely on either a distance vector or a link-state model to make routing decisions. A distance vector approach considers an estimated distance or the number of nodes to a destination. A link-state method considers real-time statistics (e.g., trunk usage, node congestion) to weigh the cost of selecting a specific path (Caro & Dorigo, 1998, p. 334).

Distributed routing systems are employed when the process of computing routes is shared among the network nodes to exchange information. They are commonly used in large networks.

Static routing systems, also referred to as *fixed traffic routing systems,* are used when the route assigned to a message or data packet on the network is based on the source and destination of the message without any concern for the state of the network. This approach is commonly used where routing systems are not flexible enough to share network links and switches.

Severity Level 1 Problem is a network trouble that has an extremely serious impact on the customer's service and cannot be circumvented. It may have one or more of the following characteristics: (a) a complete loss of the customer's service or the impacted business function is halted or (b) no interim restoration is possible or interim restoration is unacceptable to the customer (Penny, 2001).

Severity Level 2 Problem is a network trouble that has a large impact on a portion of the customer's service and cannot be circumvented. It may have one or more of the following characteristics: (a) causes significant loss of the customer's service, but the impacted business function is not halted and (b) no interim restoration is possible or interim restoration is unacceptable to the customer (Penny, 2001).

Severity Level 3 Problem is a network trouble that has a small impact on the customer's service or where a single user or component has trouble and it causes some impact to the customer's business but the trouble can be circumvented (Penny, 2001).

Dynamic traffic routing provides the capability for the links and switches to share resources necessary to transport data through a communication network (Ash, 1997).

Committed information rate (CIR) is the volume of traffic that a communication network customer promises to send through a telecommunication service provider's network. The CIR is used to determine the penalty levied on each party if the customer sends a higher rate or if the TSP is unable to process the volume at the specified CIR.

A *software agent* is a computational entity (i.e., an abstraction of an object, Shoham, 1993) that is able to represent a state and change it by performing some actions on it and also to communicate with other agents through message passing. An agent is different from an object because of its ability to perform autonomous actions—that is, the agent is able to perform its tasks without reliance on human input. In this research, the agent is used as a computational entity to represent the state of telecommunication network elements such as network switches, communication trunks, and ports.

An intelligent agent is a software agent that is capable of "flexible autonomous actions in order to meet its design objectives" (Jennings & Wooldridge, 1998, p. 2). Being flexible means that the agent is responsive, proactive, and communicative. A responsive agent is able to accept inputs from its environment—such as users, other agents, and systems—and respond in a timely manner. In addition to being responsive, a proactive agent is able to anticipate new opportunities and adapt its plans to achieve its goals, in contrast to the behavior of a reactive agent. An agent is communicative (i.e., social) if it can interact with other agents in an agent communication language to exchange knowledge necessary to perform its duties. Ability to learn is a key characteristic of an intelligent agent.

Autonomous agents can control how they interact with other agents. Agent autonomy means that the agent makes the decisions that guide its actions. There are three categories of autonomous agents: biological agents, robotic agents, and computational agents (Franklin & Graesser, 1996). Computational agents consist of software agents and artificial-life agents. The three categories of software agents are task-specific agents, entertainment agents, and viruses. This research focuses on task-specific agents.

Reactive agents sense changes in their environment and respond in a timely fashion.

Goal-driven agents are proactive agents that do not simply respond to their environment but also take initiative in how to achieve their goals. *Survivalist agents* are software agents in a collaborative multiagent system with built-in exception-handling strategies defined at the time the system is designed.

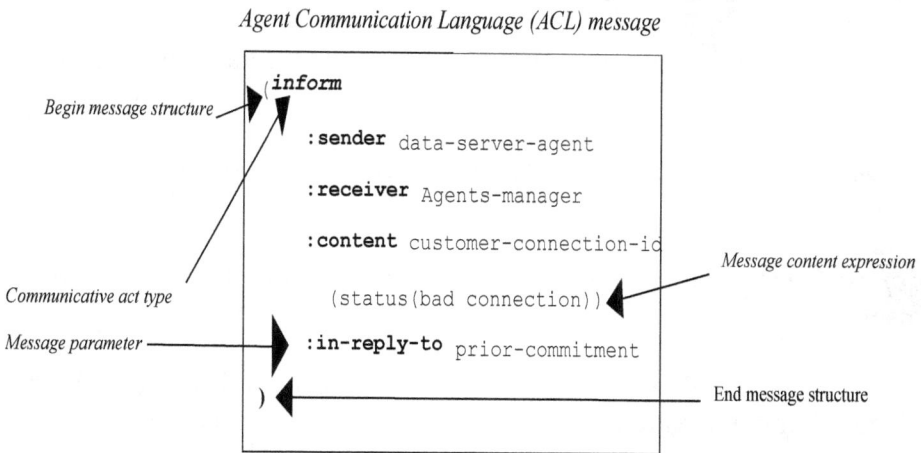

Figure 8-2: Components of an agent communication language, template available in the public domain, FIPA (1997): http://www.fipa.org.

Citizen agents are software agents in a collaborative multiagent system that employs the services of an exception-handling agent instead of relying on embedded exception-handling strategies.

Multiagent systems (MAS) are complex adaptive systems in which the agents are autonomous, social, persistent, reactive, and proactive to support emergent behavior of the MAS.

Agent communication language (Figure 7-2 and Appendix A) is a language with specific syntax and semantic rules that form the basis of communication between and among software agents.

A *communicative act (CA)* is "a special class of actions that form the basic elements of communication between agents" (FIPA, 1997, p. 1). A communicative act such as *inform* might be encoded in an ACL message performed by one agent sending a message to another agent.

Content is a component of a communicative act; it represents the domain-specific part of the communication.

A *message* is a unit of communication between two agents. The message is expressed in ACL.

An *agent platform* is the computer environment where the software agent executes its tasks.

A *proposition* states that some statement or concept in a language is true or false.

Contract net protocol is a method used to ask for bids from distributed problem-solving agents and to select winning proposals. The protocol is most suitable when the tasks are well-defined and substasks have minimal interactions (Huhns & Singh, 1997).

A *feasibility precondition* (FP) states one or more conditions that must be satisfied before an agent can perform an action. This is also known as an illocutionary effect.

A *rational effect* (RE) is a representation of a reasonable effect that an agent can expect to happen in response to an action being performed. Specifically, for a communicative act, the rational effect is called the perlocutionary effect, which an agent can expect the receiver of the communicative act to have.

Speech act theory is a theory of communication used as the basis for ACL. It is derived from analyzing human communication and assumes that every time a speaker makes a statement in any language, he or she also performs actions. The performative is the verb in a speech act that takes the form of "I hereby request" or "I hereby declare" because saying it makes it so. The verb in the statement "I hereby complete this research" does not constitute a speech act because saying it does not make it happen (Searle, as cited in FIPA, 1997).

Locutionary, illocutionary, and perlocutionary acts are the three components of communicative acts in speech act theory. Locutionary acts deal with formulating a statement, illocutionary acts involve distinguishing the utterance from the speaker's intent (e.g., Is it a question, a query, or an order?), and perlocutionary acts refer to other possible consequences of the act on the hearer.

Exceptions are system or subsystem failures that are unplanned for during system design. There are two categories of exceptions: design-time exceptions and run-time exceptions. Design-time exceptions are those anticipated during the design of the system. Run-time exceptions are exceptions that manifest themselves during the operation of the system; some may be anticipated, while others are unforeseen.

Open systems are systems whose components change over time, can be heterogeneous, and whose behaviors are unpredictable.

Heterogeneous systems are systems whose components are different in structure and exhibit different behaviors.

Thread of control is a set of actions that control the execution of a software agent.

Multithreaded programming is a method for developing a software program in which several functions within the program can execute simultaneously.

Problem Statement

A global economy depends on effective, efficient, and uninterrupted telecommunications service. Therefore, it is important that telecommunications service providers (TSPs) employ telecommunication network management tools to meet these criteria. TSPs confront many challenges in meeting service requirements of their customers due to increased competition, demand for rapid and high-quality service, network growth, and the built-in unpredictability of such an open system. Telephone calling rates have fallen from 20 cents per minute in 1997 to 3-5 cents per minute in 2005. Customers want high bandwidth communication to support their appetite for rich multimedia video and graphics that can be downloaded quickly. TSPs' problems are exacerbated if the company operates a global communication network that relies on undersea cables and terrestrial and satellite links. Therefore, to meet customer demands, TSPs need embedded and collaborating computer software tools that are responsive to customer problems, proactive in anticipating new problems, and adaptive to handling unexpected operational environments (Prouskas, Patel, Pitt, & Barria, 2000).

The most common mode of operation among TSPs is for engineers to project customer network traffic profiles; service customers' networks on the basis of these projections; and employ distributed computing software, which lacks the ability to meet the demands of the complex network. Since a telecommunication network is an open system with uncertainties in the environment and in the nature of the tasks required to manage it, will the design-time assumptions hold in real operations? If the assumptions do not hold, will the TSPs still be able to maintain customers' network connections to meet contractual service level agreements (SLAs), maintain their trust, avoid litigation, and support a global economy? Will a different approach that does not rely solely on design assumptions but accommodates changes encountered during network operations (i.e., run-time changes) address the inefficiencies inherent in design-time implementation strategies? Will the run-time approach improve the performance of the network by reducing the time to restore disrupted customers' telecommunication links?

This research attempted to provide answers to these questions by automating a global telecommunication management process with collaborative software agents that can anticipate possible problems with the aid of exception-handling strategies. This approach assumes that most business processes are open systems in which the behavior of their interacting components is unpredictable (Battram, 1998; Scott, 1998) and the software programs are adaptive.

This research extends the work of Dellarocas and Klein (2000), who investigated the development of effective multiagent systems where it is assumed that the infrastructure is unreliable and the agents are prone to fail in open-system contexts. While their research focused on the domain of bidding for contracts and contract awards using what is known as *contract net protocol*, this research focuses on a more complex domain of telecommunication network management and a consumer/producer coordination mechanism. This research develops a typology that characterizes exception-handling policies among collaborative software agents that manage complex distributed business processes. The collaborating agents constitute a multiagent system where each agent is charged with performing corresponding processing functions to improve operational effectiveness of a business process model.

Automated management of complex business processes—such as telecommunication networks, transportation networks, distributed computer systems and air traffic control systems—requires embedded computer software programs that coordinate individual functions to achieve the goal of the whole system. Each software program performs particular assigned tasks or roles and relays outcomes of its own operation to other programs within the system. When a program fails to perform or to produce its intended result (i.e., creates exceptions), conflicts between and among programs may develop within the system. As a result of this conflict, the whole system fails to meet the desired objectives.

This research tested a multiagent system approach to managing complex business processes and developing strategies to handle exceptions (i.e., role commitment violations) among software agents that manage a telecommunication network model. It employed a quasi-experimental research method to test the hypothesis that collaborative agents with exception-handling capabilities will improve operational effectiveness of a global telecommunication network model. A quasi-experimental research paradigm was used because it approximates true experimental conditions when it is not feasible to control or manipulate all variables of interest. Telecommunication network performance variables investigated in this research include average downtimes of customer connections caused by network congestion, node and trunk outages, and usage levels of customer network links (i.e., permanent virtual circuits with data from a real network).

Background

Most business processes are complex adaptive systems (Battram, 1998). Systems may be simple, chaotic, or complex adaptive. Simple systems exhibit predictable behaviors. A television set is an example of a simple but complicated system. Chaotic or crudely complex systems can assume several possible states, in which the components are widely dispersed, and can interact with neighboring components. A chaotic system exhibits largely unpredictable behavior. Clouds and weather are examples of chaotic systems. Complex adaptive systems can assume a large number of possible states with components (i.e., agents) that can interact locally and globally through a hierarchical management structure (Battram, 1998). The emergent behavior of a flock of birds flying in V formation is complex and unpredictable, but the flock is able to fly faster and longer than are individual birds. "The flock that is formed when autonomous agents—birds— interact is known as a complex adaptive system" (Santosus, 1998, p. 1). Each bird flying in a flock must obey three rules: avoid bumping into anything, keep up with the speed of other birds, and stay in close proximity to neighboring birds (Santosus, 1998, p. 1). Violating any of these rules may lead to delays in reaching the destination. Other examples of complex adaptive systems include large organizations, ant colonies, and business processes.

Figure 8-3 depicts Concert's global managed platform (GMP), a global network consisting of global points of presence (POP) connected by international private line circuits (IPLCs), which are leased from various carriers around the world. The telecommunication service platforms include frame relay switches that support Concert's frame relay service, asynchronous transfer mode (ATM) switches supporting Concert's ATM services, and voice switches that support Concert's voice network services. The GMP has over 1,000 circuits (i.e., trunks) in 52 countries. The network links can be undersea cables, terrestrial links (e.g., land lines), or satellites links. Concert was a global joint venture of AT&T and the British Telecom (BT) that provided complete global communications to about 270 multinational corporations (MNCs) and the international calling needs of individuals and businesses around the world.

The global joint venture was dissolved in June 2002 but the network is still in operation. The network is currently managed by entities of AT&T and BT.

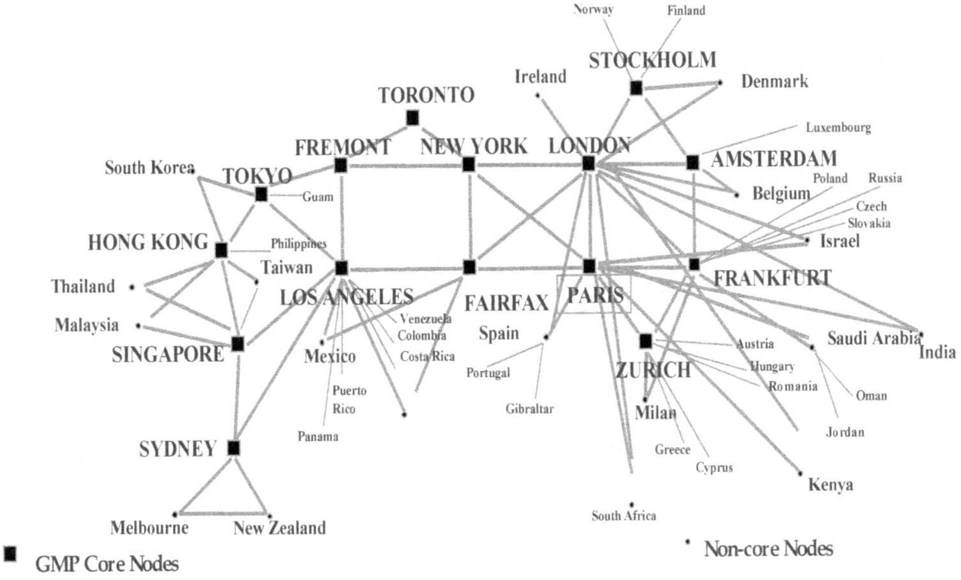

Figure 8-3: A global telecommunication network of Concert (Odubiyi, 2005).

Figure 8-4 describes the relationship among processes, functions, and data. Processes describe the sequence of activities to solve either a partial or complete business problem. Processes are typically set in motion by activators or triggers. A function is a unit of a process that can be activated by a human or automated command. As shown in Figure 8-4, each function has well-defined data inputs and outputs (Bartorsky & Deland, 1999). The diamond symbols in Figure 8-4 control the flow of functions with a process.

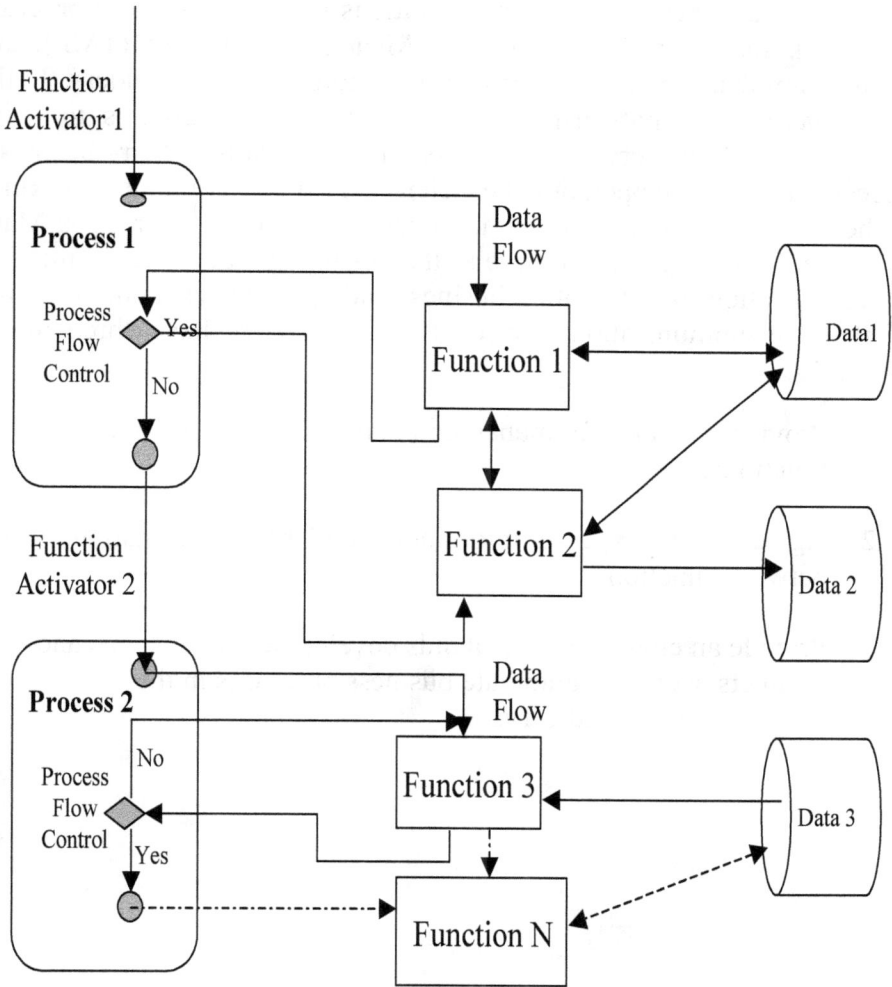

Figure 8-4: Relationship among processes, functions, and data. Adapted with permission (not required—Mike Kelly) from *TeleManagement Forum,* Bartorsky & Deland, 1999.

Figure 8-5 describes the Telecom operations map, the business process framework recommended by the TeleManagement Forum (TMF), an organization that represents telecommunications service providers. TMF is an international not-for-profit organization whose goal is to help telecommunication service providers in automating their business processes to improve operational efficiency. TMF has continued working on the TOM and has developed an enhanced Telecom Operations Map (eTOM) which, continues to serve as the business process framework for process direction for integrating business and operations support systems for the telecommunication Service Providers. They have three main objectives:

1. Provide guidance for managing communication network functions.

2. Agree on the type of information and how information flows between functions.

3. Provide an environment that aids development of systems and products needed to automate business processes in the communications industry.

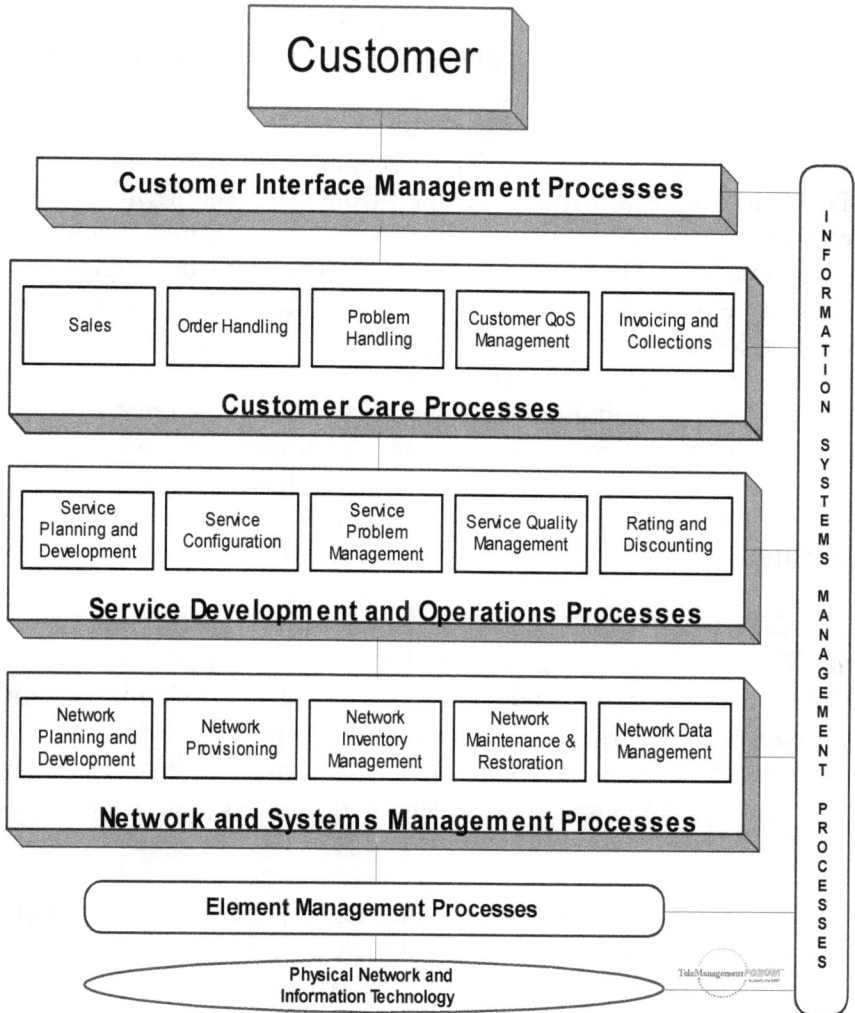

Figure 8- 5: Telecom operations map (TOM): business process framework. Adapted with permission (not required—Mike Kelly) from *TeleManagement Forum,* Bartorsky & Deland, 1999.

TMF has representatives from network service providers, operators, and software and equipment suppliers. The telecommunications industry has approved a framework for the telecommunication management network (TMN) model, which provides a logical way for viewing network service management and delivery. The telecommunications operations map (TOM) in Figure 8-5 was developed from the basic TMN model, which consists of network element management, network management, service management, and business management. The element management layer involves network components such as switches, bridges, satellites, and relay stations. The network management layer covers processes required for the connected network elements and flow processes such as network planning, provisioning, and maintenance. The service management layer involves network service development and operations processes such as service planning and configuration. The business management layer covers customer care including order handling, customer problem handling, and billing.

The TOM model in Figure 8-5 provides an overview of operations management. It can be applied to any communication service—wired or wireless. The present study focused on the network maintenance and restoration process, a subsystem of the network and systems management processes. Using a business process framework makes it easier for TSPs to analyze, evaluate, and improve the processes that can help them meet customer demands and profitability goals.

The network maintenance and restoration process and its interactions with all other subprocesses are depicted in Figure 8-6. The network maintenance and restoration process plays an important role in a customer's perception of service quality.

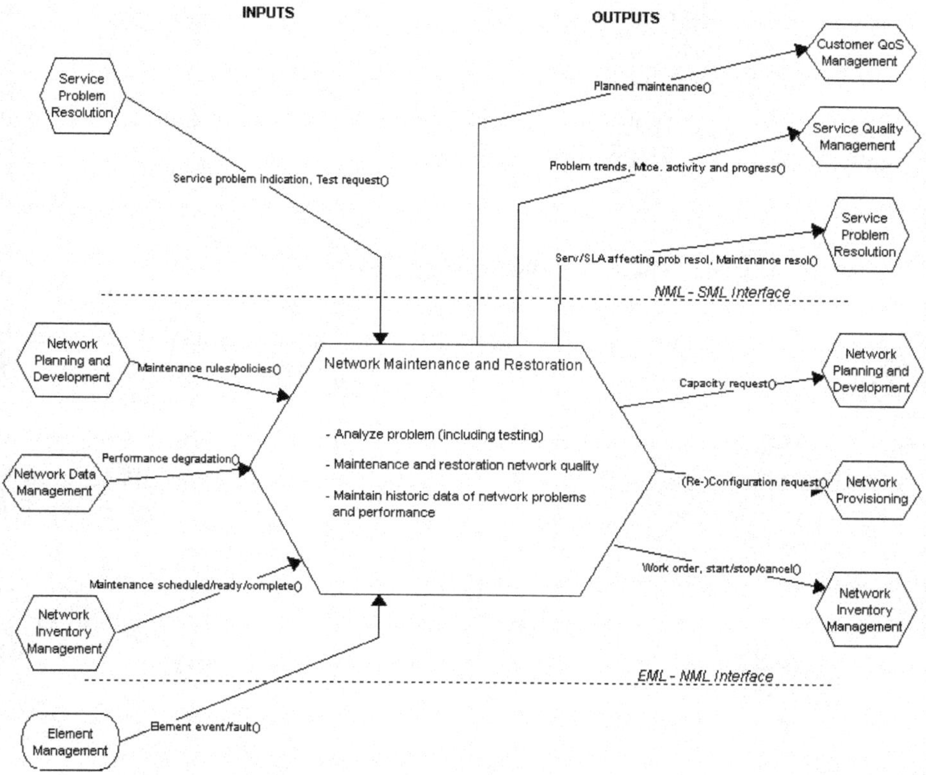

Figure 8-6: Network maintenance and restoration process. NML, SML, and EML are network, service, and element management layers respectively. QoS: Quality of Service. Adapted with permission (not required—Mike Kelly) from *TeleManagement Forum,* Bartorsky & Deland, 1999.

The efficient and timely handling of problem reports, alarms, problem diagnosis, and service restoration is a complex process responsible for identifying when customer connections are down and for managing a restoration process. This process is also important in supporting network management, service management, and customer care processes (Bartorsky & Deland, 1999). The network maintenance and restoration process is responsible for network problem analysis, maintenance, restoration of network quality, and tracking historic data of network problems and performance. As shown in Figure 8-6, to effectively support the entire business process, the maintenance and restoration subsystem must accept inputs from selected subprocesses and deliver outputs to other processes that need them.

Communication Network Topology and PVC

Figure 8-7 shows the relationship among the permanent virtual circuits (PVCs), trunks, and switches in a telecommunication network. Figure 8 depicts the interfaces between two typical switches. A typical switch holds several cards (also known as slots). Each card holds a series of ports. The trunk holding several PVCs connects two switches to enable PVCs to transfer their data via the ports. A customer connection can fail when a port is congested, a node fails, a trunk is overused, or a network transmission unit fails. Other likely causes of problems with customer connections are cut cables, power outages, faulty circuit boards or cables, and so on. All these are system variables that affect network performance.

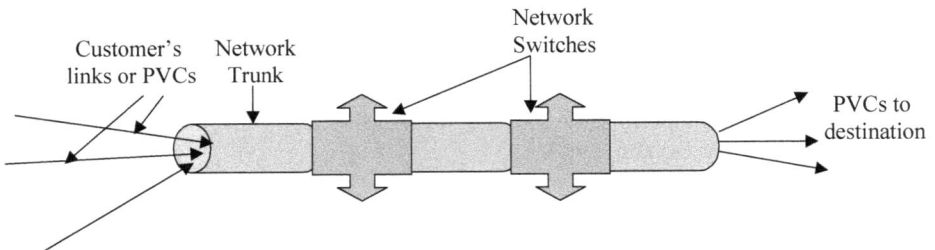

Figure 8-7: Relationships among PVCs, trunks, and switches in a network.

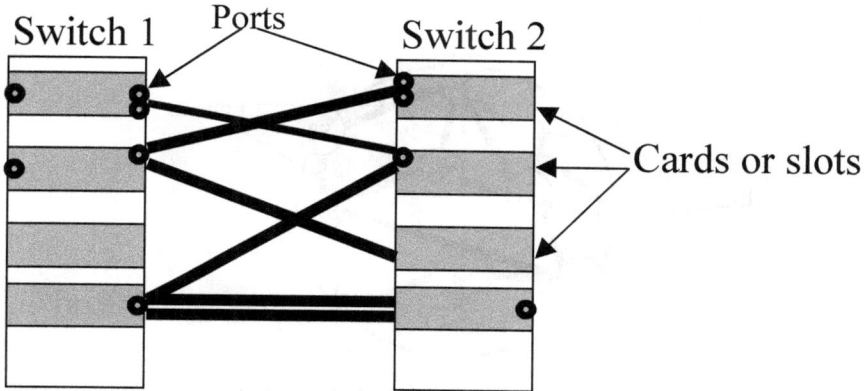

Figure 8-8: A configuration of two connected switches in a communication network.

The core nodes of Concert's global communication network (Figure 8-3) connect 30 large population centers around the world: Domingez Hills, CA; Los Angeles, CA; Sacramento, CA; San Diego, CA; San Francisco, CA; San Jose, CA; Sherman Oaks, CA; Hilburn, NY; New York, NY; Staten Island, NY; White Plains, NY; Philadelphia, PA; Potstown, PA; Sydney, Australia; Brussels, Belgium; Keybridge 1 and Keybridge 2, England; Coriander 1 and Coriander 2, England; Paris, France; Frankfurt, Germany; Munich, Germany; Dublin, Ireland; Milan, Italy; Tokyo, Japan; Amsterdam, Netherlands; Madrid, Spain; Stockholm, Sweden; Zurich, Switzerland; and Hong Kong.

Each node serves as source of customer network connections to other nodes, as shown in the global model in Figure 8-9. A scan of the topology database reveals that each node has hundreds of customer connections (PVCs) originating from it. These connections link a substantial number of other switches in the system. As depicted in Figure 8-9, connections that originate from the A-End terminate at the B-End.

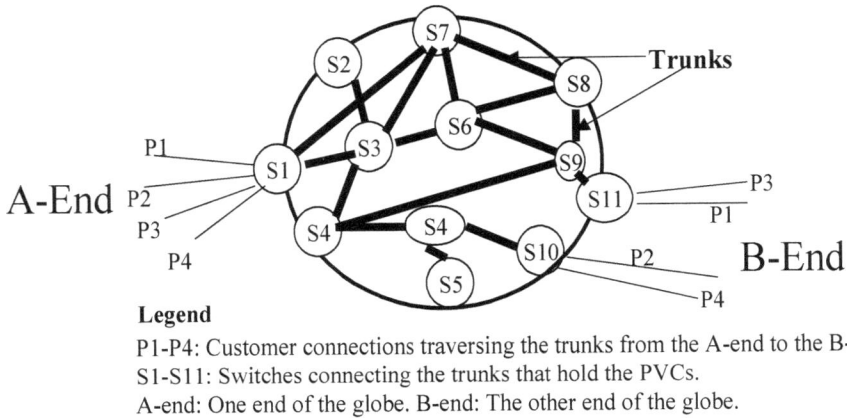

Legend
P1-P4: Customer connections traversing the trunks from the A-end to the B-end.
S1-S11: Switches connecting the trunks that hold the PVCs.
A-end: One end of the globe. B-end: The other end of the globe.

Figure 8-9: A conceptual model of a global communication network topology at node S1 at the A-end of the globe may pass through one or more switches or nodes to reach their destinations at the B-end.

According to Concert's network topology database, the node in Keybridge 1 in England has 120 customer PVCs originating from it; Staten Island, New York supports 432 PVCs; Munich, Germany supports 648 PVCs; Paris, France supports 6,408 PVCs; and Keybridge 2 near London, England manages 13,646 PVCs. An example of a PVC path originating from a switch in New York and terminating in Munich is recorded in the topology database as shown below:

Path: NYKBCR01 1.1 -- 2.8PHIBCR01 2.6 -- 6.8KEYBCR01 6.4 -- 6.2MUNBCR01

The path description shows that the connection leaves the switch in New York from Port 1 on Card 1, enters the switch in Philadelphia on Port 2 on Card 8, and connects to the switch in Munich on Port 6 on Card 2.

Any malfunction with any of the network elements (i.e., the switch, port, card, or PVC) would cause the connection to fail.

Managing Complexity in Open Business Systems

The roots of instability in complex adaptive systems can be traced to unpredictability in the behaviors of the agents within the system. Approaches used by human society to obtain conformity from its members are analogous to those used to assure conformity among the agents in an artificial system. Compliance theory, also known as social guidance theory, describes the type of power employed by elites to control lower-ranking participants in organizations in order to achieve organizational goals. Compliance is how elites maintain social order. Etzioni (1975) outlined three methods of exercising compliance: coercion, economic assets, and normative values. Elites employ coercive approaches to maintain social order in institutions such as prisons and mental hospitals. Denial of economic benefits is used to obtain compliance in industries, while denial of self-esteem or prestige is used to maintain normative values among professional organizations. Just as human society employs compliance theory, exception-handling strategies can be used to gain compliance among artificial agents such as software agents. Therefore, automating a complex adaptive system with collaborative software agents that conform to exception-handling protocols will reduce failures in the system and will enhance operational effectiveness.

To meet the demands of a complex adaptive system, embedded software agents must possess at least three basic capabilities: (a) autonomy—continuous execution without human intervention, (b) adaptiveness—ability to learn and adapt to changing environment, and (c) communication—ability to exchange information/knowledge with other agents using an agent communication language (FIPA, 2000). Software agents are different from traditional software programs such as object-oriented or procedure-oriented programs. In the object-oriented programming paradigm, when an object requests another object for a

147

service, the requestor object must specify what it wants and the method to be executed to obtain requested information. An agent-based approach employs the same paradigm that humans use. The agent simply requests another agent for a specific service, but it does not need to specify how the service could be obtained. This approach is possible due to embedded knowledge in each agent's reasoning system. The agents use speech acts such as *request, inform, propose, refuse,* and *not understood* to exchange messages (FIPA, 2000).

Categories of Exceptions

Three categories of exceptions are possible in a multiagent system: infrastructure commitment violations, agent commitment violations, and system commitment violations (Dellarocas & Klein, 2000). *Infrastructure commitment violation* refers to the commitment of the infrastructure to provide reliable agent communication and operation. The commitment could be violated if the communication links between the agents fail or the messages are lost or delayed. *Agent commitment violations* refer to the inability of agents to hold to coordination protocols that were agreed to. Agents may violate their commitments due to software bugs that limit the performance of the agent, bounded rationality (the inability of the agent to solve a problem and deliver results within acceptable time limits, possibly due to the complexity of its algorithm), poor computing resources, or death of an agent. *System commitment violation* involves the inability of the agent to obtain required resources due to an inefficient resource allocation mechanism.

The three exception types are handled in one of four classes of exception-handling processes: (a) exception anticipation, (b) exception avoidance, (c) exception detection, and (d) exception resolution. The first two exception-handling processes address exceptions prior to their occurrence, whereas the last two are aimed at exceptions after their occurrence.

Coordination, Exceptions, and Role Commitment Violation Analysis

Coordination is the process by which agents in a multiagent system make commitments to each other. Exceptions can be viewed as the ways agents in MASs can fail to meet their commitments. Role-commitment violation analysis involves (a) identifying each agent's roles, plus communication and computational infrastructures; (b) for each role, identifying the commitment that each role requires of other roles; and (c) for each commitment, identifying the ways that each commitment can be violated (i.e., exceptions). Analyzing role commitment violations does not rely on knowledge of the internal structures of each agent; therefore, it should be applicable to all domains.

Infrastructure commitments could involve commitment to message passing between agents. A commitment to send the right message to the right place at the right time would identify when wrong or garbled messages are sent to the wrong place at the wrong time or with excessive delay. The role commitment violation analysis treats each agent as a black box, while focusing on the failure modes of interaction between agents. The repository of exception-handling techniques, described in the Massachusetts Institute of Technology (MIT) process handbook and available from MIT's Center for Coordination Science (Klein, 2000; Malone et al., 1999), was assembled from multidisciplinary sources, including (a) multiagent systems (Venkatraman & Singh, 1998), (b) distributed real-time systems, (c) planning and robotics, (d) computer-supported cooperative work environments, (e) operations research, and (f) management science.

Handling Exceptions in Multiagent Systems: Collaborative Survivalist vs. Citizen Agents

Multiagent systems (MASs) have been identified as one of the most promising approaches for supporting open systems typical of telecommunication networks because they have the ability to use multiagent coordination protocols to reorganize themselves in response to changes in their problem focus and environment (Jennings, Sycara, & Wooldridge, 1998). A wide variety of implemented multiagent systems assume that distributed agents operate in a closed world where the infrastructure (i.e., computer systems and communication links) is reliable. Uncertainties in communication links and degradation of the computing environment or link failures may cause the software agents to "die" (i.e., be rendered useless) or be unable to communicate with other agents (Klein, 2000). As the number of agents in the MAS grows, possible points of failure grow geometrically.

A significant increase in the number of agents results in complex interactions among them, causing unpredictable behaviors that demand complex coordination mechanisms. When those departures from expected performance levels are not handled effectively, they can prevent the system from delivering its operational goals and can lead to the failure of the system as a whole (Dellarocas & Klein, 2000; Prouskas, Patel, Pitt, & Barria, 2000). Figure 10 depicts a basic conceptual model of traditional MASs implemented to automate the management of telecommunication networks using the survivalist agent strategy (Hayzelden & Bigham, 1998; Odubiyi, Bayless, & Ruberton, 1999; Pagurek, Li, Bieszczad, & Susilo, 1998).

These traditional MASs employ the "survivalist approach" (Dellarocas & Klein, 2000, p. 97), which, among other requirements, obliges the MAS developer to design into every problem-solving agent all skills needed to handle all possible exceptions that may develop during execution. The survivalist approach, also known as a design-time exception-handling strategy, places a significant burden on the developer, who must anticipate and plan for handling all possible exceptions.

Interactions among Survivalist Agents (SA)
and the Agent Services Manager (ASM)

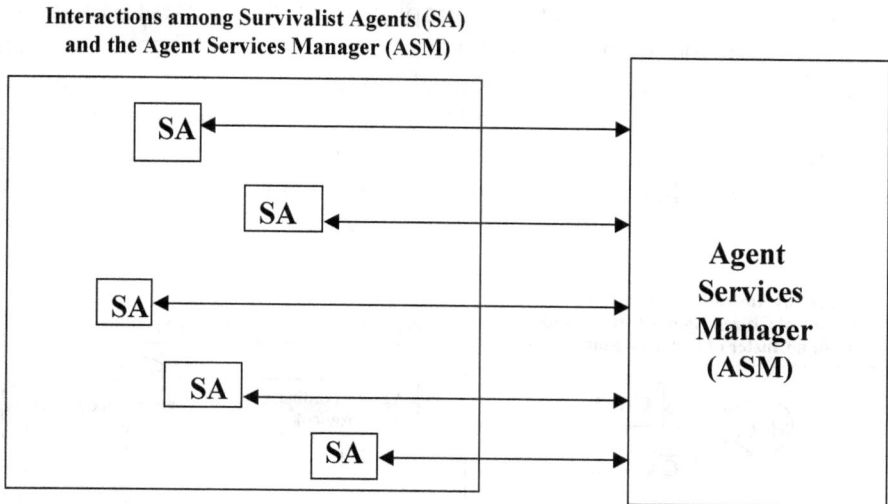

Figure 8-10: Architecture for an MAS with exception-handling strategy using the survivalist approach.

Instead of building exception-handling capability into every agent, the MAS could be implemented, to use the citizen approach, which allows exception handling to be performed by another class of agents at run-time. This citizen approach employs a societal-compliance paradigm typical of social institutions (Dellarocas & Klein, 2000; Etzioni, 1975). The paradigm emulates a law-enforcement paradigm in a community in which police officers, lawyers, and the courts enforce the law. In the citizen approach, an exception-handling agent, with the aid of sentry (i.e., sentinel) agents, is responsible for anticipating, detecting, diagnosing, and resolving failures in the operations of problem-solving agents.

151

Figure 8-10 illustrates a part of the design architecture for a MAS with the survivalist approach that was employed in the present study. The diagram shows the interactions among the survivalist agents (SA) and the ASM. A more detailed architectural model is presented in chapter 10. The agent services manager (ASM) is responsible for maintaining a directory of all the agents in the system, their capabilities, and their status. Any agent that comes into the system must register with the ASM.

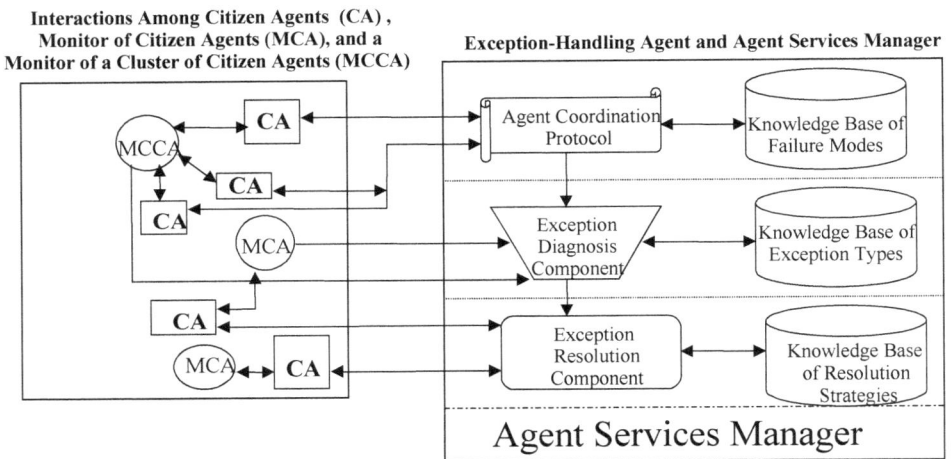

Figure 8-11: Multiagent System (MAS) architecture using citizen approach for exception handling.

The agent services manager periodically polls the survivalist agents. When it does not obtain a response after two consecutive polls, it assumes that the polled agent is dead. The ASM will generate a clone of the dead agent and reactivate it. It then sends a copy of the last message sent to the dead agent.

Multiagent Architecture and the Citizen Approach

Figure 8-11 depicts a MAS architecture that employs the citizen approach to handling the death of an agent (i.e., an exception). Just as in the survivalist approach, agents must register their skills with the ASM. As shown in Figure 8-11, in addition to supporting an agent services manager, the citizen approach also maintains knowledge bases of agent failure modes, exception types, and resolution strategies. A more detailed architectural framework for the citizen approach will be presented in Chapter 9.

In this research, the exception handler (EH) also performs the functions of the ASM. The EH is supported by a group of monitor agents that monitor communications among the citizen agents by continuously querying the status of the agents in the MAS. If a monitor agent detects symptoms of exceptions, it informs the EH, which then activates the exception diagnostic component of the exception-handling service. Each citizen agent is expected to support a set of exception-handling related messages such as "I am alive" or "My buffer is overloaded." The diagnosis component then determines the underlying cause of the exception based on the repository of exception types in its knowledge base and relays that information to the exception resolution module of the EH. The resolution module then retrieves a resolution strategy from its database of resolution strategies and recommends appropriate resolution actions. As stated above, the primary exception will be the death of an agent; however, the citizen approach may also handle other run-time exceptions such as buffer overload. When a monitor agent does not receive a response from two consecutive polls of the CA, the CA is presumed dead. This information is relayed to the exception-handling agent. The EH will clone a new CA, activate it, and reestablish its state. Some monitors will monitor individual citizen agents, while others will monitor a cluster of CAs.

Purpose of Research

The purpose of this study was to demonstrate improved effectiveness of the citizen approach for automating the management of communication networks over the traditional survivalist agent methodology. Instead of relying on the traditional survivalist software development strategy to automate telecommunication network management process, this study employed a citizen approach. The traditional approach relies on assumptions that the network design engineers make at the time they design networks. These assumptions fail during dynamic network operations environments. Very limited research has been done using the citizen approach, which supports exceptions that develop during network operations (Busuioc, Crabtree, Boyd, Sim, & Azarmi, 1996; Klein, 2000). This research advances the knowledge in applying the concept of run-time exception handling by software agents to manage complex global telecommunication network business processes. The success of this research might facilitate the development of a more effective method for building software tools that manage communication networks and other business processes.

To achieve this purpose, this researcher developed intelligent exception-handling policies using collaborative software agents to improve the performance of a business process using a model of a global telecommunication network. This researcher views business processes as complex adaptive systems where independent interactions among the agents in the system result in adaptive system behaviors (Battram, 1998, p. 28). The multiagent system is also viewed as a complex adaptive system. Exceptions among distributed and interacting agents are typically caused by role commitment violations. This approach is not in common use among researchers or practitioners who develop multiagent systems, primarily because they lack a repository of exception-handling processes. The information is usually scattered throughout the research community. This research exploits the knowledge gained from a review of a taxonomy of exceptions from a repository developed by MIT's Center for Coordination Science to ensure that distributed software agents do not violate their commitments. The feasibility of an exception-handling policy is demonstrated in a model of a global telecommunication network managed by a multiagent system. Therefore, the purpose of this research can be restated as determining if the average time it takes to restore downed customer telecommunication links is significantly reduced when the citizen agent approach, instead of the survivalist agent strategy, is employed to manage a telecommunication business process. Such an outcome would result in improved performance of the network, reduced operational costs, increased customer satisfaction, and better returns to the stakeholders.

Theoretical Framework

There has been an exponential growth in demand and supply of communications networks services (Caro & Dorigo, 1998). To meet customer demands and improve network performance, telecommunications service providers (TSPs) need to manage the flow of messages and data through the network. Effective management of telecommunications networks depends on the techniques used by TSPs to support message routing and congestion control. To achieve network performance objectives, TSPs must institute routing protocols and policies that satisfy conflicting business objectives and constraints brought about by technologies and customer demands. The following sections—telecommunications network routing, network management and design functions, and agent collaborations and agent-to-agent communications provide some theoretical perspectives for this research.

Telecommunications Network Routing

Ash (1997) considers routing an indispensable function in managing telecommunication networks because it connects a telephone call or data transfer from a source to a destination. He also views network routing as a critical part of telecommunications network architecture, design, and

155

operations. The term *network* encompasses an organization of switching systems interlinked by transmission links. The term *dynamic* describes time-sensitive routing methods, and in some situations, it may refer to real-time routing. The ability of telecommunication service providers to implement dynamic routing has improved the performance of telecommunications networks, thus improving availability of network connections and consumer cost reduction (Ash, 1997, p. 2).

Network Management and Design Functions

The three major functions of network management and design are real-time traffic management, capacity management, and network planning. *Real time traffic management* is used for optimizing network performance by reducing failures and shifting traffic loads to available routes. The tasks involved in this function—primarily traffic routing—have to be performed in minutes, seconds, or milliseconds. *Capacity management* aims to guarantee that network design and provisioning to meet performance objectives stay within acceptable budget levels. This function is typically performed within a timeframe of days and weeks. *Network planning* is a strategic function with a months-to-years timeframe. It attempts to ensure that resources for network switching and the links to transport message/data traffic are deployed ahead of time to accommodate predicted traffic growth (Ash, 1997).

In 1984, AT&T was the first telecommunications service provider to install dynamic routing when it employed preplanned hourly routing tables known as dynamic nonhierarchical routing (DNHR) and real-time network routing (RTNR) to support simultaneous routing of voice and data traffic. Nearly all established telecommunication companies—including AT&T, British Telecom, France Telecom, Japan National Telecom, Sprint, and MCI-WorldCom—employ RTNR (Ash, 1997). This research employed a real-time dynamic routing algorithm to determine new routes in a model of a telecommunication network. Collaborative agents used real-time network state-dependent routing methods in which routing patterns are defined as a result of the trunk usage levels. One set of collaborative agents used a trunk status routing map (TSRM) (Ash, 1998, p. 475) generated by another group of agents to search for new routes in a model of a communication network. The success of the routing process relies on how well the agents that are responsible for generating the TSRM perform their jobs. It is critical that the death of any agents not adversely impact the customer link restoration process. Details on the methodology are presented in Chapter 9.

The most common method used to route traffic through a communication network is called shortest-path routing. The nodes within a network are responsible for routing traffic by using a local or a global routing table. To route a message through a network, one algorithm adds a destination label to every message. When the message arrives at a switch, the switch reads the label and uses the information to select the most efficient route to a destination. In light of time of day as well as other variables such as a telethon with heavy telephone traffic, a suitable routing model is selected to achieve network performance objectives. The objectives include meeting customer's expectations and organizational profit objectives.

Collaboration among Agents

Collaboration among agents requires effective communication. The agents in this research used an agent communication language to perform communicative acts. Examples of communicative acts are *inform*—whereby one agent informs another agent about a piece of information—and *request*—whereby one agent expects a response from the message recipient agent. Additional details and categories of communicative acts are presented in Chapter 8 and Appendix A.

Quasi-Experimental Conditions and Assumptions

This research was based on the following quasi-experimental conditions and assumptions:

1. Interactions among software agents managing a model of a telecommunication network represent the behaviors and capabilities of distributed processing elements (i.e., components) that make up the network. The interacting agents within the multiagent system are used to effectively model a complex global telecommunication network maintenance and restoration process.

2. The network is an open-business process to be modeled as a complex adaptive system; thus, complexity theory applies to the mode of operation of the telecommunication network model.

3. Some agents will fail to meet the roles they had committed to; therefore, exception-handling strategies are needed to prevent inefficient agent performance. The death of an agent coupled with the recovery strategy employed by the survivalist and citizen approaches constitute the primary exception investigated in this research. During the experiment, one of the problem trunks advisor agents is selected at random to fail.

4. To qualify as an intelligent agent, software programs have three capabilities: ability to execute continuously for an extended time period, ability to acquire new knowledge and adapt to new situations, and ability to communicate with other agents.

Scope and Delimitations

The primary focus of this research was to determine the effectiveness of the MAS in the event of the death of an agent while the model is in operation. This research did not address the issues involved in automatic exception generation. The exception type and handling processes were developed prior to executing the multiagent system.

Only the network maintenance and restoration business process within the network and the systems management process depicted in Figures 11-3 and 11-6 were used to support the multiagent quasi-experimental method tested in this research. Sample data on customer network connections were used to run the experiments.

Hypotheses

The null hypothesis (H_0) for this research asserts that the use of the citizen approach for handling exceptions in an MAS where collaborative agents restore downed customer connections in a telecommunication system will not show any significant difference in restoration time with the survivalist strategy. The alternative hypothesis (H_a) is that the citizen approach will reduce the average time to restore downed customer connections, thus improving the performance of the network.

The null hypothesis implies that there will be no difference in the average time it takes the survivalist agents to restore the customer's communication links compared to the citizen agents. Instead of building exception-handling capability into every agent, the MAS could be implemented to use the citizen approach, which allows exception handling to be performed by another class of agents at run time.

The alternative hypothesis (H_a) is that the automated management of a telecommunication network with the citizen approach in a multiagent system will reduce the average downtimes of customer communication links due to a reduction in network restoration time, thus improving network performance. Other possible outcomes are explained by the null hypothesis. This hypothesis grows out of the conviction that the survivalist approach, also known as a design-time exception-handling strategy, places a significant burden on the developer, who must anticipate and plan for handling all possible exceptions prior to developing the system. In addition, embedding all possible exceptions into survivalist agents is bound to create significant overhead, thereby increasing the agent's problem-solving time and compromising MAS performance. Survivalist agents may not be as adaptive as citizen agents because if they encounter exceptions not embedded in their knowledge base at design time, they may not be able to perform their assigned tasks or may perform them poorly, thereby undermining the performance of other agents in the telecommunication network. While the citizen approach does not need to address the types of problems inherent in the survivalist approach, the damage of adding separate exception-handling agents and additional messages exchanged between the agents may outweigh the benefits derived from its efficient problem-solving abilities.

Significance of this Research

Attempts to automate business processes to improve their operational efficiency have failed because developers of those systems do not consider them as complex systems with built-in unpredictability for which the certainties of a command-and-control style of management do not apply (Battram, 1998). It is only when those systems are viewed as complex adaptive systems, where interacting agents with exception-handling capabilities prevent failures of the software systems that success can be assured (Klein, 1999). Automated management of open business processes with multiagent systems where the agents can fail has significant impact on the survival of organizations and societal health.

The negative impact of the inability of telecommunication service providers to meet their customers' service commitments is significant. In a National Public Radio Morning Edition report on September 26, 2000, Reporter Mike Shuster described the possible fines (at least $152 million) to be levied by state regulators against Ameritech, a subsidiary of Southwest Bell Corporation (SBC), for poor customer service records in five states in the Midwest. In each of the five states, hundreds of thousands of customers had to wait for weeks for telephone repairs, and several small businesses complained that delays in receiving adequate service placed them on the brink of bankruptcy. Emergency aid workers complained of their inability to reach critically sick patients because they were unable to get priority repair service (Shuster, 2000).

SBC was not the only major telecommunication service provider unable to meet customer network service demands. A 2000 *Washington Post* article reported how the loss of network connections by UUNet customers disrupted 18 area businesses in metropolitan Washington, DC (El Boghdady, 2000). One business was on contract to supply local grocery stores, but because of the disruption, trucks could not be dispatched and shelves at the stores could not be stocked.

It is standard practice among telecommunication service providers to execute a service-level agreement or guarantee (SLA/SLG) promising network availability, with significant penalties for poor service. If the thesis of this research is applied, it would be possible for telecommunication service providers to meet their customer demands with automated network management tools that model the systems as complex adaptive systems using collaborative software agents that handle exceptions. In addition, disseminating the results of this research among researchers and practitioners of multiagent systems could improve the strategies used to develop automated software for business processes.

Conclusion

A global economy relies on effective, efficient, and uninterruptible telecommunication service. Therefore, it is critical that telecommunication service providers manage the network to meet these criteria. Implementing appropriate routing algorithms is key to developing successful automated network management systems. Unfortunately, many researchers and practitioners that develop distributed software or multiagent systems to automate the management of business processes develop inefficient software systems that are unable to perform in real-world environments (Klein, 1997). The poor performance has been attributed to the assumption that business processes are closed systems where the computing infrastructures are reliable. No allowances have been made for failures in the agents' performance or for unreliable interagent communications.

In this chapter, I have presented the nature of business processes as open systems; as such, the agents in the multiagent systems developed to manage them can fail, thus preventing the system from achieving its performance objectives. Agent failures are known as exceptions. Knowledge of exception-handling strategies is scattered in the published research, making it difficult for researchers to exploit. This chapter has identified an approach for exploiting exception-handling strategies and developing robust multiagent systems, to enhance the maintenance and restoration processes in a model of a global network management system. The benefits of incorporating exception-handling strategies to manage open-business processes to support the survival of organizations and other societal benefits have been discussed.

The success of this research will have a significant social impact by equipping telecommunication service providers with automated tools that will help them implement effective network management policies. This will lead to customer satisfaction, growth in employment, increasing revenue, good returns to stakeholders' equity, and robustness of the global economy. The method could be applied to other business processes such as transportation systems and air traffic control systems. The next chapter will provide a review of the literature, to explain current developments in automating business processes, exception-handling strategies, collaborative agents, and related research to real-world applications of software agent technology.

CHAPTER 9: LITERATURE REVIEW ON EXCEPTION HANDLING STRATEGIES AND MULTI-AGENT SYSTEMS

This literature review covers the rationale for using software agents and multiagent systems (MAS) in telecommunication networks. The discussion of rationale includes some foundational knowledge of MAS and their applications to a variety of systems, as well as the applicability of complexity theory, complex adaptive systems theory, intelligent agents, business process reengineering, research design, quasi-experimental design, telecommunication networks, hypothesis testing, factor analysis, multivariate statistics, sampling theory, and statistical analysis. A review of the literature on weaknesses of current research in MASs, which does not address the critical issues of exceptions in multiagent systems that manage open business processes, will be presented. The literature review includes current research activities on commitments and commitment protocols among agents in an MAS, agent roles, commitments, role commitment violation analysis, and generic conflict management strategies. This review will be followed by a discussion of current attempts at developing systems that support exception-handling strategies to manage open systems.

Literature Search Strategy

After deciding on the topic for this research, this student identified the technical areas, which included telecommunications network domain, traffic routing in telecommunication network, complexity science, software agent technology, distributed computing, research design, management science, exception handling, and multiagent systems. These subject areas were used to guide the literature search process.

The set of literature reviewed for this research were collected in part through a full online text search of the Academic Search Elite over two summer sessions at Indiana University in Bloomington, Indiana. Additional materials were collected through online and physical access to the Montgomery County Maryland Regional library in Wheaton, Maryland. The research library at British Telecommunications, PLC in Martlesham, England (http://sss.info.bt.co.uk) provides full-text online access for a substantial number of technical journals including *Management Science, Communications of the ACM, Sloan Management Review,* and the *Journal of Artificial Intelligence.* The rest of the materials were obtained from conference proceedings, monthly professional journals obtained through subscriptions, and textbooks. Membership in the American Association for Artificial Intelligence and the Association for Computing Machinery provided access to refereed journals and conference proceedings. National Public Radio news reports (Shuster, 2000), the *Washington Post* (El Boghdady, 2000), and the *Financial Times* (Westbrook, 2000) served as valuable sources.

Rationale for Using Software Agent Technologies in Telecommunication Networks

Software agents have characteristics that make them suitable for supporting distributed open systems. Among those characteristics are agent autonomy, trustworthiness, ability to communicate with other agents (thus making them effective distributed problem solvers), ability to survive in difficult real-time environments, and their advantages over object-oriented programs (DeLoach, 2000; Gross & Strand, 2000; Jennings, Faratin, Norman, O'Brien, Odgers, & Alty, 1998; Nwana, 1996; Plu, 1998; Shoham, 1993; Wooldridge & Jennings, 1999).

Agent-Oriented versus Object-Oriented Thinking

A common confusion among researchers new to the agent-oriented method is the distinction between agents and objects in software development and application. According to Jennings, Sycara, and Wooldridge (1998), object-oriented programmers do not see anything new about agent-oriented programming. The authors define objects as computational entities that represent some state and that are able to change the state by performing some action on them and then communicating with other objects through message passing. While object characteristics seem similar to agents, the authors identified three major differences between the two models.

First, an agent has autonomy (i.e., control over its state), whereas an object does not. When an object sends a request to another object, the sending object is responsible for invoking the method (i.e., functions) that the receiving object must use. Therefore, the decision whether to execute an action lies with the object that invokes the method (i.e., the sending object). In this regard, the object that makes a request specifies what to do about a request and how to perform the request. In agent-oriented thinking, the decision on what to do comes from the requestor, while the agent that receives the request decides on how to perform the action. Autonomy as defined here is not a fundamental object-oriented model (Jennings, Sycara, & Wooldridge, 1998, p. 15).

A second attribute of agents that distinguishes them from object-oriented systems is the concept of "flexible (reactive, proactive, and social) autonomous behavior" (Jennings, Sycara, & Wooldridge, 1998, p. 15). The authors admitted that one could argue that software objects could be developed to incorporate flexible autonomous behaviors, but they pointed out that such a component is not standard to object-oriented programming.

A third distinction between standard-object and agent-oriented models is the absence of a thread of control in the object-oriented method, whereas each agent has its own thread of control (Jennings, Sycara, & Wooldridge, 1998, p. 16). With the advent of the Java programming language, with its multithreaded programming capability, objects can be developed with their own thread of control. In this writer's view, the first and second distinctions listed above are the most valid. The third distinction could be wrapped into the second attribute.

Distributed Computation and Cooperation among Processing Entities

While telecommunication networks consist of heterogeneous and distributed processing elements with distributed expertise, each network is expected to provide a common access to all its services. Such a situation demands that distributed and heterogeneous information systems interoperate (Plu, 1998). Plu observed that telecommunication networks have inherently distributed computation and cooperation among multiple authorities (i.e., consumers and telecommunication service providers), each with its own policies. Plu recommended autonomous software agents as the most appropriate software technology for effectively meeting the needs of consumers and service providers because autonomous agents can embed their control policy to act on behalf of service providers and consumers. While acting as service-provider agents, autonomous agents can control their policies because they are free to refuse requests for service, to set the cost of a service, and to select the type and quality of resource to be allocated for any request. Acting on behalf of the consumer, consumer agents are free to choose a telecommunication service provider based on the quality and cost of service.

In Plu's view, agent autonomy means the agent makes the decisions that guide its policies. It cannot rely on a human user who may be unavailable or unable to help. To succeed in telecommunication network management, autonomous agents must have all the knowledge or know where to acquire the information to fill the gaps in their knowledge and perform the tasks assigned to them. Although Plu's focus is on applying agent autonomy to the telecommunication network domain, the technology could be applied to any process-control system that supports real-world environments, such as complex business process management (Jennings, Faratin, Norman, O'Brien, et al. 1998 and Jennings, Sycara, & Wooldridge, 1998, p. 8).

In addition to agent autonomy, an agent's trustworthiness (i.e., its ability to deliver a desired quality of service within acceptable timeframe and cost of service) is critical to its application to open systems (Plu, 1998). An agent's trustworthiness can be assured only if the agent is autonomous—responsive, proactive, and social (Jennings, Sycara, & Wooldridge, 1998).

Agents' Distribution

Plu (1998); Weihmayer (1998); and Jennings, Sycara, and Wooldridge (1998) identified several challenges faced by researchers interested in applying distributed agents to networked systems. In a network environment, especially telecommunication networks, agents are expected to be physically distributed throughout networked computing equipment. As a result of their distribution, they must rely on network communication protocols such as the transmission control protocol/internet protocol (TCP/IP) to exchange data and information. Since the ability to communicate among agents rests on the availability of the network, failure or overload of the network would result in delays. In addition, confidentiality and security must be addressed when communicating over a network. Another important issue is the system's inability to maintain a global clock because each computing system maintains its own clock. Given that situation, exchange of information among the agents must be asynchronous.

Agent Communication

To achieve cooperation among distributed software agents, they must be able to communicate efficiently (Wooldridge & Jennings, 1999). In a heterogeneous open system such as a telecommunication network, all the agents must use application-independent communication protocols and communication languages. To enable effective communication, well-defined messages must be exchanged in order for each agent to update its internal state.

Agents' Persistence or Temporal Continuity

To keep track of their changing environments and at the same time be able to offer their services at any time, each agent must be persistent. Being persistent demands that each agent is able to execute continuously, to accept and send requests at any time (Plu, 1998). The agents must execute asynchronously because they cannot stop and wait for responses to their requests while they have other tasks or requests to process. During the life of the agent, its environment may change without its control. Examples of such changes include failure of resources, changes in the capability of the agent, or degradation in the utility of information available to it. Agents must adapt to accommodate those changes in their environment (Plu, 1998, p. 245).

Agents in Open Systems

Plu (1998) and Jennings, Sycara, and Wooldridge (1998, p. 23) recommended that MAS developers consider agents' survivability in an open system. Plu viewed agents operating in a networked environment as interoperating in an open system. Asserting that in an open system changes are unpredictable, he identified breakdown in communication capabilities, loss of required services, and multiple demands from other agents as critical issues that agents must address. In addition, agents that operate in open systems are expected to be flexible in responding to other agents' demands, adaptive to unforeseen events, and cognizant of new opportunities or resources that may improve their performance. Plu concluded that learning capability, self-organizing properties, message passing, and translation are some of the additional skills required by agents operating in open systems.

To meet their designers' objectives, MASs that operate in open systems require the ability to coordinate with each other (Jennings, Sycara, & Wooldridge, 1998). To be able to coordinate their activities, the agents must be able to locate other agents in an open environment and communicate, since agents may disappear and reappear without any warning.

Commitment Protocols in Multiagent Systems

This section will review ongoing research in approaches used to establish and enforce commitments among agents in multiagent systems. Jain, Aparicio, and Singh (1999) viewed agents' autonomy and their ability to perceive, reason, operate in their environment, and communicate with other agents as the key elements that make MASs effective in supporting open systems. The authors argued that autonomy is the most critical capability of a software agent built to operate in open environments. They viewed the challenge for researchers as how to manage autonomy—how to give the agent the freedom it deserves with adequate constraints to prevent it from devolving into chaos. They concluded that the best approach for managing autonomy is to formulate commitment protocols that enable the agents to voluntarily control their actions. They recommended viewing a multiagent system as spheres of commitment that define the promises and obligations agents may have for each other and the scope within which the commitments apply.

Commitment among agents is similar to the relationships among a debtor, a creditor, a context, and a proposition. In such a situation, the debtor promises a creditor to keep a promise (i.e., a proposition). The context can be viewed as a witness who is responsible for adjudicating in disputes. Jain, Aparicio, and Singh claimed that commitments are synonymous with legal reasoning. They theorized that commitment can be ensured in information-based systems by closely monitoring the integrity and flow of data exchanged among agents, monitoring the relationship between agents or the structure of the multiagent organization, and establishing a strategy to preserve autonomy among heterogeneous agents.

The rest of the review of commitment protocols will cover the views of Venkatraman and Singh (1999), as presented in their paper that explored verifying compliance with commitment protocols. Other relevant research includes Teague and Sonenberg (2000), who investigated commitment flexibility in multiagent contracts; Singh (2000), who described an ontology for commitments in multiagent systems; and multiagent systems as spheres of commitment—commitment-based interoperation for e-commerce (Xing, Rustogi, & Singh, 1999). Coen (2000) viewed a multiagent system as an artificial social system in which its constituent agents obey common social laws and are free to behave as they please as long as they avoid conflicts between agents. Using probability distributions, Coen attempted to formulate social laws and pertinent algorithms. The review will analyze the efficacy of such approaches in dealing with inter-agent conflicts.

Exception-Handling Strategies

Klein and Dellarocas (1999); Jennings (1998); and Musliner, Goldman, Pelican, and Kreobsbash (1999) agree that business environments are inherently unstable because the environments generate exceptions that are not apparent until their consequences become unbearable. At that point a typical response is to react to resolve the new situation, causing delays in meeting operational goals of the enterprise. When monitoring and control of business processes are manual, managers must locate underlying causes of a new problem through observing and reviewing records, holding discussions with employees, and spending valuable time resolving the problem before they recommend corrective actions (Klein & Dellarocas, 1999). Klein (1997) claimed that there has not been a preferred standard process for dealing with exceptions because exceptions are unanticipated problems that require nonstandard approaches to address them. He argued that poor performance, system shutdown, and adverse impacts on costs and schedules are the consequences of inconsistent exception handling process.

Dellarocas and Klein (2000) presented some popular approaches for handling exceptions in business processes and their limitations. One of the approaches is model-based fault diagnosis, which employs a generic algorithm to determine the origin of the fault in a system without demanding prior knowledge of failure mode and resolution heuristics from the manager. Dellarocas and Klein (2000) cautioned researchers that model-based fault diagnosis could be ineffective under certain situations because it assumes a complete and correct model of the system, whereas that information may not be attainable. Another approach for exception handling suggested by the same authors is the use of failure-mode analysis to describe a systematic process, which must be developed by people with in-depth knowledge of the domain. Reliance on experts makes the approach expensive (Dellarocas & Klein, 2000). Klein (1997) provided a list of disciplines with approaches for exception handling. The list includes planning, distributed systems, and manufacturing process control.

171

The planning and robotics research community emphasizes strategies that deal with unexpected states of the robot, but they focus only on the exceptions in the environment while the robot itself is excluded from their observation. Work on exception-handling strategies in computer-supported cooperative work has been applied only to very limited domains (Dellarocas & Klein, 2000). Garvin (1998) provided a uniform framework for analyzing organizational processes as work, behavioral, and change processes. Dellarocas and Klein (2000) described domain-independent exception-handling services that increase robustness in open multiagent systems. Klein and Dellarocas (1999) noted that there is a push towards developing a systematic repository of knowledge about managing multiagent system exceptions. Bourne, Excelente-Toledo, and Jennings (1999) described run-time selection of coordination mechanisms in multiagent systems to handle exceptions among the agents. Marriott and Sloman (1996) described their implementation of a management agent for interpreting obligation policy. Bell, Sethares, and Bucklew (2000) discussed coordination failure and congestion in information networks. Murphy (1999) presented some approaches for handling sensing failures in autonomous mobile robots.

O'Leary and Selfridge (1999) summarized different approaches for handling business process reengineering (BPR). They viewed BPR as a process of using new technologies to change business processes to realize significant performance improvements. They reviewed the roles of information technology tools—specifically, artificial intelligence (AI) approaches and several software tools suitable for BPR—but concluded that few organizations embed AI-based tools such as agent-oriented approaches to support BPR. The concept of exception handling did not feature in their reviews except in citing the works of Klein and Dellarocas (1999), who reported on a knowledge-based approach to handling exceptions in workflow systems.

Research in Agent-Oriented Approaches to Exception Handling

Dellarocas and Klein (2000) identified several research efforts that employ agent-oriented approach to exception handling. A major drawback is that research activities did not support an exception-handling service that can be applied to different domains. The researchers cited included Hagg, Kaminka and Tambe, Horling and Lesser, and Decker and Williamson (cited in Dellarocas & Klein, 2000). Hagg's work involved monitor agents that monitor problem-solving agents. When a problem-solving agent encounters an exception, the monitor agent intervenes by submitting an alternative problem-solving method, replacing the regular agent. This approach must be built into the system at design time and the implementation is not domain independent (cited in Dellarocas & Klein, 2000).

Kaminka and Tambe used an exception-handling approach called social attentive monitoring (SAM), where agents attempt to sense commitment violations among neighboring agents and employ their knowledge of the system to diagnose and fix the problem. This approach requires domain-dependent exception-handling strategies. Research by Horling, Lesser, and others evaluated a domain-independent exception-handling strategy in which the agents have inaccurate contextual knowledge of the dependencies among agents. This approach can handle only one exception (cited in Dellarocas & Klein, 2000). Venkatraman and Singh (1999) described a generic approach to identify the agents that do not comply with their commitment protocols. Their approach simply addresses one subset of exception handling and does not deal with exception resolution.

Related Research on Applying MAS to Real-World Business Processes

In a *Financial Times Information Technology Review* article, Perkin (2000) reported on the popularity of AI in the automotive industry. She began with a reminder of the early days of AI: "In the 1980s, AI was the Holy Grail of computer research, but it largely failed to deliver promised benefits. Today, new and more narrowly focused AI techniques are improving design and control processes" (p. 1). One of the narrowly focused techniques involves software agents, which used to be called distributed AI. Perkin described the work of Kurt Sundermeyer and his research team at DaimlerChrysler in Berlin, Germany. The research involved implementing a leading-edge materials flow control system entirely based on autonomous software agents. The system is used to produce cylinder heads of automobile engines. The research team focused on software agents' approach because traditional software systems are monolithic and hard to scale up. An MAS assigns each autonomous agent to a small part of the problem, and since there is no limit on the number of agents, the system can scale up effectively. Perkin also described how applications of software agents to real-time problems are benefiting Caterpillar Corporation for just-in-time management of factory orders, as well as Computer Associates, whose Neugents software product can predict failure in telecommunication networks.

Prouskas, Patel, Pitt, and Barria (2000) described how agent technology can be applied to intelligently control message traffic on telecommunication networks. Their research employed autonomous agents that used a market-based algorithm to control delivery of communication network resources from suppliers to consumers. The operating scenario is synonymous with supplier sites such as the Web sites of Amazon and Barnes and Noble as service control points (SCP) along with the buyers' site such as an Internet service provider (ISP) as the service switching point (SSP). The research described how a coordinator agent could be modeled to use a market-based approach to control user access to the supplier's site. The primary objective is to please customers by granting them access to the supplier's site without negatively impacting service. The consumer agents represent the customers of the ISP who must gain access to the network. Since it may not be feasible for all consumer agents to gain access to the network, the researchers used the coordinator as an auctioneer to handle bids for access from consumer agents. The coordinator agent selects acceptable bids based on market-based criteria such as the type of service, connection speed, and so on.

Prouskas et al. (2000) concluded that using a market-based approach provides better load control on the network than does an approach that selectively permits users into the network. However, the authors could not determine whether the added benefit of the agent-based approach compensates for the heavy computational overhead. Given the performance and low price of computing resources, that concern is insignificant. The authors expressed optimism regarding the merits of agent-based approach to control communication network traffic load.

Wolper, Kirshner, and Merz (1999) claimed that agents' adaptive capabilities are critical to the success of multiagent systems that operate in complex and unstable environments. The authors compared two systems: (a) routing data packets through a telecommunication network by employing adaptive agents using a reinforcement learning algorithm, and (b) agents that use a traditional routing algorithm. Shortest-path routing (i.e., a routing algorithm that selects the shortest path from an origin to a destination to route message traffic) was the traditional algorithm employed. An important finding was that their MAS, where the agents can adapt to the actions of other agents, showed a 25% performance improvement over another MAS in which the agents' interactions are not adaptive. However, given the limited number of nodes (about 10) in the network modeled, scalability of the approach to very large networks would require further investigation.

Mudgal and Vassileva (1999) studied how agents can negotiate with other agents on behalf of their owners to get the best deals in the

175

marketplace. Rather than having human users connect to the Internet and personally present their tenders, their agents do the work. The strategy involves training the agents to learn the behaviors of other agents. The authors concluded that agents that can learn the behaviors of other agents could negotiate more effectively than could those agents without the ability to learn. The application is suitable to electronic commerce sites such as eBay, where agents could be used to represent buyers and sellers and negotiate a price acceptable to their human counterparts. While the research holds promise, when there are hundreds of agents in the MAS, it is impractical to expect every agent to effectively model the behaviors of other agents due to prohibitive computational resource demands by each agent. The approach could be feasible if the agents were organized into clusters and each agent needed to know only the behaviors of the agents within its cluster.

Faratin, Jennings, Buckle, and Sierra (1999) described the design and implementation of an MAS in which agents collaborate to provide virtual private networks. The research focused on the negotiation algorithms the agents used. The MAS consists of three categories of agents: (a) personal communication agents (PCAs) to support the end users, (b) service provider agents (SPAs) that model the network services domain, and (c) network provider agents (NPAs) to simulate network connection process. Using ContractNet protocol and the Foundation for Intelligent Physical Agents (FIPA) standard for inter-agent communication and management, the researchers implemented automated negotiation among agents to provide telecommunication access to users. They concluded that it is feasible to realize automated negotiation among distributed agents that operate in dynamic environments.

Odubiyi, Bayless, and Ruberton (2001) described an MAS (Proteus) where collaborative agents interact to proactively track and resolve faults in a model of a global telecommunication network. The research focused on eliminating the labor-intensive approach of tracking and resolving faults in customers' network connections. It addressed one of the research challenges in implementing an MAS in hard real-time environments: dealing with rapidly changing data in a dynamic telecommunication operational environment.

Jennings, Faratin et al. (1998) reported on the design and implementation of an MAS research prototype that modeled the British Telecommunications business process for generating and delivering customer quotes for provisioning communication network connections. The network-provisioning process includes network service specification, configuration, and installation. The research demonstrated the feasibility of deploying agents with negotiation ability to support a business process. It also gave the researchers some insights on the application of MAS to a real-world situation. The service provisioning process requires negotiation among different participants on price, duration, penalty, and volume of service. The participants were modeled as customer agents and service-provider agents. This seems to be the most common implementation strategy used by developers of multiagent systems (Dellarocas & Klein, 2000; Prouskas, Patel, Pitt, & Barria, 2000). The problem is usually framed to allow the application of ContractNet protocol for bidding and auctions. A unique contribution of this research is its support of exception handling that resolves communication failure, functional failure, resource failure, and service exception. The survivalist agent strategy is used to handle exceptions. When information between agents is corrupted or lost, the message is resent. When a task fails, another task is restarted. When a resource such as network designer is unavailable to complete a task, the task is rescheduled. When there is the possibility that the service level agreement cannot be met, a decision is made to proactively renegotiate.

Musliner, Goldman, Pelican, and Kreobsbash (1999) sought to identify necessary agent skills to operate effectively in real-time environments. They affirmed that a real-time environment constrains an agent's ability to sense, process, and respond to inputs from its environment; therefore, agents that operate in such an environment must have self-adaptive capabilities. Again, these agents were built with the survivalist agent paradigm, with its demand for built-in capability established at design

177

time, which may limit the agent's ability to effectively adapt to unforeseen run-time situations.

Conclusion

Research on the use of agent and multiagent system technology demonstrates the effectiveness of an agent-based approach to system management problems in open business systems. The MAS approach is recommended for automating the management of business processes with heterogeneous and distributed processing elements and distributed expertise, such as those found in the operations of telecommunication networks.

This literature review also covered agent attributes such as the ability to communicate with other system entities, to run autonomously for extended time periods (i.e., temporal continuity), and to adapt to changing and unpredictable influences of the external environment. The literature review also evaluated commitment protocols necessary for handling exceptions among the agents in a multiagent system. These agent and MAS attributes were employed in the present study. The approach for using them is described in the presentation of research methods in the next chapter.

The last part of the literature review identified related research on applying MAS to real-world business processes. Research at DaimlerChrysler in Berlin, Germany, documented success in applying software agent technology to material flow control and automobile engine cylinder manufacturing processes. This example demonstrates the maturity of software agent technology and its utility in supporting automation of business processes. However, most of the multiagent systems still employ the survivalist approach to handle exceptions that develop during the operation of an MAS. The next chapter describes the research methods used to investigate the feasibility of implementing an MAS that incorporates exception-handling service and improves the performance of a business process over a traditional survivalist agent approach.

CHAPTER 10: RESEARCH METHODS FOR EXCEPTION HANDLING STRATEGIES TO ENSURE SYSTEM SURVIVABILITY

Open distributed business processes are characterized by nonroutine tasks in unpredictable environments. Such business processes are known as complex systems (Coveney & Highfield, 1995; Pascale, 1999). "Because complex systems have built-in unpredictability, the certainties of a command-and-control approach to management no longer hold true" (Battram, 1998, p. 11). Therefore, for open business processes to survive, they must be managed as complex adaptive systems (Battram, 1998).

Telecommunications service providers confront many challenges in meeting service requirements of their customers due to increased competition, demand for rapid and high-quality service, and network growth. To meet customer demands, telecommunications service providers need embedded and collaborating computer software tools that are responsive to solving customer problems, proactive in anticipating new problems, and adaptive to handling unexpected operational environments (Prouskas, Patel, Pitt, & Barria, 2000).

Multiagent systems (MASs) have been identified as one of the most promising approaches for supporting open systems typical of telecommunication networks because they have the ability to use multiagent coordination protocols to reorganize themselves in response to changes in their problem focus and environment (Jennings, Sycara, & Wooldridge, 1998). A wide variety of implemented MASs assume that distributed agents operate in a closed world where the infrastructure (i.e., computer systems and communication links) is reliable. Uncertainties in communication links and degradation of the computing environment or link failures may cause the software agents to "die" (i.e., be rendered useless) or be unable to communicate with other agents (Klein, 1997). As the number of agents in the MAS grows, possible points of failure grow geometrically. A significant increase in the number of agents results in complex interactions among them, causing unpredictable behaviors that demand complex coordination mechanisms. These departures from expected performance levels are called exceptions, and, if not handled effectively, they can prevent the system from delivering its operational goals and can lead to the failure of the system as a whole (Dellarocas & Klein, 2000; Prouskas, Patel, Pitt, & Barria, 2000).

The MAS described above is typical of traditional distributed software systems implemented to automate the management of telecommunication networks (Hayzelden & Bigham, 1998; Odubiyi, Bayless, & Ruberton, 1999; Pagurek, Li, Bieszczad, & Susilo, 1998). These traditional MASs employ the *survivalist approach* (Dellarocas & Klein, 2000, p. 97), which, among other requirements, obliges the MAS developer to design into every problem-solving agent all skills needed to handle all possible exceptions that may develop during execution. The survivalist approach, also known as a design-time exception-handling strategy, places a significant burden on the developer, who must anticipate and plan for handling all possible exceptions.

The null hypothesis (H_0) for this research asserted that the citizen approach for handling exceptions in a MAS, where collaborative agents restore downed customer connections in a telecommunication system, would not show any significant difference in the restoration time over the survivalist strategy. The alternative hypothesis (H_a) predicted that the citizen approach would reduce the average time to restore downed customer connections, thus improving the performance of the network. This hypothesis was based on a one-tailed test because the assertion specifies a direction.

This study extends the work of Dellarocas and Klein (2000), which investigated the development of effective MASs where it is assumed that the infrastructure of the open system under investigation is unreliable and the agents are prone to fail. Their research focused on the domain of bidding for contracts and contract awards using Contract Net (CNET) protocol (Huhns, & Singh, 1997). They assumed that it is feasible to characterize reusable domain-independent exception-handling expertise that describes the modes of failure for a variety of MAS coordination methods and exception-handling strategies. Instead of building exception-handling capability into every agent, exception handling is performed by another class of agents. Their approach permits survivalist agents to renege on their commitments and accept the penalties. The MAS manager is notified by the problematic agents ahead of time to reduce the negative impacts of their actions. On the other hand, the citizen agent strategy employs the following process: (a) identifying a target exception at run time, (b) examining the repository of exceptions to identify a process for resolving a target exception, (c) determining the root cause of the exception, (d) determining the process for fixing the exception, (e) fixing the exception, and (f) learning from the exception handling process.

This research addressed some challenges that were not investigated by Delarocas and Klein (1997). In their research, as is typical of any contract bidding process where the focus is on a single task, several agents are available to work on the task at hand because the agents possess similar skills. It is therefore feasible to send the task of a dysfunctional or dead agent to another agent. Such an approach was not feasible in the current study because the problem-solving agents have unique skills not possessed by other agents. They are specialist agents and must collaborate with other agents to restore the downed communication link. In dealing with the death of an agent, Busuioc and Crabtree (1996) distributed the task of the dead agent among other agents. That approach assumes that the task is decomposable. Delarocas and Klein (2000) used a similar approach. The present study did not assume that each task is decomposable nor did it assume that any agent can take over the task of a dead agent. When an agent died, a new agent was cloned to replace the dead agent.

The rest of this chapter covers the research process, beginning with a description of the architecture for an MAS that employs the survivalist agent strategy, followed by a discussion of architecture that uses the citizen agent approach for handling exceptions. Additional components described include the quasi-experimental design process, identification and definition of the network system variables, and procedures to determine sample sizes for PVCs originating from the network nodes. This chapter concludes with a discussion of data sampling and data analysis, and a summary of the chapter.

Research Process

This research focused on one independent variable—the average time to restore downed customer network connections, and two strategies--the survivalist strategy and the citizen approach for handling exceptions or role commitment violations among agents in an MAS. The primary objective was to determine which of the two multiagent system strategies is more effective in restoring downed customer connections.

Telecommunication service providers (TSPs) typically provide three types of message traffic to their customers: (a) interactive message traffic for basic terminal-to-host or telephone applications, (b) client-server applications where the processing is done in the background such as in database retrieval, and (c) batch processing such as email with attachments. A service level agreement (SLA) is signed between the parties. The TSPs incur financial penalties if they are unable to meet their commitments. The PVC connects the customer (e.g., a multinational corporation with offices in several countries) from an office at one location to a destination office at another location through a set of switches. It is the responsibility of the TSP to ensure that the telecommunication connections (i.e., PVCs) are up so that message traffic can be relayed between the offices. When the connection or link fails, a PVC restoration process is activated.

Each PVC is measured in bits-per-second, also known as bandwidth. Network trunks hold several PVCs and connect the switches. The data collected from the network elements help determine when a customer has violated its committed information rate (CIR), when the link is down, or when the trunk that a PVC traverses is congested and the PVC needs to be rerouted.

This research followed the seven steps in experimental research proposed by Isaac and Michael (1989). The first three steps are (a) a survey of the literature for problem related topics, (b) definition of the problem, and (c) formulation of problem hypothesis and definition of basic terms and variables. Isaac and Michael's (1989) fourth step— develop a plan for the experiment—was achieved as follows:

1.   Identifying all the non-quasi-experimental variables that may influence the outcome of the research. Ten of these system-related variables are described below.

2.   Selecting a research design: quasi-experimental. This design was chosen because it was not feasible to control all the factors that might affect the validity of the research results. This approach is appropriate because this research employs real network operations data and rather than simulated data.

3.   Selecting a sample of subjects to represent the population. Samples of PVCs (Table 10-1) from 15 of the nodes in the global communication network were selected using cluster-sampling approach. The samples are representative of the

population N of the PVCs in the network with 95% confidence level.

4. Selecting and validating the instruments required to measure the outcome of the experiment. The main measurement performed in this experiment was done by the data server agent that reads network statistics on customer connections from a database, reads the computer clock, and reads the clock again from the same computer after the connection has been restored by other agents.

5. Developing a procedure for collecting the data and validating the instruments required to measure the outcome of the experiment. The data for this research represent 3 days of communication network results. The network data include customer connections (PVCs), port congestion, trunk usage, network topology, and the names and locations of switches.

6. Stating the null hypothesis for the research variables. The null hypothesis for this research was that there will be no significant difference in the average time it takes a group of collaborative agents to restore customer connections, whether they use the survivalist or the citizen agent approach to handle exceptions in the operation of the MASs.

Isaac and Michael's (1989) fifth step is actually conducting the experiment(s). Those procedures are discussed in the section that describes the multiagent testbed architectures for the survivalist and the citizen approaches.

Internal Validity of the Multiagent Agent System

The software programs used in this research has been developed according to the software agent design and development standard proposed by the Foundation for Intelligent Physical Agents (FIPA). The multiagent system framework employed in this research reused software components that have been used successfully in two previous research efforts directed by this researcher. The two research projects for which this researcher served as the Principal Investigator are: (a) SAIRE – A Scalable Agent-based Information Retrieval Engine (Odubiyi, Wakim, Kocur, Weinstein; et. al., 1997) and (b) Victor – Proactive Fault Tracking and Resolution in Broadband Networks using Collaborative Intelligent Agents (Odubiyi, Bayless, & Ruberton, 2001). Results from these research activities have shown that the software agents collaborate to generate data outputs that are deemed reasonable.

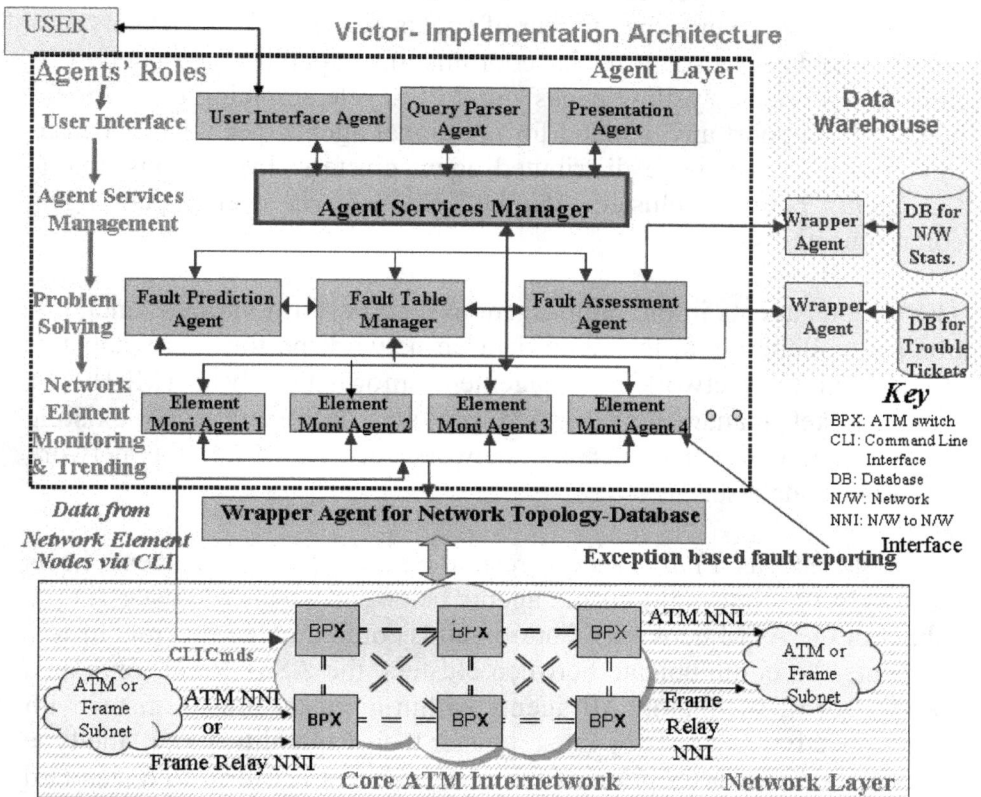

Figure 10-1: Victor System Implementation Architecture

Figure 10-1 depicts the system implementation architecture for Victor followed by a brief description of the system. The core of the Victor system is the agent layer. The agent layer consists of a number of agents that provide the control mechanism for achieving the desired objectives of the Victor system. Figure 10-1 illustrates the design architecture of Victor system prototype. The agent layer has a hierarchical structure consisting of groups of agents with different high level roles or sub-layers: *User Interface, agents-services management, problem solving, network monitoring and performance trending, and interfaces with heritage-network operations data sources.* The agent services and management sub-layer has only a single agent, the Agent Services Manager (ASM), since the number of agents required for the prototype is small. The layer also provides coordination capability for supporting directory services, "yellow pages", and life-cycle servicing tasks for the agents. To support any demand for additional agents, peer ASMs can be implemented to manage distributed agent clusters. Interactions among the agents between clusters can be achieved via peer-to-peer agent communications.

The various agents in the multi-agent system perform various functions, often in collaboration, to obtain data on network performance statistics residing in the network's management information base (MIB). A trouble-ticket management system provides information on existing faults on network elements and network topology from the network operations database.

The ASM acts as a name server, resource server for all the agents in its cluster. In the first build all the agents belong to a single cluster (i.e., a subnet of the ATM network). Future builds could include several clusters of agents. To communicate between clusters, the ASM could serve as a coordinator or facilitator. All agents within a cluster must register with their respective ASM. They must register their capabilities, (i.e., the type of services). The description of the services must conform to a standard service description template such as:

<agent-name, request(ASM,
  (:register (:agent-name <name of agent>))
  (:service-description (:service-name <name-of-service>))
  (:service-ontology <the ontology-of-service---a list of actions-the agent can
  perform such as get, compute, retrieve, etc.>))
  (:communication protocols < [e. g., TCP/IP sockets, CORBA IIOP]>,
  (:address <e.g., IP address>) (:message-format <a format>)))>.

Tables A1, A2, and A3 in Appendix A provide additional details on service types and the Agent Communication Language.

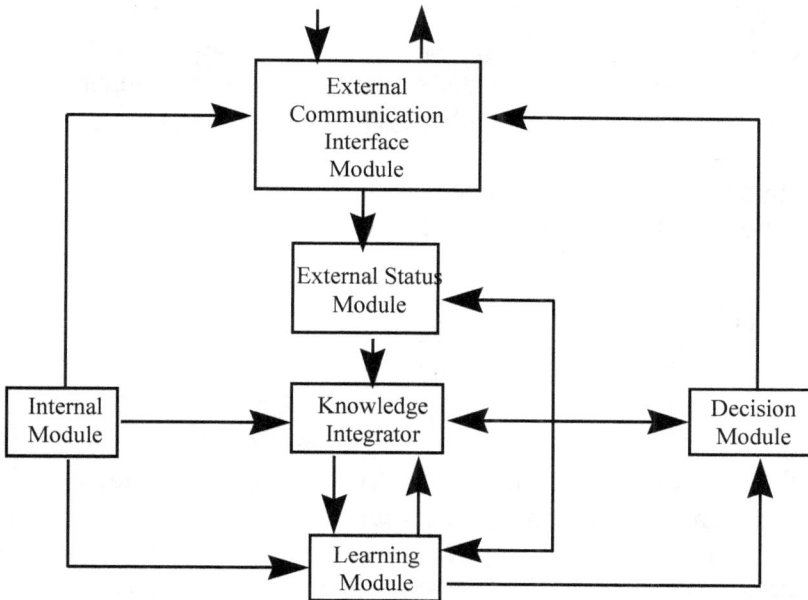

Figure 10-2: Architecture of an Agent in Victor

Architecture of a Victor Agent

Figure 10-2 depicts the major structural components of each agent in Victor as described below:

189

- *The Decision Module* is the planning and inference engine used to make decisions based on the information provided by the Internal and External Modules, and based on the decision rules stored in the Knowledge Base
- *The Knowledge Base* maintains the decision rules
- *The Learning Module* changes the existing rules and derives the new decision rules through learning
- *The Internal (Model) Module* gathers information from the local environment.
- *The External Status Module* exchanges environment information with other agents within the multi-agent system
- *The Communication Interface* facilitates the communication link between agents and other system components.

The following paragraphs describe specific functions of each component within each knowledge-intensive intelligent (Jones and Wray, 2006) agent:

The Decision Module: This module takes input from the Knowledge Base Integrator and the Learning Module to make the following decisions:

- When to initiate communication/collaboration process,
- Which agent to communicate with,
- When to request a change,
- Whether to increase/decrease the VPC bandwidth, and
- When to execute an action.

The Knowledge Base Integrator: This module takes inputs from the Internal (Model) Module and External Status Module to analyze system performance parameters. The results of this analysis could be a set of rules or control parameters, which can be forwarded to the Decision

Module. The Knowledge Base Integrator also gets input from the Learning Module to modify old rules or old knowledge.

The Internal (Model) Module: This module in some of the agents collects the following network performance parameters to support other modules.
- Traffic type,
- Quality of service,
- Communication direction,
- Average VPC bandwidth usage.

The External Status Module: This module in some of the agents collects the following information from other agents:
- VPC bandwidth utilization,
- Network performance,
- System configuration, and
- Agent status.

The External Interface Communication Module: This module collects the following information for use by other modules:
- Message exchange between agents,
- PVC bandwidth utilization,
- Incoming connection, and
- Network performance.

The Learning Module: The main task of this module is to learn from new information and new knowledge about changes occurring within the system. It uses knowledge gained to modify the rules in the Knowledge Base Integrator or to influence the decision making process of the Decision Module. This module employs a reinforcement-learning paradigm (Kaelbling, Littmann, and Moore, 1996). Appendix A provides an overview of this paradigm and the rationale for its selection.

The multi-agent framework and the agent structure and functions described above provide the foundation for the agent architectures employed in this research. The remainder of this chapter provides additional information on the domain, experimental design, and implementation of the survivalist and citizen multiagent framework.

Table 10-1: Global Communications Network Topology Data

Network Node Count and Alias	Location of Network Node	Number of Customer Connections (PVCs) Originating from Node	Number of Sampled PVCs	Region of Network Nodes (A, B or C) depicted in Figures 11 and 12
1. AMS	Amsterdam, NE	1552	229	A
2. BRU	Brussels	416	200	A
3. COR1	Coriander 1 UK	1081	283	A
4. COR2	Coriander 2 UK	1158	289	A
5. DOH	Domingez Hills, CA	460	210	C
6. FRK	Frankfurt GE	758	255	B
7. HKG	Hong Kong	404	197	C
8. KEY1	Keybridge 1 UK	837	263	A
9. MUN	Munich, GE	674	245	B
10. PAR	Paris, FR	783	258	B
11. POT	Pottstown, PA	238	121	C
12. SAC	Sacramento, CA	290	146	C
13. STK	Stockholm, SE	211	106	B
14. SYD	Sydney, AU	159	80	C
15. TOK	Tokyo, JP	205	103	A
Total Number of Customer Connections		**9,226**	**2985**	

Note. Sum of sampled customer connections by region: Region A: 1167, Region B: 1064, Region C: 754. The process for generating the sample sizes in column 4 in Table 10-1 is described below. Table B1 in Appendix B depicts a sample of customer network topology data used to support both the survivalist agent and the citizen agent approaches.

Isaac and Michael's (1989) sixth step involved determining the time it took the agents to restore simulated downed customer connections for different samples of the connections and for the two approaches (survivalist and citizen). This step is also discussed below.

Quasi-Experimental Design

A quasi-experimental research design was used because it was not feasible to determine all possible variables (both internal and external) that might influence the system. Therefore, some compromises were made regarding external and internal validity of the research design. The multiagent system model of the communication network was not connected directly to the physical network elements but was fed by data previously collected from the network.

Cluster Sampling

Cluster sampling was employed to randomly sample sets of customer connections (Table 10-1) for specific nodes to include in this experiment. Cluster sampling was employed because it is suitable for this situation, where successive random sampling was performed on units that successively decreased in size. In order to ensure that selected samples were representative of the PVCs originating from a switch, a sample size that reduces the standard error was obtained using the method described in the following paragraphs.

Sample Size Estimation

The standard procedure for choosing a sample size is to pick a bound B, on the error and a confidence coefficient $(1-\alpha)$ or level of confidence, and solve the equation for the sample size n. It was assumed that the estimate of the difference in mean times to restore customer connections would be accurate to within 2 seconds (i.e., B=2) with a probability of 0.95.

The value for n can be generated from the equation $Z_{\alpha/2}\sigma_\theta = B$ where σ_θ = square root of $[(\sigma_s^2/n_s) + (\sigma_c^2/n_c)]$ is the standard deviation of the parameter to be estimated or the difference in the means of restoration times, and σ_s^2 and σ_c^2 are the variances for the survivalist and the citizen strategy respectively (Mendenhall and Beaver, 1991, pp. 268-271).

The sample sizes for the two strategies are identical, therefore,

$$n = n_s = n_c, \text{ then } B = 1.96 * \text{ square root of } [(\sigma_s^2/n) + (\sigma_c^2/n)].$$
$$n = (Z_{\alpha/2} / B)^2 * (\sigma_s^2 + \sigma_s^2)$$

Assuming that the variability of each strategy were the same, then

$$\sigma_s^2 = \sigma_c^2 = \sigma^2$$

Since the exact value of σ is not known, the best approximation could be obtained using empirical rule of thumb that the range is approximately equal to 6σ (R. A. Maurer private communication, Dec. 17, 2002). Mendenhall and Beaver (1991, p. 269) suggest a more relaxed range approximation of 4σ. Using 6σ as the range and 90 seconds as the range between the minimum and maximum mean restoration times, then, $\sigma = 90/6 = 15$.

The sample size $n = (1.96/2.0)^2 * (\sigma_s^2 + \sigma_c^2) = 0.96 * (225 +225) = 432$.

I used a pseudo-random number table to generate 632 customer connections as the sample of failed customer connections for this research. The sample size used in the experiment has 200 connections more than required by the sample size calculation. This is the basis for the sample size used in the experiments reported in Chapter 11.

Quasi-Experimental Procedure

Prior to running the experiment, a sampling strategy was used to select samples of customer network connections. The sampled data were used to drive the model at run time. The research was based on data from Concert/BT's global telecommunication network, which consists of asynchronous transfer mode (ATM) switches, network trunks, ports, cards, and customer connections otherwise known as permanent virtual connections (PVCs). The ideal situation for this research was for each agent to reside within each switch being monitored, thereby reducing the time between when the switch generates status information and when the agent receives that information.

Agent Death Exception

Periodically, one of the problem trunk advisor agents (PTAA, PTAB, or PTAC) shown in Figures 10-3 and 10-4 was disabled (i.e., killed) to determine the effectiveness of the survivalist strategy over the citizen approach. The values of the following system variables were obtained from the network data stored in the global network operations database (i.e., the network performance statistics and alarms databases). Samples of the format of the network data are presented in Appendix B. The format includes network topology, trunk statistics, customer connections, and switch port statistics.

Communications Network System-Related Variables

The system-related variables employed were PVC utilization, PVC bandwidth, number of switches (i.e., nodes), network trunk size, trunk usage, congestion rate, customer's committed information rate, and execution traces or processing times. Each of these variables is defined as follows:

1. PVC utilization is the usage level (i.e., fraction) of a customer connection. A PVC transmits bits of data. There is a limit on the volume of data that can be transmitted through a specific PVC. When transmitting at its upper limit, the PVC is said to be 100% utilized. A customer's connection is usually defined in committed information rate (CIR), which also transmits in kilobits or megabits per second. A PVC is analogous to a pipe that transfers water with a limit on the volume of water it can transfer per time period. The value of this variable was obtained from the database maintained by the communication network system. The knowledge of a PVC's usage is valuable in deciding when to reroute the PVC and whether a customer is keeping within its CIR.

2. A PVC's bandwidth (in kilobits per second) is the size of the PVC or the maximum volume of data that it has been designed to transmit. The value of this variable is available in the communication network's database. This value is useful in selecting appropriate network trunks during a PVC rerouting process.

3. Number of nodes is the number of switches that any customer's PVC traverses. The value is available from the network topology database. It helps an agent determine an optimum path to reroute a PVC that is experiencing a problem. Data on 15 nodes were used in this research. These 15 nodes provide a 95% confidence level as representative of all the nodes in the communication network.

4. Nodes traversed by PVCs are the switches that a customer's PVC traverses. A network topology agent (described below) read the alarms database and the network topology database to generate the value for this variable.

5. The size of the trunks (in kilobits/second) in a network is its maximum bandwidth, which translates to the maximum volume

of PVCs it can hold. Knowing the size of a trunk and its current usage level helps an agent decide when to include or exclude the path of the trunk in routing other PVCs or rerouting the PVCs that currently use the trunk. The size of the trunks will be obtained from the network elements' statistics database.

6. Trunk usage (i.e., usage percentage) is the proportion of the network trunk in use. It is the sum of the usage levels or utilization of the PVCs that pass through it.

7. Congestion rate (in kilobits per second) of each input port on the switches is the rate at which the input buffer of the switch port fills up with customer data. Knowing the congestion rate of the input port helps agents determine which ports to avoid and which ones to select when routing or rerouting the PVC.

8. Congestion rate of each exit port on the switches is the rate at which the exit buffer of the port fills up with customer data. It has a direct relationship with the rate of congestion of the network trunks. If the exit port is congested, it is not feasible to route the PVC through its corresponding trunk.

9. A Customer's committed information rates in kilobits per second are described in the first item above. CIR is useful in determining whether a service-level agreement between the network service provider and the customer is being met.

10. Processing times or execution traces are used to check the reasonableness of the nine variables described above as well as rerouting times. The time it takes to locate a new path to reroute a downed customer link has a direct impact on the link's restoration process and the performance of the network.

These 10 system-related variables helped determine the average time to restore customer communication links. In restoring customer links, the agents must determine the severity of the fault and the source of the problem; if rerouting the link is required, they must recommend a cost-efficient routing path (Murakami & Kim, 1997; Xiong & Mason, 1997).

Multiagent Testbed and the Survivalist Agent Architecture

The MAS architecture depicted in Figure 10-3 has been used to model agents that collaborate to restore downed customer connections in a telecommunication network. The database component depicted in Figure 10-3 holds 3 days of hourly data of customer network connections and trunk statistics collected from Concert's global communication network. The architecture consists of a database of customer network links; a data server agent (DSA); an agent management server (AMS); a user interface agent (UIA); a new route search agent manager (NRSAM); plus one new route search agent, with its search algorithm. The communication network is divided into three regions—A, B, and C.

There is a problem trunk advisor (PTA) agent for each corresponding region. The PTAs are responsible for monitoring the trunk congestion in their regions and displaying the trunk identification numbers for those trunks with usage levels greater than 50% on a trunk status routing map (TSRM). The new route search agent uses the TSRM to know which trunks to avoid when searching for a new route in the network. The diagram in Figure 10-3 is for an MAS using the survivalist agent approach to handle exceptions. Each agent is a piece of software code written in CLIPS (C-Language Integrated Production System), an artificial intelligence development software for rule-based processing and expert system reasoning. The MAS software was executed on a Pentium computer with the Linux operating system.

The experiments employed two MAS architectures operating with survivalist and the citizen agents, as shown in Figures 10-3 and 10-4 respectively. The experiment considered only three agents in Figure 10-3 (PTA-A, PTA-B, and PTA-C) as citizen agents. The primary independent variable was the average customer link restoration time by the MAS operating in each of the two operating modes (i.e., the survivalist and citizen architectures). A software program (i.e., a multiagent system, described below) read a record of each customer link stored as a PVC from a database of PVCs previously populated with data retrieved from the networks' database, and presented it to the MAS for processing. Each record included the PVC's bandwidth and the number of network nodes and the trunks it traversed, including their sizes and rates of congestion at each entry and exit port for each switch. During the run of the experiments, customer connections (i.e., PVCs in the database) were selected at random, and one or more network elements along the path were made to fail. It is important to note that data feeds to the MAS were not directly connected to the global network. This approach was necessary to guarantee that the same data samples fed the MAS for each operating mode, thereby eliminating possible errors from varying network data values.

The experiments were run in sequence. The MAS software program with the survivalist approach was run first until all the PVCs were processed. The survivalist MAS model was then shut down. This was followed by a run of the MAS software with the citizen approach, with the same set of PVC data. The transit time for the PVCs was tallied, and at the end of the experiment the mean, variance, and standard deviation of the restoration time were computed for each strategy. The experiment was run with a sample of PVCs (described earlier). Sample statistics are analyzed in Chapter 11.

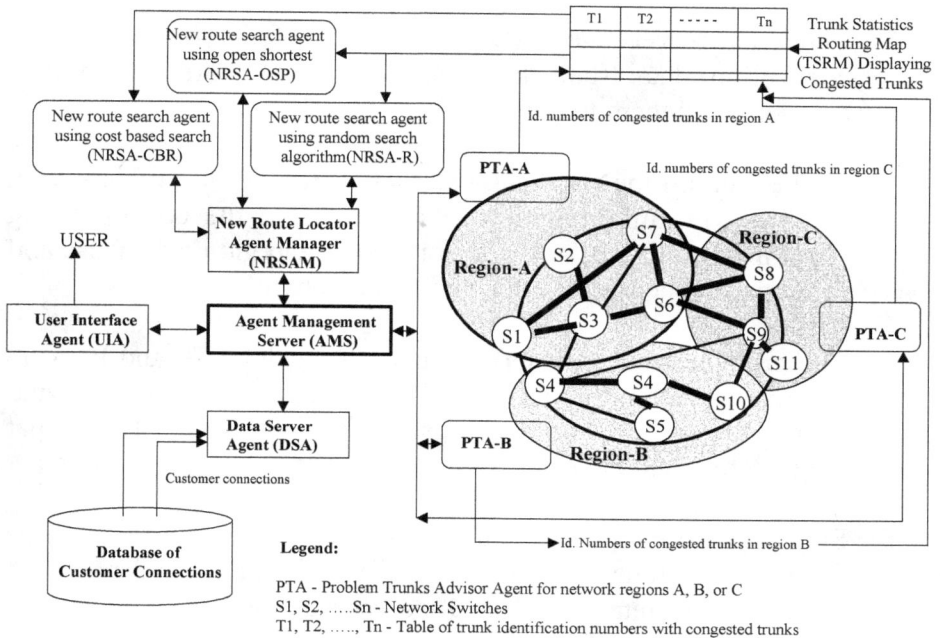

Figure 10-3: Multiagent system architecture using the survivalist agent approach to handle exceptions.

Customer Link Failure Identification and Restoration Process

Each quasi-experimental run consisted of the following steps (also depicted in Figure 10-5):

1. The system started by executing the Linux shell software scripts shown as exhibits C1 and C2 in Appendix C. The scripts built and activated the agent management server (AMS) shown in Exhibit C3 in Appendix C. The AMS in turn built and sequentially activated the other agents and loaded the database.

201

2. The data server agent (DSA) read the PVC (i.e., customer connection) data, trunk statistics, and other network system data, and delivered them to the AMS.

3. If the data on the PVC showed that there was no problem with the PVC, the information was forwarded to the corresponding agent in region A, B, or C for storage in the region's database and for updating the status of the simulated network.

4. The problem trunk advisor agents (PTA-A, PTA-B, and PTA-C) continuously monitored usage of the trunks and their regions and posted the identification of those trunks with usage levels that were higher than 50%.

5. Steps 2-4 were repeated until a customer connection read by the DSA was the one randomly picked to fail (i.e., it did not meet customer requirements). The DSA recorded the current time from the computer and forwarded the PVC's information to the AMS.

6. The AMS then forwarded the information on the PVC to the New Route Search Agent Manager (NRSAM), a second copy to a corresponding PTA, and another copy of the information to the user interface agent (UIA) for display to human users. Every 5 seconds, the NMA polled all the PTAs cyclically to verify if they were still functioning. If it did not receive a response after two consecutive polls, it considered that agent dead and restarted the agent. All prior information about the agent (since the last PVC was sent to it) was considered lost. This is the agent death exception-handling process with the survivalist agent strategy.

7. The NRSAM forwarded the information on the downed PVC to the new route search agent (NRSA) that employed the open shortest path (OSP) algorithm, and requested it to find an acceptable route within the network. The NRSA was instructed that acceptable routes were routes on network trunks with less than 50% usage.

8. The NRSA checked the trunk status routing map to identify the trunks to avoid; then, it used its algorithm to determine an optimal route and delivered it to the NRSAM.

9. The NRSAM accepted the route, recorded it, and forwarded the results to the AMS. The AMS read the current computer time and subtracted from it the time that DSA entered the PVC into the system. The resulting time is the PVC restoration time.

10. The AMS then forwarded the information on the new route and trunk to the UIA for display and recording.

11. The DSA read the computer clock and recorded the current time. It then subtracted the recorded time in Step 5 from the current time. The result is the restoration time for the downed customer connection.

12. Steps 1-11 were repeated for the single sample of customer connections until all the connections were processed.

The Citizen Agent Approach and Exception-Handling Strategy

Figure 10-4 describes the citizen agent approach to exception handling by the agents. Instead of equipping every agent with citizenship properties, only three agents are granted citizenship and monitored accordingly. The three are the problem trunk advisor agents. This decision was made to simplify the experiment and to demonstrate the impact of agent death exception. Accordingly, only one of the three agents was disabled at a time to trigger the exception-handling process. The MAS architectures in Figures 10-3 and 10-4 are identical except for the presence of three monitor agents—PTA-A, PTA-B, and PTA-C—and the AMS with its exception-handling service.

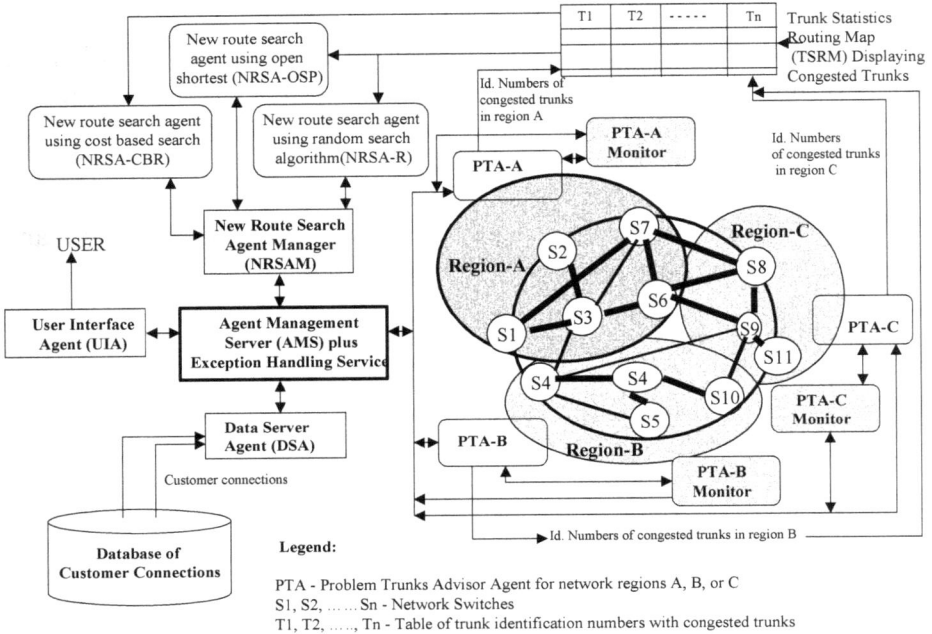

Figure 10-4: Multiagent system architecture using the citizen agent approach to handle exceptions.

The process of executing the citizen model is similar to that described above for the survivalist approach. The primary difference is the function of the AMS in step 6. Instead of monitoring the health of the three PTA agents, their corresponding monitor agents monitor them and store their states during execution. That way if any of the agents die, a corresponding monitor agent sends the state of the dead agent to the AMS to help it clone the dead agent and ascribe the properties of the dead agent to it. This is significant because, unlike the survivalist approach, where the AMS may not be aware of the death of an agent until after two polling cycles, the AMS is informed of the exception by

204

the monitor agent and a new PTA agent would be in place without much loss of time. The longer any one of the three PTAs is out of service, the more inaccurate the trunk status routing map would be. If the information contained in the routing map was inaccurate, the new route search agent was bound to run into trunks with usages higher than the acceptable 50%. This meant that the agents had to backtrack, causing the affected agent to lose precious time in finding new routes. Figure 10-4 depicts the interactions among agents to restore a downed customer connection with the survivalist agent strategy.

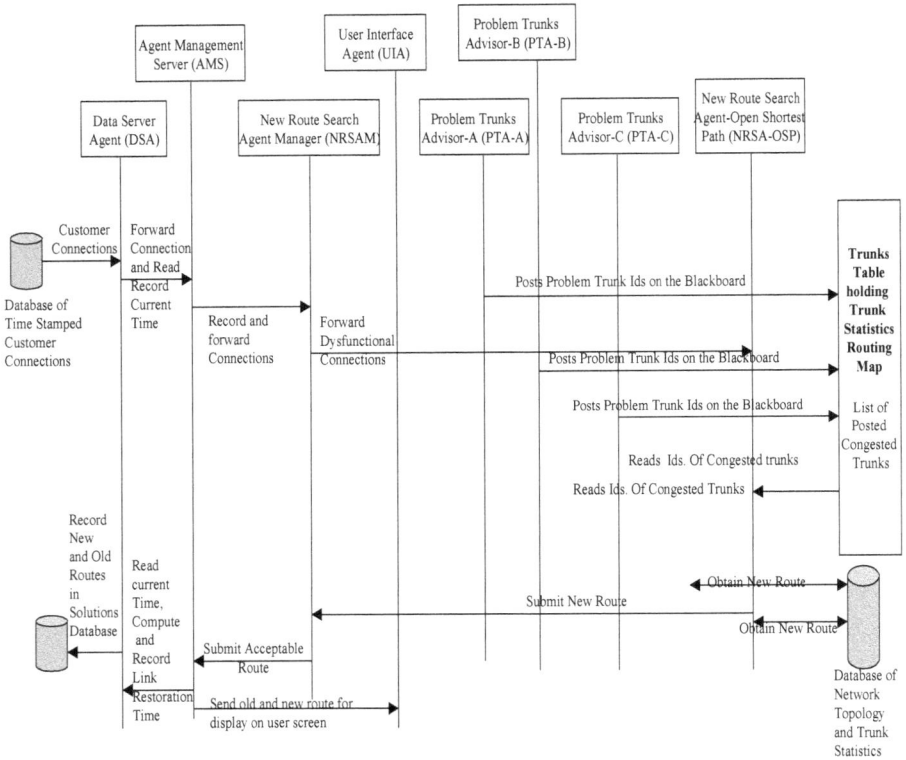

Figure 10-5: Interactions among agents to restore downed customer connections.

Measurement of Quasi-Experimental Variables

The quasi-experimental variables consisted of one independent variable—customer link restoration time (R) and two treatments—the survivalist strategy (S) and the citizen approach (C). The purpose of the experiment was to determine the effects of each strategy or treatment on link downtimes and the pace of system restoration in the face of agent death. The independent variable R was measured by summing the execution traces of the agents involved in restoring downed PVCs. As explained above, the network topology data server agent read the computer clock when it sent the attributes of a downed customer connection (i.e., a PVC) to the agent services manager (AMS). The AMS read the clock after receiving restoration parameters information about the PVC. By subtracting the previous clock time taken by the data services agent (DSA) from the new time, the network topology agent obtained the restoration time for the PVC. The time values were forwarded to the user interface agent (UIA) for storage.

Hypothesis testing in this research consisted of two steps:

1. Two mutually exclusive hypothesis statements were formulated, which together represented all possible outcomes.

2. One set of hypotheses was tested so that one was accepted and the other rejected.

The set of hypotheses was tested to avoid making two types of errors—Type I or Type II. A Type I error is caused by accepting the alternate hypothesis when it is in fact false, while a Type II error results in rejecting the alternate hypothesis when it is actually true. The experiments on the samples of customer connections were driven by the assertions of the null hypothesis (H_0) and the alternate hypothesis (H_a):

H_0 : Link restoration time with survivalist R_S = Link restoration time with citizen R_C

H_a : Link restoration time with survivalist R_S > Link restoration time with citizen R_C

The alternative hypothesis is based on a one-tailed test, and the Student *t* statistic is used to test the difference between the two means. I considered the following measurement characteristics: (a) type of measure—discrete or continuous, (b) realism of the measurement, (c) level or specificity of the measurement, (d) measurement biases or variances in the measures that are unrelated to the construct of interest, (e) sensitivity of the measurement, and (f) dimensionality—the clarity of definition of the construct of interest (Tracey & Glidden-Tracey, 1999, p. 307). The system variables such as PVC usage, trunk usage, and port congestion apply equally to both approaches. The software that supports the communication network generates the values for the system variables. The telecommunication network system employs precise measuring instruments or computing software to collect all the network system variables; therefore, the values are realistic and precise. This research assumed that the underlying population of customer connections and the restoration times were normal. The pairs of execution traces were generated from the same sample; thus, the sample customer connections had the same variance.

Summation of the execution times spent by the agents to restore the customer's network connection was based on the time read from a computer. This process is very robust and repeatable. If the computer crashes during the experiment, all the data taken during that run of the experiment could be discarded and the experiment repeated. Other researchers can readily replicate the data gathering and measurement process in this research.

Quasi-Experimental Conditions

The experiments were run under two quasi-experimental conditions: (a) the survivalist approach with agent death exception, and (b) the citizen approach with agent death exception. The experiments for each of the operating modes were run in sequence. The MAS model with the survivalist approach was run first, followed by the model that employed the citizen agent strategy. In determining the lifespan of an agent, this research investigated the suitability of the approach used by (Delarocas and Klein, 2000; Klein, Rodriguez-Aguilar, and Dellarocas, 2003), who defined the variable as the mean time between failures (MTBF). MTBF is viewed as a geometric distribution, with the MTBF equal to 100 times the duration of the shortest task or 10 times the duration of the longest task. In this research, each of the three problem trunk advisor agents was assigned a set of random numbers. Whenever one of the random numbers was selected, a corresponding agent was disabled, thus simulating the death of an agent.

Data analysis presented in Chapter 11 involved presenting the means of execution traces of the time to restore downed connections for the survivalist and the citizen strategies for a single sample of 632 connections. The analysis also included statistical tests on the time it took the system to recover after the death of an agent for each of the two strategies.

Conclusion

This chapter describes the research methodology used to test the performance of a model of a telecommunication network using two types of multiagent systems as the measurement instrument. One approach employed agents that apply the survivalist approach whereby all exception-handling strategies are built into each agent (i.e., design-time exception handling). The citizen approach (i.e., run-time exception handling) employed a separate exception-handling agent that supports problem-solving agents to manage exceptions.

CHAPTER 11: RESEARCH RESULTS AND SUMMARY OF FINDINGS

Summary and Integration of Results

The experiments on a sample of customer connections in this research were driven by the null hypothesis (H_0) and the alternate hypothesis (H_a):

H_0 : Link restoration time with survivalist R_S = Link restoration time with citizen R_C

H_a : Link restoration time with survivalist R_S > Link restoration time with citizen R_C

The results indicate that there was a significant difference between the times to restore customer connections regardless of which multiagent system strategy (survivalist or the citizen) was used. The results from this research do not support the null hypothesis. The results support the alternative hypothesis; therefore, it is concluded that the use of the citizen approach to restore downed customer connections will reduce the restoration time at a faster pace than when the survivalist strategy is employed.

211

Explanation for Findings

Pairs of times of execution traces for restoring customer connections are presented in Table B2 in Appendix B. The statistics presented in the following tables were generated from the data contained in Table B2. These tables were generated with the Statistical Package for the Social Sciences (SPSS).

Table 11-1 shows descriptive statistics on restoration times for downed customer network links for the survivalist and citizen approaches (i.e., T1SURV and T1CITZ). The statistics show that the mean of system restoration times for the citizen approach is lower than that of the survivalist approach. The data for the system restoration times for both approaches show a more defined spread, as demonstrated by the standard error of the means, the standard deviation, and the variances. The statistics on skewness and kurtosis for the citizen approach support assumption of normality of the sample distribution (i.e., short tails are not longer than for a normal distribution). To reject normality, the ratio of each of the two statistics to their respective standard error need to be less than -2 or greater than $+2$. These ratios are -6.2 to 2.2 for the survivalist strategy (non-normal) and -0.55 to 10.6 for the citizen approach (which violates the limit on the positive side), therefore, this researcher decided not to make any claim on the normality of the data.

Table 11-1: Statistics on Restoration Times for Failed Customer Connections for the *Survivalists (T1SURV) and the Citizen (T1CITZ) Agent Strategies*

		T1SURV	T1CITZ
S	Valid	632	632
	Missing Cases	0	0
Mean		56.819	54.977
Std. Error of Mean		.5220	.4109
Median		58.000	51.000
Mode		40.00	48.00
Std. Deviation		13.123	10.330
Variance		172.221	106.715
Skewness		.212	1.028
Std. Error of Skewness		.097	.097
Kurtosis		-1.196	-.107
Std. Error of Kurtosis		.194	.194
Range		45.00	45.00
Minimum		36.00	42.00
Maximum		81.00	87.00

Note. S: Sample size.

The statistics for the raw data on customer connection restoration times depicted in the appendix as Table B2 are presented in Table 11-2.

The sum of the system restoration times listed in Table 11-2 shows a time saving of 1164 seconds or 3.4 percent in favor of the citizen approach over the survivalist strategy.

Table 11-2: Sum of Link Restoration Times

Descriptive Statistics: Sum of Link Restoration Times

	S	Sum	Mean
T1CITZ	632	34746.0	54.977
T1SURV	632	35910.0	56.819
Sample Size	632		

Table 11-3: Statistics on Link Restoration Times for the Survivalist and the Citizen Agent Approaches

One-Sample Test

					95% Confidence Interval of the Difference	
	t	df	Sig. (2-tailed)	Mean Difference	Lower	Upper
T1SURV	108.846	631	.000	56.8196	55.7945	57.8447
T1CITZ	133.793	631	.000	54.9778	54.1709	55.7848

Note. SURV: Survival Approach; CITZ: Citizen Approach; t: Student's t statistic; df: degree of freedom.

The test results of the Student's t statistic and the mean difference for one-sample t-test are shown in Table 11-5. Let $R_{smean} = 56.819$, (i.e., the mean restoration time for the survivalist approach) and $R_{svar} = 172.221$, (i.e., the variance of the restoration time for the survivalists approach) as shown in Tables 11-3 and 11-5. Let $R_{cmean} = 54.977$ represent the mean and $R_{cvar} = 106.715$ represent the variance for the restoration time for the citizen agent approach respectively. Can one conclude at a 5% level of significance that there is a difference between the average link restoration times of the two approaches?

$$H_0 : \mu_{surv} - \mu_{citz} = 0 \text{ or } H_a : \mu_{surv} - \mu_{citz} \neq 0.$$

Using a decision rule that $\alpha = 0.05$ (level of significance) and 631 degrees of freedom, the null hypothesis should be rejected if calculated t falls outside the range of $-1.96 \leq t_{critical} \leq 1.96$. Since the degree of freedom is very large and the population standard deviation is unknown, Student's t test for single samples could be calculated (Pagano, 1997, pp. 277-282; Fogiel, 2002, pp. 650-651).

$$t = ((R_{smean} - R_{cmean}) - (\mu_{surv} - \mu_{citz})) / \text{(SD of the difference of the means--Sddiffmean)}.$$

The standard deviation (SD) of the difference of the means can be obtained from the following equation (Fogiel, 2002, pp. 650-651):

$$Sddiffmean = \sqrt{(((n_{surv} - 1) \text{ variance}_{surv} + ((n_{citz} - 1) \text{ variance}_{citz})) / (n_{surv} + n_{citz} - 2))} * \sqrt{(1/n_{surv} + 1/n_{citz})}$$

After appropriate substitutions, the value for Sddiffmean = 0.664.
$$t = (56.819 - 54.977)/0.664 = 2.77.$$

The Student's *t* test of hypothesis concerning the difference between two means for a single sample suggests rejecting the null hypothesis because the calculated *t* statistical value of 2.77 is larger than *t* value obtained from tables of critical *t* values. From the table of critical values of Student's *t* distribution with $df > 30$ and $\alpha = 0.05$ for one-tailed test, $t_{critical}$ ranges from -1.645 to 1.645. The critical values for t is not very different from the critical values for Z for a large number of degrees of freedom (Fogiel, 2002, p. 250).

The time sequence plots in Figure 11-1 support the same observation reported in the paragraph above. The downed connections are restored more quickly with the survivalist strategy (as depicted in Figure 11-1 with by the first 157 restoration times) while the reverse is true for most of the remainder of restoration times (i.e., 158 through 632). A possible explanation for this effect is provided later in this chapter where convergence of findings is discussed.

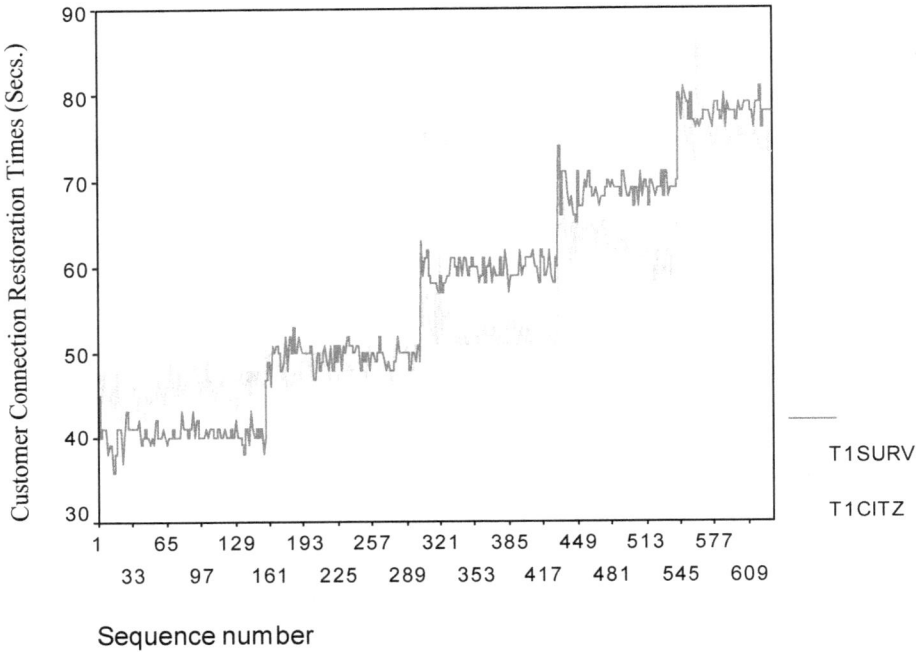

Figure 11-1: Sequence plots of restoration times for the citizen (CITZ-Bottom) versus the survivalist (SURV-Top) approaches from a sample of 632 customer connections.

While the previous section covers restoration times for downed customer connections, the following paragraphs and Table 11-4 and Figure 11-2 present the response of the system to recover to 15 random instances when one of the agents failed.

216

Table 11-4: Descriptive Statistics of System Recovery Times for the Survivalist and Citizen Approaches: RECSURV vs. RECCITZ (Single Sample of Size 15)

Statistics

		RECSURV	RECCITZ
S	Valid	15	15
	Missing	0	0
Mean		117.133	84.000
Std. Error of Mean		12.058	4.980
Media		115.000	91.000
Mode		53.00[a]	85.00[a]
Std. Deviation		46.702	19.287
Variance		2181.123	372.000
Skewnes		-.115	-1.196
Std. Error of Skewness		.580	.580
Kurtosis		-1.662	1.014
Std. Error of Kurtosis		1.121	1.121
Range		122.0	67.00
Minimum		53.00	38.00
Maximum		175.0	105.0
Sum		1757.0	1260.0

a. Multiple modes exist. The smallest value is

<u>Note.</u> RECSURV: Recovery time for the Survival Approach; RECCITZ: Recovery time for the Citizen Approach; S: Sample size.

Descriptive statistics of recovery times after the failure of respective survivalist and citizen agents are displayed in Table 11-4. The mean multiagent system recovery time for the citizen agent approach is smaller than that of the survivalist approach. All the measures of variability (i.e., standard error of the mean, standard deviation, and variance) are consistently lower for the citizen agent strategy than are those of the

217

survivalist approach. The sum of recovery times for the survivalist agent approach is considerably higher than that of the citizen approach (1,757 seconds against 1,260 seconds). These figures show that application of the citizen approach to support system recovery in the event of the death of an agent could save 39% of the time over that of the survivalist agent strategy.

Table 11-5: Statistics of System Recovery Times for the Survivalist and Citizen Approaches

One-Sample Statistics

	S	Mean	Std. Deviation	Std. Error Mean
RECSURV	15	117.1333	46.7025	12.0585
RECCITZ	15	84.0000	19.2873	4.9800

Note. SURV: Survival Approach; CITZ: Citizen Approach; S: Sample size.

The Time Sequence Plots of the MAS recovery times shown in Figure 11-2 demonstrates that the citizen approach took a longer time to recover from system failure until the 7th sequence. This change can be attributed to the fact that the citizen approach is more efficient at processing large volumes of information and long tasks, while the survivalist approach is less efficient in such an environment.

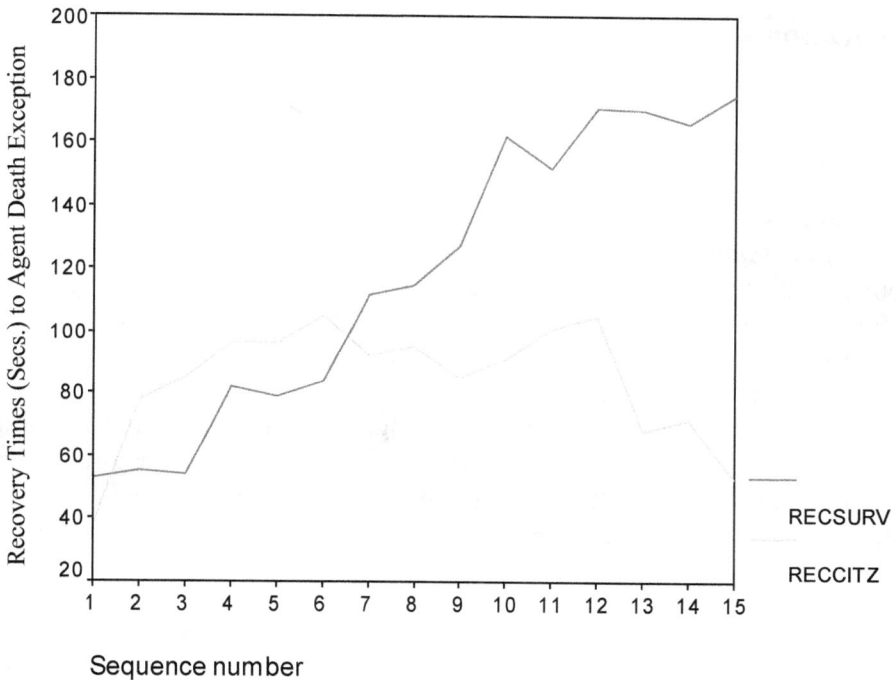

Figure 11-2: Sequence plots of system recovery times from agent death exception.

Note. SURV: Survival approach; CITZ: Citizen approach; RECSURV: Recovery statistics for the Survival Approach; RECCITZ: Recovery statistics for the Citizen Approach; t: Student's t statistics, df: degree of freedom.

Calculated t given the values reported on Table 7 (t = (117.133 – 84.00)/9.225 = 3.59) with df = 14, and α =0.05$_{2\ tail}$. From a table of t-values, for one-tailed test, t $_{critical}$ = 1.761. This is another reason for rejecting the null because there is a significant difference between the system recovery times for the two strategies.

219

Integration of Findings with Literature

Convergence of Findings

The findings of this research are consistent with those of Dellarocas and Klein (1997) and Klein, Rodriguez-Aguilar, and Dellarocas (2003), who reported "citizen agents with exception handling clearly outperformed survivalist agents". They found that for small tasks, the survivalist agents performed better due to timely detection of agent death. However, for long tasks, the citizen agents outperformed the survivalists because the probability of multiple agent deaths is higher while processing a single task. This created a problem for the survivalist agent because it had to start from the scratch while the citizen agent did not, thus reducing the task completion times. The graphs in Figure 11-2 support this explanation.

Divergent Findings

Only a single agent was disabled during the processing of a single task, while Dellarocas and Klein (2000) permit the death of multiple agents during the execution of a single task. This research tracked task execution times (i.e., customer link restoration times) and identified the restoration times as a whole, as well as actual recovery times when the agents were disabled. This helps explain the influence of the MAS architecture on the connection restoration times for the two strategies. The MAS architecture for the citizen approach demonstrates that when a task can be decomposed and assigned to multiple specialist agents, the overall restoration time for the customer connection can be shorter than that obtained when the task is assigned to a single agent. This assumes, however, that the agents do not need to contend for scarce resources.

Contributions of Findings to the Literature

This research contributes some evidence for the superiority of the citizen approach to exception handling under certain conditions. When the tasks to be performed are short, the survivalist agent approach produces shorter task completion times than does the citizen approach. Also, for short tasks, the survivalist agent approach recovers faster after the death of an agent. In the domain of network management and restoring connections, a short task is a task that requires very little searching to determine a new path for a downed customer connection.

The agents in Dellarocas and Klein's (2000) research had identical skills so that in the event of agent death, it was fairly easy to clone a new agent to replace the dead one. The agents employed in this research were specialists, each possessing its own unique skills. Therefore, this researcher cannot conclude that the use of specialist agents (i.e., heterogeneous agents) improves the system recovery times over an architecture that employs agents with identical skills (i.e., homogeneous agents).

The approach used to monitor agent death in this research differs according to the MAS architectures. In the survivalist agent strategy, the agent management server (AMS), in collaboration with the network-monitoring agent (NMA), monitors the problem trunk advisor agents (PTAs). This is performed through periodic polling of the PTAs. In the citizen MAS architecture, corresponding PTAs, in collaboration with the AMS, are responsible for checking the health of the PTAs by polling them periodically. Since polling was used to detect the health of the PTAs, the polling intervals would affect experimental results. This researcher kept the same polling intervals for the NMA and the PTA monitor agents. It is possible that using some optimum polling intervals may affect the speed at which an agent's death is detected, which could affect task completion times and improve system performance. While this researcher did not attach any priority to the polling message,

221

assigning it a top priority may influence the speed at which the death of a PTA is detected.

The approach presented in this research could be applied to other business operations such as transportation networks and air traffic controls to support the free flight initiative. In the free flight program, pilots are responsible for generating clear flight paths, which change periodically due to changes in weather conditions and restricted air spaces.

CHAPTER 12: CONCLUSIONS

Automated management of complex business processes—such as telecommunication networks, transportation networks, distributed computer and air traffic control systems—requires embedded computer software programs that coordinate individual functions to achieve the goal of the whole system. Automated software systems that rely on design-time assumptions without contingencies to manage open business processes are bound to fail when design-time assumptions fail during business operations. This research tested a multiagent system framework using citizen agents and survivalist agents as automated software to restore failed customer network connections in a global network management domain. Results led to a rejection of the null hypothesis, which predicted that the citizen agent strategy would not reduce the time to restore a customer network connection compared to the traditional survivalist strategy. Under specified situations, the citizen agent approach improved the restoration times of failed customer network links.

By applying this approach to the telecommunication network management domain and obtaining results similar to those obtained by Dellarocas and Klein (2000) in their application to contract bidding, this research validated the use of multiagent systems and exception handling for open business processes. The framework for repeating this research has been documented. To improve on the work reported in this research, future researchers and practitioners need to consider multiple exceptions and additional open business processes.

Limitations of Findings

The results of this study are limited by the focus of the research. Since the purpose was to test the hypothesis that there would be no significant difference in the performance of a multiagent system (MAS) using the survivalist or the citizen agent strategy, only one search algorithm (open shortest path) was used to determine a new path for a downed customer connection. Other network search algorithms such as least cost routing or least number of hops may show different results.

This research focused on one exception—agent death. There are several other mechanisms, such as agent clusters and application servers with inherent high availability and fail-over support, which could be used to address this exception. Also, this research did not address exceptions caused by failed communication links among agents, or lost or incomplete messages. The research reported here was limited to the telecommunications network management domain. While the approach is generic and potentially applicable to other domains, its generalizability would have to be tested.

The data used in this research were collected and processed prior to the experiments to ensure consistency and reliability of the input data. In an operational environment, it would be ideal to co-locate each agent with the switch that it is managing. That approach would make it difficult to implement in a research environment that demands the same input data be used for the two MAS strategies. It would affect the measurement accuracy of the system variables and the reliability of the results.

Suggestions for Future Research

Several components of this research warrant further investigation. This researcher did not recommend any agent control and coordination mechanisms, which would impact the performance of the MAS. Future research should address the impact of multiple exceptions to improve the robustness of the research output. To improve the generalizability of this research, future researchers should apply the citizen agent strategy to other domains beyond those of network management and calls for proposals (i.e., bidding on contracts).

Additional research is needed to investigate optimum mechanisms for detecting agent deaths. If a polling mechanism is used, then the polling interval will directly affect the experimental results. There is a need to determine an optimum set of polling intervals. This research relied on a set of nonoptimal polling intervals. Other approaches for detecting agent death could be to request the dying agent (in situations where it is possible to identify parameters that show degradation of agent performance) to use a signal to indicate the agent's demise to either the agent services manager or the agent monitor. Some systems set up a *heartbeat* mechanism also known as *ping* to communicate life. The choice and implementation of these or other mechanisms directly affect the experimental results and conclusions.

Research Conclusions and Recommendations

Open distributed business processes are characterized by nonroutine tasks in unpredictable environments. Such business processes are known as complex systems (Coveney & Highfield, 1995; Pascale, 1999). "Because complex systems have built-in unpredictability, the certainties of the command-and-control approach to management no longer hold true" (Battram, 1998, p. 11). Therefore, for open business processes to survive, they must be managed as complex, adaptive systems (Battram, 1998). This research has demonstrated the practicality of the citizen agent MAS approach for restoring failed customer connections in telecommunication networks. This study showed that compared to an approach relying on design-time assumptions, which may not hold in open business processes. It demonstrated that the citizen agent approach, which focuses on resolving run-time exceptions by outsourcing exception-handling services to another group of agents, improves operational performance of business processes. Both strategies can support the system's survivability goals.

This study confirmed the findings of Dellarocas and Klein (2000) as applied to contract bidding. It shows the importance of viewing business processes as open systems. Therefore, methodologies that can cope with system exceptions at run time will help improve operational performance of business processes. This research has demonstrated the feasibility of a successful application of multiagent systems and exception handling methodologies to an open system domain beyond contract bidding. Future researchers can explore the feasibility of the same technologies to several other open business processes such as transportation, air traffic control, battle management, and manufacturing systems.

Social Significance of this Study

The November 1999 annual network product performance report of Concert (a global joint venture of AT&T and BT) issued by the Network Services division shows that in Europe and Asia Pacific, fewer than 50% of severity 1 (Penny, 2001) faults are cleared within 5 hours or less. In the Americas, only 20% of the faults are cleared within 5 hours from June through November. During the same period fewer than 50% of Severity 2 (Penny, 2001) faults are cleared in 12 hours or less in the three regions (i.e., Europe, Asia Pacific, and the Americas). Reports on network performance statistics from other TSPs are not better (Khan,

2001). Telecommunication network fault management involves the physical monitoring of network elements, fault assessment and fault mitigation. The StrataView network element management software system used today on Cisco switches still presents a never-ending stream of alarm information to the operator console in real time. In several situations, alarms are presented in chronological order without filtering or prioritization. Depending on the state of the network, the volumes of alarms can range from tens to hundreds of messages per minute. The research reported in this dissertation could help network operators at network management centers identify network problems, reduce information overload, resolve network problems, and improve network performance. In the telecommunication industry, business success does not lie in the ability to providing only the communication bandwidth but in managing the connections to ensure that customers receive guaranteed services (El Boghdady, 2000; Shuster, 2000).

The ability of an organizational business manager to deploy systems that meet customer expectations is particularly critical to the survival of the organization. For example, in the telecommunication industry, the inability of automated systems to meet service level guarantees can result in substantial financial penalties to the telecommunication service providers. In addition, since a global economy depends on effective, efficient, and uninterrupted telecommunications service, it is important that telecommunications service providers employ network management tools that do not rely on design-time assumptions because those assumptions cannot be relied on in open business processes.

The consequence in the air traffic control business process can be fatal if the automated system used to manage aircraft in-flight separation requirements fails to handle real-time exceptions. The Air Traffic Control department of the Federal Aviation Administration (FAA) can apply the research reported here to support pilots in planning their flight paths in the FAA sponsored initiative called *Free Flight*. In addition to handling these scenarios, the research methodology demonstrated in this study can be extended to improve the performance of open business processes in other

227

organizations with the mission to provide reliable and efficient services to their customers.

Concluding Remarks on Building Survivable Systems

In Part I of this book, I presented the requirements and methodologies for building complex product, process, and business systems for survival. Survivability is defined as the ability of a system to provide essential services in the event of any failures of its components. The premise for system survivability is based on my assertion that the system developer can build a survivable system if s/he has access to approaches that provide the ability to investigate a variety of operational scenarios during the design stage. Three system-building approaches: finite element modeling for product innovation, modeling and simulation science for process innovation, and complex adaptive systems theory for business process modeling were presented. It is my hope that the presentation of the applications of the principles will help the business leader, the researcher, the decision maker, or the practitioner identify ways to build survivable systems. The in-depth research presented in Part II demonstrates the feasibility of building survivable systems and suggestions for future research.

REFERENCES

Antony, J., & Kaye, M. (1997). Design of experiments for improving the product and process integrity. *Total Quality Management, 8*(2/3), 75-79.

Aramayo, G. A., & Bobrek, A. (2001). Development of a Finite Element Model of a 1998 AUDI A8 for Crash Analysis. Computer Science and Mathematics Division, Oak Ridge National Laboratory, TN. USA.

Aronson, J., Manikonda, V., Peng, W., Levy, R., & Roth, K. (2000). An HLA Compliant Agent-Based Fast-Time Simulation Architecture for Analysis of Civil Aviation Concepts. SAIC and NASA Ames Research Center, Moffet Field, CA 94035-1000.

Ash, G. R. (1997). *Dynamic routing in telecommunications networks.* New York: McGraw-Hill.

Avison, D., Lau, F., Myers, M., & Nielsen, P. A. (1999). Action research. *Communications of the ACM, 42*(1), 94-97.

Bacharach, S. B. (1989). Organizational theories: Some criteria for evaluation. <u>Academy of Management Review</u>, 14(4), 496-515.

Banks, J., Carson II, J. S., Nelson, B. L., & Nicol, D. M. (2001). *Discrete-event system simulation* (3rd ed.). Upper Saddle River, NJ: Prentice-Hall, Inc.

Battram, A. (1998). *Navigating complexity: The essential guide to complexity theory in business and management.* Dover, NH: The Industrial Society.

Batorsky, D., & Deland, D. (1999). Telecom Operations Map Evaluation Version 2.0. TeleManagement FORUM. Retrieved November 10, 2000 from the World Wide Web: http://www.tmforum.org.

Bell, A. M., Sethares, W. A., & Bucklew, J. A. (2000). Coordination failure and congestion in information networks. AGENTS. American Association for Artificial Intelligence. Retrieved April 21, 2001 from the World Wide Web: http://www.aaai.org. 9-14.

Beer, M., & Eisentat, R. A. (2000). The silent killers of strategy implementation and learning. Sloan Management Review, 41(4), 29-40.

Beinhocker, E. D. (1999). Robust adaptive strategies. Sloan Management Review, 40(3), 95-109.

Birnberg, J. G. (1998). Some reflections on the evolution of organizational control. Behavioral Research in Accounting, 1998 Supplement, 10, 27-46.

Blechar, M., J., Sinur, J. (2006). "Magic Quadrant for Business Process Analysis Tools 2006" Gartner Research, February, 2006.

Bourne, R. A., Excelente-Toledo, C. B., & Jennings, N. R. (1999). Run-time selection of coordination mechanisms in multiagent systems. *Proceedings of the 14th European Conference on Artificial Intelligence (ECAI-2000), Berlin, Germany,* 1-5.

Brynjolfsson, E., & Renshaw, A. A. (1997). The matrix of change. Sloan Management Review, 38(2). 37-54.

Burrus, D. (1993). *Technotrends: How to use technology to go beyond your competition.* New York: HarperBusiness.

Busuioc, M., Crabtree, B., Boyd, I., Sim, S. & Azarmi, N. (1996). Global network management using distributed software agents. *BT Technical Journal, 18.* Adastral Park Martlesham Heath, Ipswich, Suffolk UK, IP5 3RE. Kluwer Academic Publishers.

Busby, J. S. (1999). The effectiveness of collective retrospection as a mechanism of organizational learning. Journal of Applied Behavioral Science, 35(1), 109-130.

Campbell, D. T., & Stanley, J. C. (1966). *Experimental and quasi-experimental designs for research.* Chicago: Rand McNally College Publishing Company.

Capra, F. (1996). *The web of life: A new scientific understanding of living systems.* Doubleday. New York.

Caro, G. D., & Dorigo, M. (1998). AntNet: Distributed stigmergetic control for communication networks. *Journal of Artificial Intelligence Research, 9,* 317-365.

Casti, J., Kauffman, S., Epstein, J., & Meyer, C. (1998). Colloquium: Complexity science. *Complexity, 3,* 27-36.

Casti, J. L. (1999). The computer as a laboratory: Toward a theory of complex, adaptive systems. Complexity, (4)5, 12-14.

Carroll, J. S., & Hatakenaka, S. (2001). Driving organizational change in the midst of crisis. MIT Sloan Management Review, 42(3), 70-79.

Coen, M. H. (2000). Nondeterministic social laws. Agents, American Association for Artificial Intelligence. MIT Artificial Intelligence Lab, Cambridge, MA. DARPA Contract number F30602-94-c-0204. 15-21.

Cohen, P. R. (1995). *Empirical methods for artificial intelligence.* Cambridge, MA: The MIT Press.

Collins, J. (2001). *Good to great: Why some companies make the leap and others don't*, HarperCollins Publishers Inc., New York, NY.

Concert. (1999). Human Resources Initiative. http://insiteremote.concert.com/humanresources/hrint.asp.

Coveney, P., & Highfield, R. (1995). *Frontiers of complexity: The search for order in a chaotic world.* Fawcett Columbine, New York.

Covey, S. R. (1991). Principle-centered leadership. Simon & Schuster, New York.

Creswell, J. W. (1998). *Qualitative inquiry and research design: Choosing among five traditions.* Thousand Oaks, CA: Sage Publications.

Creswell, J. W. (1994). *Research design: Quantitative & qualitative approaches.* Thousand Oaks, CA: Sage Publications.

Davenport, T. H. (1992). Process Innovation: Work Through Information Technology. Harvard Business School Press, Cambridge, MA.

DeLoach, S. A. (2000). Multiagent systems engineering: A methodology and language for designing agent systems. *Proceedings of the Fourth International Conference on MultiAgent Systems-ICMAS-2000, IEEE Computer Society, Boston,* 1-9.

biodegraded or transformed. It has been observed that pesticide sorption to soil organic matter can either enhance or decrease the microbial degradation rate in soil (Aislaibe and Jones, 1995).

Also, degradation of some pollutants like pesticides and PCBs may proceed under alternating aerobic and anaerobic conditions.

Critical conditions for bioremediation include the following:

- Host microbial contaminants that provide fuel and energy to parasitic microbes
- Parasitic microbes that feed off their harmful hosts and destroy them
- Oxygen in sufficient amounts to support aerobic biodegradation (studies have revealed that bacteria like *Escherichia coli* are chemotactic to oxygen; Adler, 1966)
- Water, either in liquid form or in soil moisture content, that creates soil conditions favorable for microbial/plant growth and enzymatic activity
- Carbon as the foundation of microbial life and its energy source; some pesticides, such as carbofuran, serve as carbon sources for bacterial growth, but in the presence of alternative readily degradable carbon sources, bacteria are less likely to degrade the pesticide (Aislaibe and Jones, 1995)
- A temperature range that allows microbial life to flourish; based on their temperature requirements, microbes are classified as psychrophiles (e.g., *Bacillus*) mesophiles (e.g., *Escherichia coli*), thermophiles (e.g., *Thermus aquaticus*), extreme thermophiles (e.g., *Thermoproteus*), and hyperthermophiles (e.g., *Pyrobaculum*)
- Nutrients like nitrogen, phosphorus, potassium, and sulfur to support microbe growth
- pH in the range of 6.5 to 7.5; based on their pH tolerance, microorganisms are classified as acidophiles, neutrophiles, and alkaliphiles

A typical bacterial cell is 50% carbon, 14% nitrogen, 3% phosphorous, 2% potassium, 1% sulfur, 0.2% iron, and 0.5% each of calcium, magnesium, and chloride. If there is a limited supply of any of these essential elements relative to carbon in organic contaminants, overall microbial growth will be affected, which will lead to slow contaminant removal. Thus, the bioremediation system must be designed to supply proper concentrations and ratios of these nutrients. Aislaibe and Jones (1995) also discuss that the availability of essential nutrients may limit the rate at which bacteria degrade a pesticide.

10.5.1 Biodegradation of the Dirty Dozen

The Dirty Dozen are the POPs that are banned worldwide due to the risks they pose to the environment and life. Biodegradation of these contaminants is a major concern. Purnomo (2017) reviewed the microbe-assisted degradation of aldrin and dieldrin, and found that around 22 strains of soil bacteria, including *Bacillus*, *Micromonospora*, *Mycobacterium*, *Nocardia*, *Streptomyces*, and *Thermoactinomyces* species, degrade aldrin. Aldrin disappears more quickly in moist soil than in dry, since microbes are more active in moist soils (Adi et al., 2017). Patil et al. (1970) also report the ability of 20 microorganisms, including *Bacillus* and *Pseudomonas* species, to degrade DDT, aldrin, and endrin. Organochlorines like DDT are highly persistent in the environment and have proven to be recalcitrant. Although DDT is a persistent pollutant, it does appear to undergo slow degradation (Chaudhry et al., 1991). Studies show that biodegradation of DDT residues involves cometabolism, which means that an alternative source of carbon is required so that degrading organisms are able to transform DDT without deriving any nutrient or energy from the process (Porto et al., 2011). Although this cometabolism may not result in complete mineralization of the molecule to inorganic chloride, carbon dioxide, and water, it does eliminate the toxicity of the pesticide in the environment (Raymond, 1972). Roles for *Pseudomonas putida*, *Escherichia coli*, *Enterobacter aerogenes*, and *Bacillus* species in degrading DDT in soil have also been reported (Sharma et al., 2016). Porto et al. (2011) found that anaerobic conditions are beneficial for dechlorinating DDT, and that addition of hydrogen peroxide and carbon favors the biodegradation of some organochlorines. Studies also report that irrigation of soils enhances degradation of DDT to DDD, which could be due to the creation of anaerobic microsites (Aislaibe and Jones, 1995). Hepatochlor is another organochlorine that can be degraded, by *Phlebia* species and *Phanerochaete chrysosporium* (Porto et al., 2011).

Dioxins and furans are groups of planar tricyclic compounds containing one to eight chlorine atoms, and they have very similar structures and properties. They are produced as by-products of other chemical productions. It has been reported that they can be subjected to reductive dehalogenation, leading to less-halogenated congeners which can be degraded efficiently by fungal and bacterial oxidases and dioxygenases (Wittich, 1998). Studies reveal success in degrading these toxic compounds, but a lot of work still needs to be done in filling the gaps in laboratory and field studies.

10.6   OBSTACLES TO BACTERIAL CLEANUP

Bioremediation involves natural processes and is a publicly accepted treatment of polluted soil, because in situ bioremediation can result in complete degradation of pollutants into harmless products on-site. It also poses fewer risks involved with transportation for treatment and elimination of contaminated substances, and consumes less energy than incineration and landfills. But there are still many hurdles encountered in field application of the process, including the following:

- A given polluting compound's degradation pathway is determined by the physical, chemical, and microbiological aspects of its ambient environment (Chaudhry et al., 1991).
- Only biodegradable compounds can undergo bioremediation, and not every compound is capable of fully degrading quickly.
- Bacterial growth on pollutant mixtures is an important aspect of bioremediation (Heinaru et al., 2005).
- The products of biodegradation may potentially be even more persistent or toxic than the original contaminant.

- Biological functions are usually extremely specific and require the presence of microbes that are capable of metabolizing the contaminants. In order for the correct microbes to be present, the appropriate environmental conditions and levels of nutrients and contaminants need to be in place.
- Real environments contain contaminants that are mixed, unevenly distributed, and in different phases (solid, liquid, gas). More research needs to be completed to create technologies that can adapt.
- The bioavailability of pollutants in the natural environment is limited.
- In nature, pollutants are mixed, some requiring aerobic digestion and others requiring anaerobic digestion, so a bacterium that tests well in the lab may not generate positive results in the field. Most of the time, pesticide degradation is achieved by a consortium of microbes rather than a single species (Aislaibe and Jones, 1995).
- Bacterial adaptation to contaminants might be different under natural conditions.
- Contaminated soil may need to be treated to promote contact between microbes and the substrate. To this end, surfactant treatment may well prove useful (Aislabie et al., 1997).
- Compared to other treatment technologies, bioremediation often takes more time.
- Problems with ensuring adequate contact between the microbes and the contaminant's preferential pathway and soil structure can leave uncertainty in remediation dispersal.

10.7   CONCLUSION

Bioremediation or biological waste treatment is a very old technique and taps the great capacity of microorganisms to absorb, accumulate, and detoxify a variety of toxic compounds; but our knowledge of the microbial world is not very deep, which prevents us from using them to their complete ability. The process has technical and cost advantages, although it can often take more time than traditional methods. Many times, physical conditions like mixing of wastes and nutrient and electron acceptor species are suboptimal and affect the rate of the process. If we are able to tailor the process to the needs of a polluted site and use specific microbes or consortia to break down the pollutants, we can achieve better results with degrading organic pollutants. For future studies we can look into preadaptation of bacteria to the pollution conditions in which they have to work and try improving their on-field efficiency.

REFERENCES

Adi, P.S. 2017. Microbe assisted degradation of aldrin and dieldrin. *Microbe Induced Degradation of Pesticides.* Springer International Publishing.

Adler, J. 1966. Effect of amino acids and oxygen on chemotaxis in *Escherichia coli. Journal of Bacteriology.* 92(1). 121–129.

Agamuthu, P. and Y.L. Kee. 2016. Persistent organic pollutants management and remediation. *Procedia Environmental Sciences*. 31: 842–848.

Agrawal, N. and A.K. Dixit. 2015. An environmental cleanup strategy – Microbial transformation of xenobiotic compounds. *International Journal of Current Microbiology and Applied Sciences*. 4(4). 429–461.

Aislaibe, J. and L.G. Jones. 1995. A review of bacterial degradation of pesticides. *Australian Journal of Soil Research*. 33(6). 925–942.

Aislabie, J.M., K.N. Richards, and H.L. Boul. 1997. Microbial degradation of DDT and its residues – A review. *New Zealand Journal of Agricultural Research*. 40(2). 269–282.

Alexander, M. 1964. Biochemical ecology of soil microorganisms. *Annual Review of Microbiology*. 18: 217–250.

Ang, E.L., H. Zhao, J.P. Obbard. 2005. Recent advances in bioremediation of persistent organic pollutants via biomolecular engineering. *Enzyme and Microbial Technology*. 37. 487–496.

Blasco, R., Mallavarapu, M., Rolf, M.W., Timmis, N.K. and Pieper, D.H. 1997. Evidence that formation of protoanemonin from metabolites of 4- chlorobiphenyl degradation negatively affects the survival of 4- chlorobiphenyl-cometabolizing microorganisms. *Applied and Environmental Microbiology*. 427–434.

Brusseau, M.L. 2019. Soil and groundwater remediation. *Environmental and Pollution Science*, 3rd ed. 329–354.

Chaudhry, R.G. and S. Chapalmadugu. 1991. Biodegradation of halogenated organic compounds. *Microbiological Reviews*. 55(1), 59–70.

Cutright, J.T. and E. Ziya. 2012. Overview of the bioremediation and the degradation pathways of DDT. *Journal of Adnan Menderes University, Agricultural Faculty*. 9(2), 39–45.

DeRosier, J.D. 1998. The turn of the screw: The bacterial flagellar motor-mini review. *Cell*. 93, 17–20.

Deziel, E., G.Paquette, Villemur, R., F. Lepine, and J. Bisaillon. 1996. Biosurfactant production by a soil pseudomonas strain growing on polycyclic aromatic hydrocarbons. *Applied and Environmental Microbiology*. 62(6), 1908–1912.

Gale, E.F. 1951. *The Chemical Activities of Bacteria*, 3rd ed. London: Academic Press.

Heijman, C.G., E. Greider, C. Holliger, and Schwarzenbach. 1995. Reduction of nitroaromatic compounds coupled to iron reduction in laboratory aquifer columns. *Environmental Science and Technology*. 29, 775–783.

Heijman, C.G., C. Holliger, M.A. Glaus, Schwarzenbach, and J. Zeyer. 1993. Abiotic reduction of 4-chloronitrobenzene in a dissimilatory iron reducing enrichment culture. *Applied Environmental Microbiology*. 59, 4350–4353.

Heinaru, E., M. Merike, V. Signe, et al. 2005. Biodegradation efficiency of functionally important populations selected for bioaugmentation in phenol- and oil-polluted area. *FEMS Microbiology Ecology*. 51, 363–373.

Imae, Y., K. Oosawa, T. Mizuno, M. Kihara, and R.M. Macnab. 1987. Phenol: A complex chemoeffector in bacterial chemotaxis. *Journal of Bacteriology*. 169(1), 371–379.

Jahangeer and V. Kumar, 2013. An overview on microbial degradation of petroleum hydrocarbon contaminants. *International Journal of Engineering and Technical Research*. 1(8), 34–37.

Lebeau, T. 2011. Bioaugmentation for insitu soil remediation: How to ensure success of such a process. *Bioaugmentation, Biostimulation, Biocontrol, Soil Biology*. 28, 129–186.

Mateju, V. 2016. Lecture on pollutants-Characteristics, fate and availability at IMETE, 2016.

Megharaj, M., B. Ramakrishnan, K. Venkateswarlu, N. Sethunathan, R. Naidu. 2011. Bioremediation approaches for organic pollutants: A critical perspective. *Environment International*. 37, 1362–1375.

Megharaj, M., K. Venkateswarlu, R. Naidu. 2014. *Bioremediation, Encyclopedia of Toxicology*, 3rd ed., 485–489.

Pandey, G. and R.K. Jain. 2002. Bacterial chemotaxis toward environmental pollutants: Role in bioremediation. *Applied and Environmental Microbiology*. 68(12), 5789–5795.

Patil, K.C., F. Matsumura, and M.G. Boush. 1970. Degradation of endrin, aldrin and DDT by soil microorganisms. *Applied Microbiology*. 19(5), 879–881.

Porto, A.L.M., G.Z. Melgar, M.C. Kasemodel, and M. Nitschke. 2011. Biodegradation of Pesticides. *Pesticides in the Modern World – Pesticide Use and Management*, Margarita Stoytcheva (ed.). ISBN: 978-953-307-459-7.

Purnomo, A. S. 2017. Microbe assisted degradation of aldrin and dieldrin. In Singh S. (ed.) *Environmental Science and Engineering*. Springer:1–22.

Raymond, H.S. 1972. Microbial co-metabolism and the degradation of organic compounds in nature. *Bacteriological Reviews*. 36(2), 146–155.

Robert, K.A. and H. Shigeaki. 2000. Biodegradation of high molecula weight polycyclic aromatic hydrocarbons by bacteria. *Journal of Bacteriology*. 182(8), 2059–2067.

Rashed, M.N. 2013. Chapter 7. Adsorption techniques for the removal of persistent organic pollutants from water and wastewater. *Organic Pollutants – Monitoring, Risk and Treatment*. London: Intech.

Ratnakar, A., Shikha, S. Shankar. 2016. An overview of biodegradation of organic pollutants. *International Journal of Scientific and Innovative Research*. 4(1), 73–91.

Romantschuk, M. 2014. Insitu bioremediation: Possibilities and limitations. Proceedings of the 4th International Conference on Environmental Pollution and RemediationPrague, Czech, August 11–13.

Rozgaj, R., 1994. Microbial degradation of xenobiotics in the environment. *Archives of Industrial Hygiene and Toxicology*. 45(2), 189–198.

Stanley, M.E. 2005. *Environmental Chemistry*, 8th ed. CRC Press.

Shackelford, C.D. 2013. Geo environmental engineering. *Reference Module in Earth Systems and Environmental Sciences*.Elsevier.

Sharma, A., Pankaj, P., Khati, S., Gangola and G. Kumar. 2016. Microbial degradation of pesticides for environmental cleanup. *Bioremediation of Industrial Pollutants*. 178–205.

Sjoding, A., D.G. Patterson and A. Bergman. 2003. A review of human exposure to bro- minated flame retardents – Particularly polybrominated diphenyl ethers. *Environment International*. 29, 829–839.

Smith, J.L. and H.P. Collins. 2007. Management of organisms and their processes in soils. *Soil Microbiology, Ecology and Biochemistry*, 3rd ed., 471–502.

UNEP. 2001. *United Nation Environmental Program. Stockholm convention on persistent organic pollutants*. Stockholm, Sweden, 2001.

Urbánek, J., K. Brabec, L. Dušek, I. Holoubek, J. Hřebíček, and M. Kubásek. 2010. Monitoring and assessment of environmental impact by persistent organic pollutants. Conference paper.

WHO. (2003). Report of Joint WHO, Europe/Convention Task Force on the Health Aspects of air pollution. Health risk of persistent organic pollutants from long range trans- boundary air pollution.

Wittich, R.M. 1998. Degradation of dioxin like compounds by microorganisms. *Applied Microbial Biotechnology*. 49, 489–499.

Ying, G.-G., 2018. Remediation and mitigation strategies. *Integrated Analytical Approaches for Pesticide Management*. Academic Press, 207–217.

Zacharia, T.J. 2019. *Degradation pathways of persistent organic pollutants (POPs) in the environment. Persistent organic pollutants*, Stephen Kudom Donyinah (ed.).

11 Remediation of Organic Pollutants Using Biobased Nanomaterials

*Solomon E. Shaibu[1], Edu J. Inam[1],
Eno A. Moses[2], Nsikak A. Abraham[3], and
Nnanake-Abasi O. Offiong[4]*

[1]Department of Chemistry, University of Uyo, Uyo, Nigeria and International Centre for Energy and Environmental Sustainability Research (ICEESR), University of Uyo, Uyo, Nigeria
[2]Department of Chemistry, University of Uyo, Uyo, Nigeria
[3]International Centre for Energy and Environmental Sustainability Research (ICEESR), University of Uyo, Uyo, Nigeria and Department of Microbiology, University of Uyo, Uyo, Nigeria
[4]International Centre for Energy and Environmental Sustainability Research (ICEESR), University of Uyo, Uyo, Nigeria and College of New Energy and Environment, Jilin University, Changchun, P.R. China

11.1 INTRODUCTION

Given their potential for environmental persistence, bioaccumulation, and long-range transport, persistent organic pollutants receive vehement scrutiny from environmental scientists, engineers, and policy makers. Recent research trends have shifted to monitoring in environmental matrices, regions, and biota that were hitherto inaccessible or not considered for technical reasons, as well as advanced remediation approaches for polluted sites. If the source of pollution is identifiable and disposable, it can be removed; if not, levels of release must be regulated to safeguard the receiving environment. In the event that the pollution status is unacceptable, the site must be remediated.

Several remediation approaches have been experimented with and deployed in field trials and projects, including adsorption, flocculation, coprecipitation, reverse osmosis, chlorination, oxidation, ozonization, membrane filtration, and ion exchange (Awad et al., 2019; Jiang et al., 2017; Momčilović et al, 2011). Interestingly, most of these techniques are nondestructive—the contaminants are only transferred onto another material (adsorbent) to form a sludge, giving rise to a new type of pollution which requires further treatment (Chen, 2006). Though Awad et al. (2019) and Fatoki et al. (2013) consider adsorption comparatively economical, versatile, and simple, Chen, 2006 has proposed biological treatment as an effective alternative to conventional physical techniques. All these techniques have their inherent advantages and drawbacks, so sometimes they are employed concomitantly.

The remediation approaches adopted depend on several factors, including the physicochemical properties of the individual pollutant, the environmental matrix of concern, cost, and technical feasibilities. The underlying chemistry of these approaches may include one or more of the following mechanism of actions: oxidation-reduction, adsorption-desorption, absorption, immobilization, solubilization, mobilization, or other reactive transformations and biodegradation.

The advent of nanotechnology, which is largely based on the unique properties of materials on the scale of 10^{-9} m, has brought a new dimension to the arsenal of remediation techniques. Although wide deployment of large-scale nanoremediants in the field is still in a developmental stage, it remains a viable research endeavor for the near future. Even more, because of the flexibility to combine several materials of different forms at nanoscale, it has become attractive for remediation studies. This could be attributed to the fact that the cost of remediation would be greatly reduced if smaller amounts of active remediant ingredients could be deployed for remediation of multiple different pollutants. The desire for these multifunctional materials stems from the complex nature of the environment, which often requires more than one approach to achieve remediation goals.

Furthermore, in the wake of resource depletion, the choice of feedstock for the preparation of multifunctional hybrid nanomaterials has come to the attention of researchers and practitioners. Therefore, current remediation efforts attempt to re-engineer natural processes that would not just remediate contaminated sites but also aid in ecological restoration for other ecosystem functions, such as agriculture. This development has introduced several remediation techniques under the purview of green and sustainable technologies. Among this array of approaches is biobased nanotechnology.

Essentially, biobased nanocomposites, also referred to as bionanocomposites, nanobiocomposites, or green composites (Arora et al., 2018), are materials with multiple phases; one is in the nanometer range and another is a biomass (starch, cellulose, lignin, chitosan, biochar, polylactic acid, etc.). Biodegradability, recyclability, and renewability are some of the indispensable features of a typical biobased nanocomposite (Sharma et al., 2017). A number of processing techniques can be used to fabricate biobased nanocomposites; the choice is highly dependent on the biomaterial. Solution casting, compression molding, twin screw extrusion, tape casting, thermal molding, and melt blending are regular methods used to develop starch-related nanocomposites, thanks to their simplicity, flexibility, and tunability (El Miri et al., 2015; Sreekumar et al., 2012; Thomas et al., 2019). Chitosan-based nanocomposites are processed via physical techniques such as mechanical stirring and melt blending, as reported by Thomas et al. (2019). Bionanocomposites' eco-friendly nature, mechanical (Orue et al., 2014) and thermal stability (Li et al, 2011a), and adsorptive properties (Gomes et al., 2015) give them a wide application range, but they are reliant on their individual components (Thomas et al., 2019).

11.2 BIOBASED ADSORBENTS AND NANOMATERIALS FOR REMEDIATION OF ORGANIC POLLUTANTS

In recent times, eco-friendly research has been on the front burner in many fora—and rightly so, because of the global concern for environmental sustainability and protection. The abundance of biomass provides a major feedstock for natural biopolymers; they could be synthesized, but not without major environmental impact, which gives more credence to natural sources. Sourcing for biopolymers (cellulose, starch, chitosan, lignin, etc.) from biomass is more sustainable, more economical, simpler, and greener than the alternative synthetic route (Shaghaleh et al., 2018).

The use of synthetic sorbent materials in remediating contamination has been limited by their high cost, the initial concentration of the synthetic materials, the prevailing temperature and pH, biomass, and time (Pattnaik et al., 2018). This has led to the development of biological-equivalent sorbent materials such as chitosan, cellulose, zeolites, clay, coal, and some microbial biomass products. These natural products (biosorbent materials) have been intensively used as sorbents for removing heavy-metal ions from water and industrial effluents (Khan et al., 2011). However, the need to improve the adsorption capacity and separation rate of these biomaterials has led to the development of nanoparticle-biopolymer composites, which have been shown to be effective in wastewater treatment (Liu et al., 2009; Pattnaik et al., 2018). At nanometer scale, it is established that materials exhibit exceptional properties, and incorporation of these extremely small particles into different matrices enhances the intrinsic features of the resulting compound, consequently increasing its utility (Mahfoudhi and Boufi, 2017; Zhou et al., 2011).

11.2.1 STARCH-BASED NANOCOMPOSITES

Starch, a readily abundant natural polymeric material, possesses versatile features that make it an ideal candidate for impregnation with various nanosized fillers (nanomaterial) to make bionanocomposites (Zhao et al., 2008). Among natural biopolymers, starch stands out for its combination of vital properties from ubiquity to low cost (Zakaria et al., 2017), but particularly nonoxicity, biodegradation, renewability, and tunability (Sharma et al., 2017; Duarah and Karak, 2019; Namazi et al., 2019; Olad et al., 2014), along with biocompatibility (Petersson and Stading, 2005; Olad et al., 2014). Generally, starch is a semicrystalline polysaccharide composed of branch amylopectin and linear amylase, as depicted in Figure 11.1 (Masina et al., 2017). It can be extracted from different sources, which primarily imparts its composition. Starches derived from cassava, banana, and sorghum are reported to contain more than 70% amylopectin by weight and less than 30% amylose (Zakaria et al., 2017). In contrast, waxy starch from maize is composed almost entirely of amylopectin, and this compositional variance affects its inherent stability (texture) and appearance (García et al., 2009; Zakaria et al., 2017). Functionalization of starch through a number of chemical modifications (Sui and BeMiller, 2013; Xiao, 2012) enhances its properties, creating a plethora of application windows (Masina et al., 2017). Each modification method imparts distinctive surface features to the starch moiety. Esterification (Paulos et al., 2016),

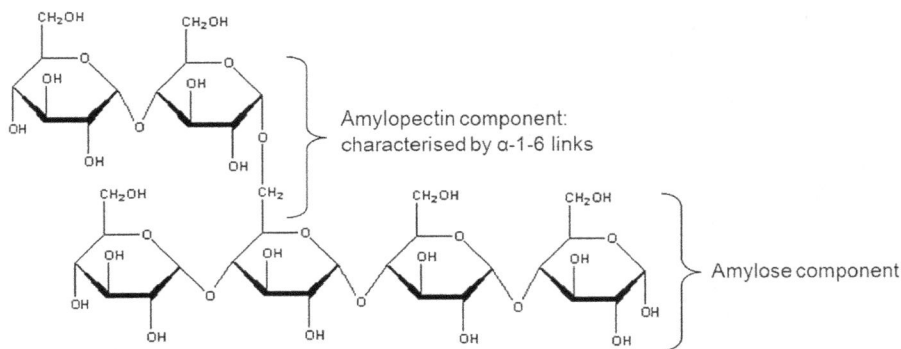

FIGURE 11.1 Starch copolymer chain with amylase and amylopectin component (Masina et al., 2017; reprinted with permission from Elsevier BV).

etherification (Heinze et al., 2004), oxidation (Li et al., 2011a), carboxymethylation (Lawal et al., 2009; Heinze et al., 2004), hydroxypropylation (Singh et al., 2007), and hydroxyethylation (Chen et al., 2010) are some of the chemical methods used to enrich starch (Mostafa, 1997 and Zakaria et al., 2017).

Lately, researchers have been exploring avenues to improve the structural and mechanical properties and wettability of starch biopolymers, and modifications toward this goal have been made by intermingling different organic and inorganic fillers (Zakaria et al., 2017). Though many inorganic and organic fillers (e.g., montmorillonite, polyacrylamide, silica, kaolinite, and polysodium acrylate; Al et al., 2008; Singh and Mahto, 2017; Li et al., 2018; Mbey et al., 2012; Spagnol et al., 2012) have been incorporated into the starch matrix, nanofillers are more promising (El Achaby et al., 2017; Kim et al., 2013; Dorathi and Kandasamy, 2012). Impregnation with nanofillers yields improved overall properties of the resulting bionanocomposite as compared to the raw starch biopolymer; synergistic interplay between the nanofillers and biomaterials is often posited by researchers to be responsible for their enhanced performance in treating different effluent streams (Zhao et al., 2019; Zakaria et al., 2017; Shaibu et al., 2014; Teow et al., 2019; Vikrant and Kim, 2019).

The effects of loading flax cellulose nanocrystals with plasticized starch on the general properties of the resulting nanocomposite film were studied by Cao et al. (2008), who assert that it significantly affects the mechanical and water-related properties of the starch-based nanocomposite among all the properties investigated. Duarah and Karak (2019) attempted to photocatalytically degrade organic contaminants (dodecylbenzylsulfonate and commercial detergent) using a starched modified hyperbranched polyurethane and a nanocomposite of reduced carbon dots and zinc. It was proposed that this nanocomposite is a robust, recyclable, and efficient solar-assisted photocatalyst synthesized via an easy, green approach. Prior to the degradation of organic contaminants, optical studies revealed that the reduced optical band gap of the nanocomposite played a major role in the high degradation efficiency of the organic contaminants by the bionanocomposite—but only the strength and heat stability of the bionanocomposite can be tuned through alteration of the synthesis process and nanohybrid loading, not all the parameters investigated, as might have been speculated.

The recalcitrant nature and health implications of organic contaminants, especially synthetic dyes, are highly documented (Abe et al., 2017; Yusuf, 2019; Oz et al., 2011; Abe et al., 2019), but they still enjoy wide application. Gomes et al. (2015) evaluated the adsorption of methylene blue (one of the most studied synthetic dyes) from aqueous media onto a hydrogel composite of starch and cellulose nanowhiskers. The proposed mechanism of the adsorption, shown in Figure 11.2, suggested electrostatic attraction between the negatively charged surface groups of the bionanocomposite and the dimethylamino groups of methylene blue, coupled with weak intermolecular forces as corroborated by other reports (Erdem et al., 2016; Cheng et al., 2018; Albadarin et al., 2017). Variation of the adsorption parameter showed a very high percentage of removal, about 90%, under the experimental conditions, but the highlights of the study are the biodegradable nature and rapid adsorption kinetics of the bionanocomposite (Gomes et al., 2015).

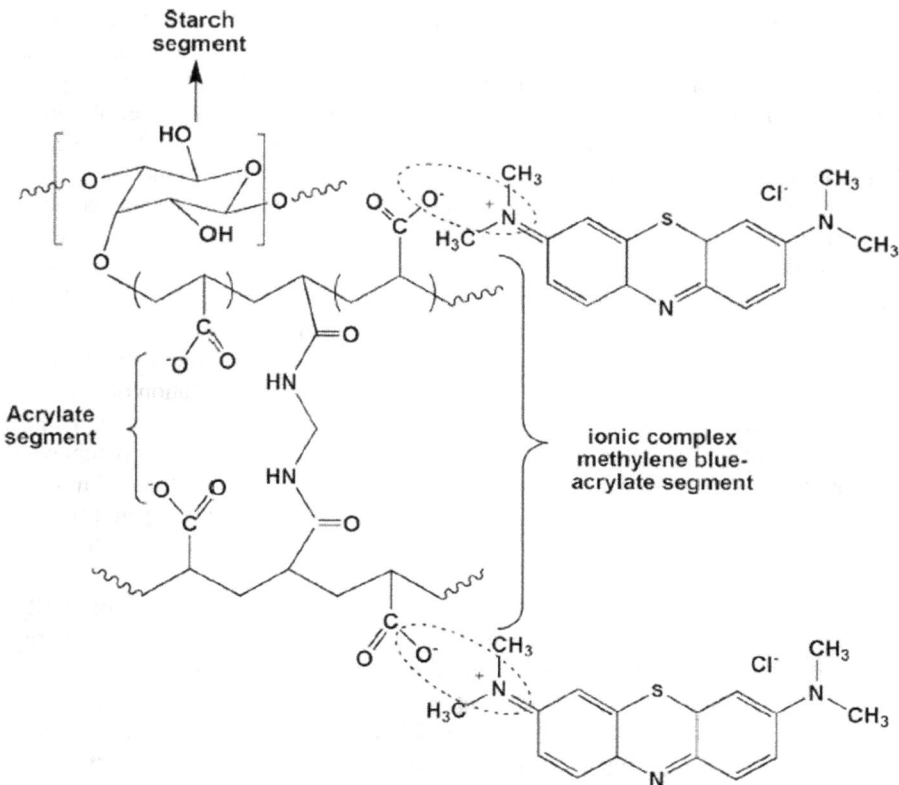

FIGURE 11.2 Proposed scheme for the adsorption mechanism of methylene blue onto a hydrogel nanocomposite of starch-g-polyacrylic acid and carbon nanowhiskers (Gomes et al., 2015; reprinted with permission from Elsevier BV).

Incidentally, a major drawback to the use of nanocomposites is the high agglomeration tendency of the nanomaterials, which affects the resulting properties and applications. However, a number of mitigation measures have been attempted, including use of stabilizing agents and synthesis in volatile solvents, with reasonable success (Lin et al., 2010; Liu et al., 2014; Kim et al., 2013; Dorathi and Kandasamy, 2012; Shaibu et al., 2014). Closely related to the study by Gomes et al. (2015) is the removal of Coomassie Brilliant Blue R-250 dye, another persistent organic contaminant, by Sharma et al. (2017) using a starch/poly(alginic acid-cl-acrylamide) nanohydrogel. Though the synthesis of this bionanocomposite was done by copolymerization, it was still reported to be an efficient adsorbent for removing the dye, and the adsorption process was both spontaneous and chemical in nature.

11.2.2 CELLULOSE-BASED NANOCOMPOSITES

Cellulose, chemical formula $(C_6H_{10}O_5)_n$ (Mohamed et al., 2017; Mahfoudhi and Boufi, 2017), is reported to be the most abundant renewable polymeric material, with both hydrophobic and hydrophilic properties and a yearly estimated production from nature of about 75 billion tons (Thomas et al., 2018; French et al., 2018). Aside from its relative abundance, its physical and chemical properties from its high surface area, aspect ratio, and stability (Mahfoudhi and Boufi, 2017) have found diverse applications in industry for cellulose-based materials (Sun et al., 2016; Nogi et al., 2013; Faruk et al., 2014; Li et al., 2015; Atalla et al., 2005; Milwich et al., 2006; Ferraz, Carlsson & Hong, 2012). Many important materials, each with specific features for different applications, can be derived from cellulose, including cellulose nanofiber (Abe et al., 2007 and Teixeira et al., 2010), nanocrystalline cellulose (Mohamed et al., 2015), cellulose acetate (Jogunola et al., 2016 and Fischer et al., 2008), bacterial cellulose (Zhijiang et al., 2012, Dal'Acqua et al., 2015; Huang et al., 2017), regenerated cellulose (Wang et al., 2016; Soheilmoghaddam et al., 2014), and cellulose hydrogel (Shen et al., 2016; Kimura et al., 2015). The feedstock (source of cellulose) influences the type of isolation used to tune certain properties. Isolation of cellulose nanofiber from wood powder using mechanical treatment produces particles with an average size of 15 nm, whereas Kim et al. (2006) used electrospinning to achieve a size of 250–750 nm from fibrous cellulose and surgical cotton batting. Similarly, nanocrystalline cellulose—nanometric rodlike particles—is usually prepared by acid hydrolysis of cellulose microfibrils under specific conditions (Grishkewich, et al., 2017; Teixeira et al., 2010).

According to Mohamed et al. (2017), bacterial cellulose has superior purity, affinity for water, biological congruence, and mechanical and textural properties compared to plant-derived cellulose. However, it is expensive to procure. Though regenerated cellulose is prepared by simple dissolution due to environmental concerns, it is still widely reported to possess high physical, chemical, and aqueous properties, thereby enjoying extensive applications (Mohamed et al., 2017; Algarra et al., 2014). In the formation of regenerated cellulose nanocomposites, Mohamed et al. (2017) propose that there exists a chemical interaction between the nanofiller and biomaterial, as depicted in Figure 11.3, rather than just physical mixing of the different components.

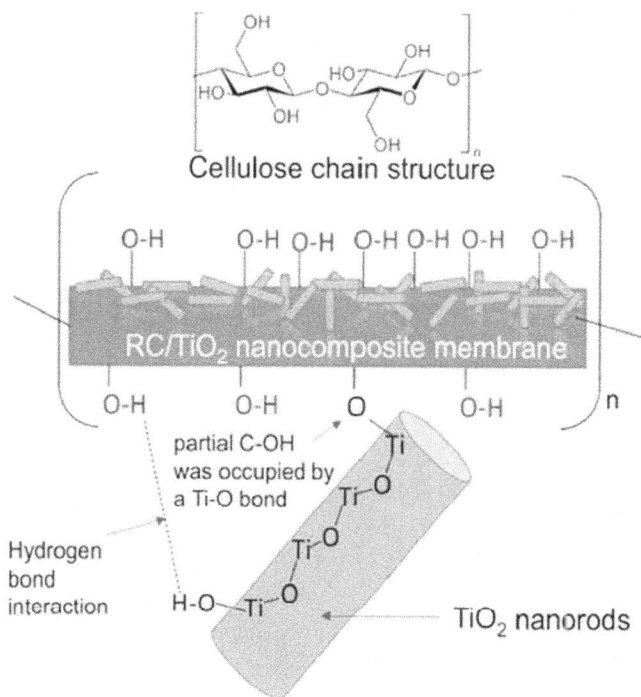

FIGURE 11.3 Schematic illustration of the interaction between the hydroxyl groups of regenerated cellulose (RC) and the titanium dioxide particles in an RC/TiO$_2$ nanocomposite membrane (Mohamed et al., 2017; reprinted with permission from Elsevier BV).

The effects of different synthesis parameters during the preparation of a series of nanocomposite hydrogels of moderately hydrolyzed polyacrylamide and cellulose nanocrystals were investigated by Zhou et al. (2014) for the removal of methylene blue dye. About 90% of methylene blue was removed from aqueous solution, as evident from the clear solution formed after contact with the nanocomposite. A simple thermal treatment was used to fabricate the absorbent, and its efficiency was attributed to the synergistic effect of acid-hydrolyzed cellulose nanocrystals and hydrolyzed polyacrylamide. Adsorption is broadly accepted as a preferable treatment technique in view of its comparative attributes (Shaibu et al., 2014), however, as shown in Figure 11.4, the mechanism of selective photocatalytic degradation of organic contaminants was explored by Zhao et al. (2019) using biomass and titanium dioxide as a reaction center for the mineralization of the target contaminants. Here, the biomaterial mainly acts as a support for the photoactive titanium dioxide.

Suman et al. (2015) attempted in situ synthesis of silver nanoparticles and subsequent impregnation into concrete pebbles prior to embedding nanocellulose in a column. Adsorption studies of the single- and multicomponent systems of methylene blue, heavy metals, and microorganisms showed that the efficiency of the process highly depended on pH, surface area, and the presence of negatively charged surface groups. A higher removal percentage was observed at alkaline pH

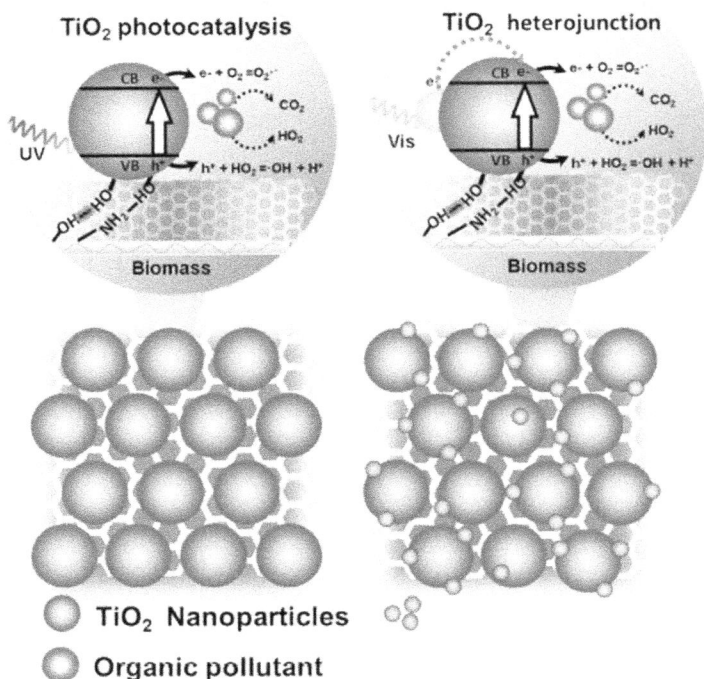

FIGURE 11.4 The mechanism of biomass/titanium dioxide nanocomposites for the degradation of trace organic pollutants (Zhao et al., 2019; reprinted with permission from Elsevier BV).

values, as supported by results from previous studies (Li et al., 2014; Wang et al., 2017; Kumari et al., 2016), but the reusability of the bed column (which purifies after desorption in an acidic medium) did not exceed six cycles, which contrasts with some other reported results (Giri et al., 2017; Urbina et al., 2018; Meera and Arunbabu, 2019; Kumar et al., 2019). Also, crystal violet dye—another organic pollutant similar to methylene blue—was successfully adsorbed onto a carboxymethyl cellulose-based nanocomposite by Saber-Samandari et al. (2016) at different loadings of bentonite. Different physicochemical parameters, from contact time to pH, were reported to play significant roles in the adsorption process, with indications of thermodynamic favorability and spontaneity.

In a different study (Jin et al., 2015), a graphical representation was presented of the removal by a nanocellulose-based nanocomposite of three different anionic dyes (acid red GR, Congo red 4BS, and reactive light yellow K-4G). The nanocellulose was collected from wood pulp. The highest removal efficiency was at a pH of 3.5, and the swelling ratio was also highly influenced by hydrogen/hydroxyl ion concentration.

As reported by Verma et al. (2012), almost 70,000 cubic meters of untreated wastewater laden with organics is discharged daily by the textile industry. Janaki et al. (2013) attempted to apply a nanocomposite of cellulose and polyaniline to remove dyes from simulated textile wastewater. A batch adsorption process was able to remove more than 90% of all the dyes studied, but efficiency was negatively affected by the presence of salts in the simulated effluent. Basically, cellulose-based nanocomposites have shown promise for the degradation and removal of organic pollutants as adsorbents or support systems for photocatalysis.

11.2.3 CHITOSAN NANOMATERIALS

Chitosan is a biopolysaccharide obtained via *N*-deacetylation of chitin, the primary structural polymer in arthropod exoskeletons (Kim, 2018; Park and Kim, 2010; Younes and Rinaudo, 2015; Islam et al., 2017). As illustrated in Figure 11.5, it is formed from the alkaline deacetylation of chitin, composed of 2-amino-2-dedoxy-glucose and 2-acetamino-dedoxy-d-glucose units linked with β-(1→4) bonds (Islam et al., 2017). Being of natural origin, chitosan is highly biodegradable and bio-compatible, and has inbuilt antimicrobial properties.

According to Kim (2018), there are three types of reactive groups in chitosan: the primary amine group and the primary and secondary hydroxyl groups, respectively at the C-2, C-3, and C-6 positions. Among the three reactive groups, the primary amine at the C-2″ position of the glucosamine residues is the most considerable functional

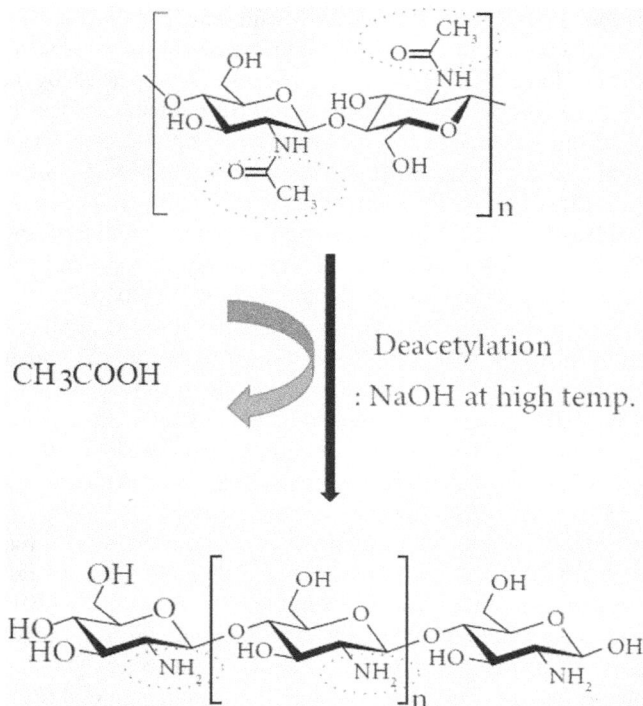

FIGURE 11.5   Schematic presentation of chitin deacetylation with alkaline (Kim, 2018).

group for the biological activities of chitosan (Aranaz et al., 2010). During the process of deacetylating chitin, the acetamide groups are transformed to the primary amino groups, which are the principal functional groups of chitosan attached to the C-2 position of the moiety. The bioactivity of chitosan is directly influenced by its degree of deacetylation. The functional amino groups are easily modified by chemical reaction, resulting in changes to the mechanical and physical properties of chitosan.

Among the various biopolymers developed for sorption processes, chitosan exhibits the highest sorption capacity for several heavy-metal ions, possibly due to the presence of the primary amine group at the C-2 position of the glucosamine residues (Malathi et al., 2014). Despites this, the efficiency of chitosan biopolymers as sorbent materials are limited by their softness, tendency to agglomerate, non-availability of reactive binding sites for biosorption of specific micropollutants, sensitivity to pH, low thermal stability, inadequate mechanical properties, and low porosity (Wang and Chen, 2014; Wan Ngah et al., 2011; Zhang et al., 2016; Pattnaik et al., 2018). To overcome this, novel chitosan-based biocomposites has been developed (Malathi et al., 2014), by cross-linking reagents such as glyoxal, formaldehyde, glutaraldehyde, epichlorohydrin, ethylene glycol diglycidyl ether, and isocyanates to stabilize chitosan in acid solutions and enhance its mechanical properties (Wan Ngah et al., 2011).

Widely applied in adsorption of trace metals, chitosan-based nanomaterials include chitosan-grafted cocoa-husk char biocomposites (Okoya et al., 2014) and chitosan-clay composite beads cross-linked with epichlorohydrin (Tirtom et al., 2012). Owing to the unique physicochemical properties of polymer nanocomposites, several researchers have studied improving chitosan's properties by incorporating nanomaterials. Nanocomposites enhance the surface area, surface functionality, morphology, and thermal stability of materials, and improve their adsorption capacities (Tran et al., 2015). Examples of blends include lignin and chitosan (Volkova et al., 2012), starch and lignin (Naseem et al., 2016), and copolymers of lignin and poly(acrylic acid) (Ma et al., 2016), whereas composites include those with metal oxides, such as titanium dioxide and lignin or titanium dioxide and chitosan (Tran et al., 2015), and magnetic composites (Kolodyńska et al., 2016).

Other nanocomposites that have been used include alumina (Sankar et al., 2013; Azlan et al., 2009; Khattak et al., 2000) and carbon nanotubes (Tjong, 2006), which are used as inorganic fillers for reinforcing or toughening polymeric materials. Masheane et al. (2016) used nanocomposite beads of alumina and functionalized multiwalled carbon nanotubes to remove nitrates from a 50 mg/L nitrate water solution over a pH range of 2–6 and reported a maximum removal rate of 96.8%, compared to 23% removal for chitosan alone at a pH of 4.

Due to their higher sorption capacity compared to closely related materials such as chitin (Xu et al., 2005), chitosan-based materials have great application in adsorption of organic pollutants. As an example, Sahithya et al. (2015) prepared nanoparticles of montmorillonite, copper(II) oxide, and chitosan and used them to remove dichlorvos, an organophosphate pesticide, from water. The chitosan-based nanocomposite performed better than a similar composite prepared from gum ghatti and polylactic acid. In further elucidation of the mechanism of action, the authors maintain that all three components of the nanocomposite were involved in the remediation process. Therefore, the effectiveness of a biobased nanomaterial depends on the biological feedstock or precursors as well as other synthetic reagents.

The suitability of a nanoremediant is also dependent on the target organic micropollutants. Again, Sahithya et al. (2016) established this by comparing the adsorptive removal efficiencies against the organophosphate insecticide monocrotophos of nanocomposites of montmorillonite, copper(II) oxide, and chitosan; montmorillonite, copper(II) oxide, and polylactic acid; and montmorillonite, copper(II) oxide, and gum ghatti. The nanocomposite derived from polylactic acid performed better than the chitosan-based material. Further analysis revealed major involvement of amines and carboxylic groups, carbon atoms, copper(II) oxide nanoparticles, and silicon in the process. The homogeneity of the composite derived from polylactic acid was said to account for its superior efficiency during monocrotophos removal from aqueous matrix.

In spite of its great adsorption capacity, the major setback in applying chitosan-based materials for removing pollutants in aqueous solution is the difficulty in separating them from the medium using conventional approaches such as filtration and sedimentation (Kadam and Lee, 2015). Therefore, the development of synthetic methods to yield magnetic adsorbents, which are more separable, is desirable. As an attempt, Kadam and Lee (2015) synthesized glutaraldehyde-cross-linked magnetic chitosan nanocomposites using an inexpensive reduction precipitation method. The nanocomposites achieved a recovery efficiency of 100% after use in the removal of some organic textile dyes.

Some other key factors that influence the efficiency of chitosan-based nanomaterials in adsorption of organic micropollutants in the environment include contact time, pH, and possible interaction between a protonated chitosan and anionic moieties of organic pollutants. Harmoudi et al. (2014) demonstrated the possible electrostatic and cation-dipole interactions between protonated chitin and chitosan (Figure 11.6).

Chitosan nanocomposites have also been used for successful remediation of organic pollutants such as polycyclic aromatic hydrocarbons (Xu et al., 2005), oily waste (Elanchezhiyan and Meenakshi, 2016), chlorinated hydrocarbons (Mohammad et al., 2017), pesticides (Carneiro et al., 2015; Sahithya et al., 2015; Sahithya 2016), and dyes (Kadam and Lee, 2015; Akar et al., 2016). Other applications of chitosan nanocomposites and their adsorption capacity, as summarized by Kanmani et al. (2017), are presented in Table 11.1.

11.2.4 BIOCHAR NANOMATERIALS

Biochar nanoremediants could be classified as biobased nanoparticles, since biochar materials are derived from biomass. Biochar, which is short for "biomass-derived char" (Xie et al., 2015), is a porous carbonaceous material prepared under thermal anoxic conditions mainly from biofeedstocks of plant and animal origin. Biochar on its own has found a wide range of applications in agronomy, energy, environmental remediation, and carbon dioxide sequestration, and as structural support for other materials (Chen et al., 2019; Jung et al., 2019; Lehmann, 2019; Mierzwa-Hersztek et al., 2018; Tareq et al., 2019; Xiao et al., 2018).

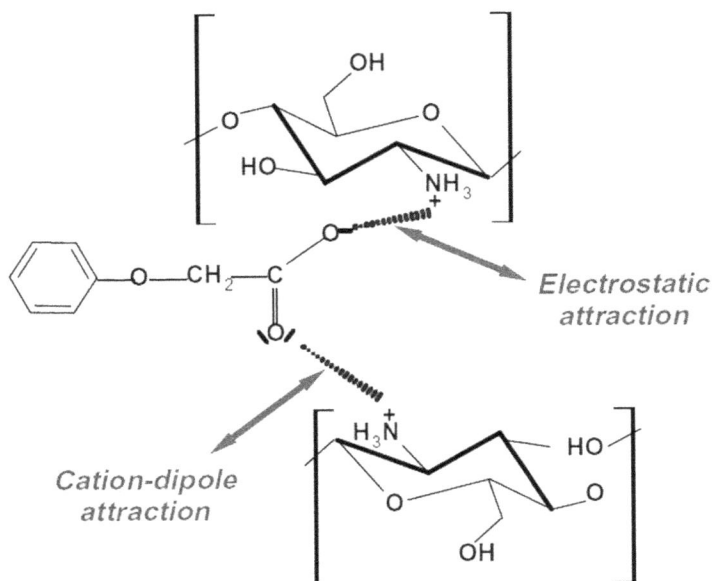

FIGURE 11.6 Attraction between protonated chitin and chitosan and anionic pesticide (Harmoudi et al., 2014; reprinted with permission from Elsevier BV).

For environmental applications, biochar materials have been used to remediate organic and inorganic contaminants in both soil and water matrices (Beesley et al., 2011; Qin et al., 2013; Zhang et al., 2013; Tan et al., 2015; Anyika et al., 2015; Chintala et al., 2014; Kumari et al., 2014; Sizmur et al., 2017; Sophia and Lima, 2018). Properties such as enhanced porosity, high surface area, surface functionality, cation exchange capacity, pH moderation ability, hydrophobicity, and polarity, are key to biochar's role in remediation of pollutants. The main mechanisms of action include adsorption, degradation, dechlorination, and hydrogenation. Owing to disparities in results of different studies on application of biochars for remediation of organic pollutants (Wu et al., 2017), scientists and engineers now consider biochar composite nanomaterials as overcoming some of the deficiencies of biochar alone. The disparities in research results are mainly due to differences in characteristics of biochar feedstocks and products, types of organic contaminants, preparation methods (such as pyrolysis temperature), and prevailing matrix conditions (Břendová et al., 2017; Gai et al., 2014; Jindo et al., 2014; Yuan et al., 2015).

Recently, extensive research efforts have been dedicated to the fabrication of advanced nano-based biochar composites for enhanced functionality, improved surface morphology, and the ability to remove multiple pollutants (Zhang et al., 2012; Bleyl et al., 2012; Inyang et al., 2014; Khatee et al., 2017; Lawrinenko et al., 2017; Mackenzie et al., 2012; Sharma et al., 2019; Tareq et al., 2019; Wang et al., 2017). Common examples of preparation methods involve preparing the biochar from its feedstock and then incorporating the nanocomponent (Figures 11.7 and 11.8). Although most of the nanocomponents are made up of

TABLE 11.1

Chitosan-based Adsorbents of Organic Pollutants (Adapted from Kanmani et al., 2017)

Type of pollutant	Pollutant name	Biopolymer adsorbent	Adsorption capacity (mg/g)	Reference
Dye	Acid red 2	Magnetic chitosan nanocomposites	90.06	Kadam and Lee (2015)
	Acid red 1 and reactive red 2	Composite of chitosan and alunite	Acid red 1: 462.74; reactive red 2: 588.75	Akar et al. (2016)
	Basic Blue 41 and Basic Red 18	Ethyl acrylate–grafted chitosan	Basic Blue 41: 217.39; Basic Red 18: 158.73	Sadeghi-Kiakhani et al. (2013)
	Methylene blue and methylene violet	Chitosan-based graphene oxide gels	Methylene blue: 1,100; methylene violet: 1,350	Deng et al. (2013)
Pesticide	2,4-Dichlorophenoxyacetate	Native chitosan	11.157	Harmoudi et al. (2014)
	Dichlorvos	Chitosan-modified composite of montmorillonite and copper(II) oxide	500	Sahithya et al. (2015)
	Monocrotophos		142.8	Sahithya et al. (2016)
	Glyphosate	Chitosan and chitosan/alginate membranes	Chitosan: 10.88; chitosan/alginate: 8.70	Carneiro et al. (2015)

metallic materials (iron, titanium, and so on), recently metal-free and graphene oxide components have been reported (Zhu et al., 2018; Huang et al., 2017). The main mechanisms by which nano-based biochar materials remediate organic pollutants are adsorption and degradation; some examples are illustrated in Figures 11.9 and 11.10. While most authors report direct adsorption and degradation, there is increased interest in the catalytic potential of nano-based biochar materials for removing organic pollutants from the environment. A typical example is the use of biochar-supported nanoscale zerovalent iron composite as a persulfate activator for removing trichloroethylene (Figure 11.9). Many examples have been reviewed and documented elsewhere (Wang et al., 2019; Xiong et al., 2017).

Table 11.2 presents a summary of feedstock materials used for preparation of nano-based biochar materials, the composites prepared, the target emerging or legacy organic pollutant, and key research outcomesTable 11.2.

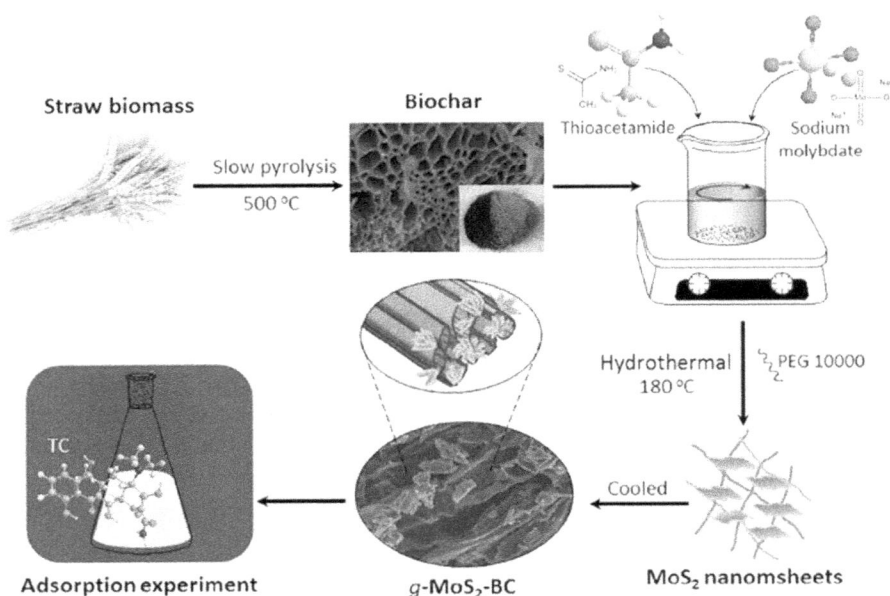

FIGURE 11.7 Schematic illustration of preparation and application of a composite of g-molybdenum sulfide and biochar for removal of tetracycline from an aqueous medium (Zeng et al., 2019; reprinted with permission from Elsevier BV).

11.2.5 POLYLACTIC ACID NANOMATERIALS

Polylactic acids (PLAs), also known as polyactides, are biodegradable and compostable aliphatic polyesters commonly made from α-hydroxy acids, which include polyglycolic and polymandelic acids (Garlotta, 2001). They are thermostable, high-strength polymers made from renewable resources that can be easily processed on standard plastic equipment to yield molded parts, films, or fibers. PLAs belong to the group of polymers whose stereochemical structures can be easily modified by polymerization in a controlled mixture of the L- or D- isomers to yield high-molecular-weight amorphous or crystalline polymers that can be used for food contents and are generally recognized as safe (Garlotta, 2001). PLAs are prepared by direct condensation of lactic acids or by ring-opening polymerization of cyclic lactide dimers (Elsawy et al., 2017). As a renewable and sustainable resource, polylactic acids have great potential to reduce dependence on petroleum-based materials, for economically and environmentally sustainable development. The ability to recycle a PLA into its monomers (lactic acid) is crucial in controlling its environmental impacts and degradation process.

Incorporation of organic and inorganic materials into a PLA matrix enhances its mechanical and thermal properties (Meng et al., 2011; Li et al., 2011c). The main advantage of nanoreinforcement is the lower quantity (0.5%–8% weight) required to produce desired properties in a PLA. Different types of nanofillers that are used

2 mmol Bi(NO$_3$)$_3$·5H$_2$O
20 mL ethylene glycol

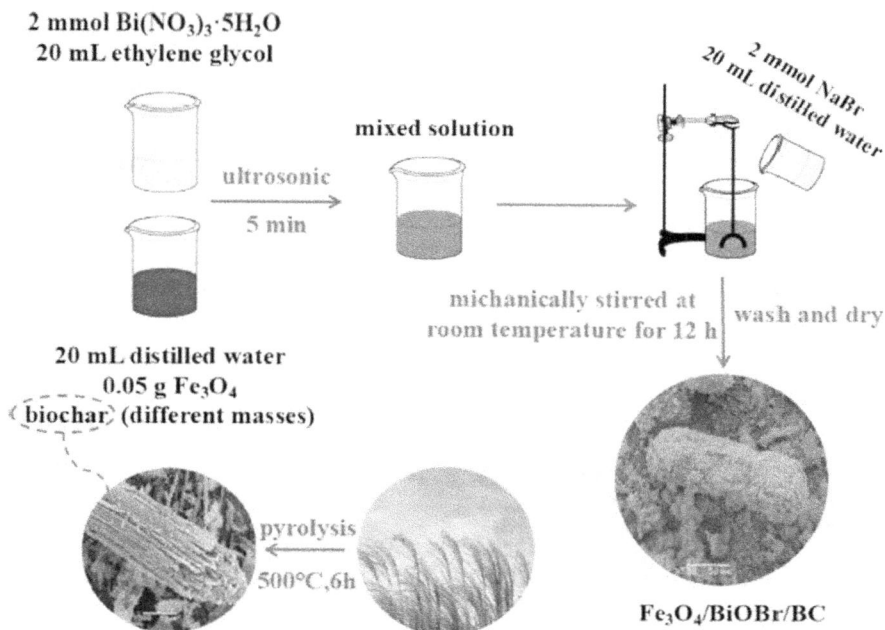

FIGURE 11.8   Fabrication of a composite of iron(II,III) oxide, bismuth oxybromide, and biochar for photodegradation of carbamazepine (Li et al., 2019; reprinted with permission from Elsevier BV).

to make PLA nanocomposites include carbon nanotubes, layered silicates, hydroxyapatite, layered titanate, and aluminum hydroxide (Sharif et al., 2019).

Typically, nanocomposites of a polylactic acid and iron(II,III) oxide have exhibited promising applications in wastewater treatment and bioseparation (Sajjadi et al., 2017; Xia et al., 2017). Nanoparticles derived from iron(II,III) oxide have also been applied in many areas, such as sorbents, flocculents, catalysts, and ion exchangers (Mu et al., 2017). Nanocomposites of a polylactic acid and titanium dioxide have demonstrated excellent degradation of organic pollutants due to their effective photostability, reusability, nontoxicity, and low cost (Sharif et al., 2019).

11.3   FUTURE PERSPECTIVES AND CONCLUSION

This chapter has given an insight into bionanocomposites and their applications for the removal or degradation of organic contaminants in environmental matrices. Globally, scientists are adopting a more sustainable, eco-friendly, and circular-economic approach to material synthesis and applications, which makes bionano-composites an ideal replacement for many unsustainable products currently in circulation. These unique materials exhibit remarkable properties besides abundance, due to the impregnation of nanofillers into the biomass matrix, which provides a platform for wide range of applications. Interestingly, the features they possess are attributable to a synergistic mechanism of the individual components

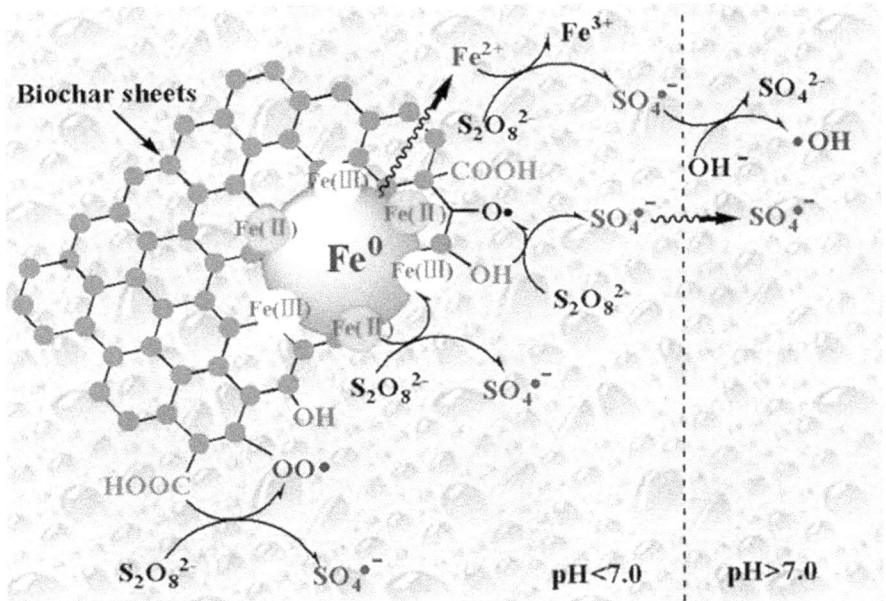

FIGURE 11.9 Biochar-supported nanoscale zerovalent iron composite used as persulfate activator for removing trichloroethylene (Yan et al., 2015; reprinted with permission from Elsevier BV).

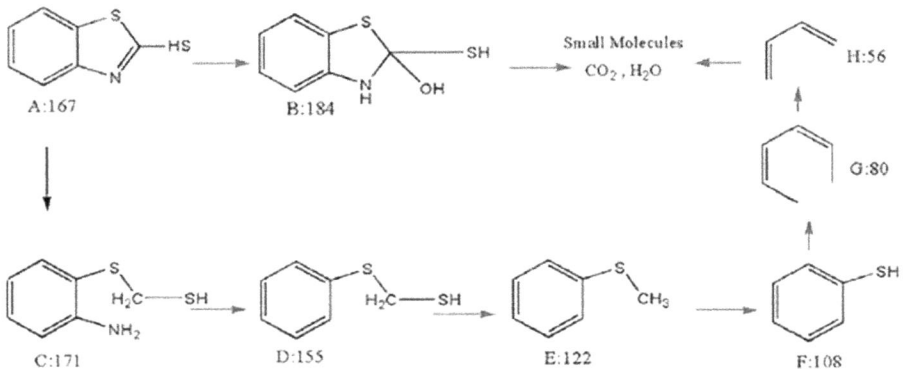

FIGURE 11.10 Mechanism for the degradation of 2-mercaptobenzothiazole by metal-free biochar-based graphitic carbon nitride (adapted from Zhu et al., 2018, with permission from Elsevier BV).

making up the composite material. It is imperative to state that much research into ideal feedstocks, synthetic methods, characterization, cost, and scaling-up implications is being explored for practical applications, even though these materials are already slowly being incorporated into many products.

TABLE 11.2

Examples of Nano-based Biochar Materials for Remediation of Emerging and Legacy Organic Pollutants

Target contaminant(s)	Biochar primary feedstock	Composite prepared	Key mechanism and outcome	Reference
Carbamazepine	Reed straw	Fe_3O_4/BiOBr stacked on biochar	95.51% photodegradation in aqueous medium	Li et al., 2019
Sulfamethazine	Bamboo sawdust	Graphene oxide–coated biochar	Sorption enhanced by 30%	Huang et al., 2017
Tetracycline hydrochloride	Rice straw	g-MoS_2-decorated biochar nanocomposites	Considerable adsorption	Zeng et al., 2019
2-Mercaptobenzothiazole	Magnolia precursor	Metal-free biochar-based graphitic carbon nitride	90% degradation	Zhu et al., 2018
Methylparaben and 2-chlorophenol	Waste pine needles	Biochar-supported graphitic carbon nitride (g-C_3N_4/$FeVO_4$)	98.4% methylparaben and 90.7% 2-chlorophenol degradation under simultaneous adsorption and photocatalysis	Kumar et al., 2017
Phenanthrene	Sawdust	Nanoscale zerovalent iron immobilized on alkali modified biochar (nZVI/MB)	Enhanced phenanthrene removal by 4.9 times versus nZVI and 1.2 times versus MB alone	Wu et al., 2019
Anthraquinone dye	Paper sludge and wheat husks	TiO_2-biochar nanocomposite	Enhanced photocatalytic degradation	Khataee et al., 2017
Reactive brilliant blue dye	Coconut shell	TiO_2-supported biochar nanocomposite	Highest decoloration efficiency (99.7%) was achieved in acidic medium after photocatalysis under UVs	Zhang & Lu, 2018

(Continued)

TABLE 11.2 (Continued)

Target contaminant(s)	Biochar primary feedstock	Composite prepared	Key mechanism and outcome	Reference
Malachite green dye	Algal biomass	Algal biochar–reinforced trimetallic nanocomposite	94% remediation via adsorption and photocatalysis	Sharma et al., 2019
Methylene blue dye	Milled cotton wool	Graphene-coated biochar	20 times better adsorption than unmodified cotton wool	Zhang et al., 2012
Methylene blue dye	Cotton wood	Biochar/AlOOH nanocomposite	Effective removal	Zhang & Gao, 2013
Methylene blue dye	Hickory and bagasse	Multiwalled carbon nanotube–coated biochar	Enhanced sorption	Inyang et al., 2014
Trichloroethylene	Lignin	Biochar/zerovalent iron composite	Effective removal from water	Lawrinenko et al., 2017
Trichloroethylene	Rice hull	Biochar-supported zerovalent iron composite (nZVI-BC)	Efficient degradation (99.4%) in nZVI/BC-persulfate system	Yan et al., 2015
Trichloroethylene	Maize stalk and maize cob	Biochar-supported nano zerovalent iron composite	100% removal in groundwater after 20 min via catalytic degradation	Li et al., 2020

Biomass is a relatively inexhaustible commodity; it ranges from wastes to materials of animal or plant origins (Eisenhauer et al., 2017). It can be deliberately grown for a particular purpose and then serve as feedstock from which bionanocomposites are synthesised. Some other precursors for biobased nanocomposites include lignin (Guigo et al., 2009), protein (Zhao et al, 2008), chitin (Kumar, 2000), and alginate (Zia et al., 2017). Most of these bionanocomposites have been extensively studied but are not covered in this chapter.

ACKNOWLEDGEMENT

This work was supported by an Institutional Based Research Grant from the Tertiary Education Trust Fund (TETFund) of Nigeria (Years 2016-2018 (merged) TETFUND Research Projects (TRP) Intervention).

REFERENCES

Abe, F.R., Machado, A.L., Soares, A.M., de Oliveira, D.P., and Pestana, J.L. 2019. Life history and behavior effects of synthetic and natural dyes on *Daphnia magna*. *Chemosphere*, *236*, 124390. https://doi.org/10.1016/j.chemosphere.2019.124390

Abe, F.R., Mendonça, J.N., Moraes, L.A., et al. 2017. Toxicological and behavioral responses as a tool to assess the effects of natural and synthetic dyes on zebrafish early life. *Chemosphere*, *178*, 282–290.

Abe, K., Iwamoto, S., Yano, H. 2007. Obtaining cellulose nanofibers with a uniform width of 15 nm from wood. *Biomacromolecules*, *8*, 3276–3278.

Akar, S.T., San, E. and Akar, T. 2016. Chitosan–alunite composite: An effective dye remover with high sorption, regeneration and application potential. *Carbohydrate Polymers*, *143*, 318–326.

Al, E., Güçlü, G., İyim, T.B., Emik, S., and Özgümüş, S. 2008. Synthesis and properties of starch-graft-acrylic acid/Na-montmorillonite superabsorbent nanocomposite hydrogels. *Journal of Applied Polymer Science*, *109*(1), 16–22.

Albadarin, A.B., Collins, M.N., Naushad, M., Shirazian, S., Walker, G., and Mangwandi, C. 2017. Activated lignin-chitosan extruded blends for efficient adsorption of methylene blue. *Chemical Engineering Journal*, *307*, 264–272.

Algarra M., Vázquez, M.I., Alonso, B., Casado, C.M., Casado, J., and Benavente, J. 2014. Characterization of an engineered cellulose based membrane by thioldendrimer for heavy metals removal. *Chemical Engineering Journal*, *253*, 472–477.

Anyika, C., Abdul Majid, Z., Ibrahim, Z., Zakaria, M.P., and Yahya, A. 2015. The impact of biochars on sorption and biodegradation of polycyclic aromatic hydrocarbons in soils—A review. *Environmental Science and Pollution Research*, *22*(5), 3314–3341.

Aranaz, I., Harris, R., and Heras, A. 2010. Chitosan amphiphilic derivatives. Chemistry and applications. *Current Organic Chemistry*, *14*(3), 308–330.

Arora, B., Bhatia, R., and Attri, P. 2018. Bionanocomposites: Green materials for a sustainable future. In C.M. Hussain, and A.K. Mishra (editors), *New Polymer Nanocomposites for Environmental Remediation*, pp. 699–712. Elsevier, Amsterdam, The Netherlands. doi: 10.1016/B978-0-12-811033-1.00027-5

Atalla, R., Beecher, J., Caron, R. et al. (2005). *Nanotechnology for the forest products industry vision and technology roadmap*. Office of Energy Efficiency and Renewable Energy EERE, Washington DC, United States.

Awad, A.M., Shaikh, S.M., Jalab, R., et al. 2019. Adsorption of organic pollutants by natural and modified clays: A comprehensive review. *Separation and Purification Technology, 228*, 115719. https://doi.org/10.1016/j.seppur.2019.115719

Azlan, K., Wan Saime, W.N., and Lai Ken, L., 2009. Chitosan and chemically modified chitosan beads for acid dyes sorption. *Journal of Environmental Sciences, 21*(3), 296–302.

Beesley, L., Moreno-Jiménez, E., Gomez-Eyles, J.L., Harris, E., Robinson, B., and Sizmur, T. 2011. A review of biochars' potential role in the remediation, revegetation and restoration of contaminated soils. *Environmental Pollution, 159*(12), 3269–3282.

Bleyl, S., Kopinke, F.-D., and Mackenzie, K. 2012. Carbo-Iron®—Synthesis and stabilization of Fe(0)-doped colloidal activated carbon for in situ groundwater treatment. *Chemical Engineering Journal, 191*, 588–595.

Břendová, K., Száková, J., Lhotka, M., Krulikovská, T., Punčochář, M., and Tlustoš, P. 2017. Biochar physicochemical parameters as a result of feedstock material and pyrolysis temperature: Predictable for the fate of biochar in soil? *Environmental Geochemistry and Health, 39*(6), 1381–1395.

Cao, X., Chen, Y., Chang, P.R., Muir, A.D., and Falk, G. 2008. Starch-based nanocomposites reinforced with flax cellulose nanocrystals. *Express Polymer Letters, 2*(7), 502–510.

Carneiro, R.T., Taketa, T.B., Neto, R.J.G., et al. (2015). Removal of glyphosate herbicide from water using biopolymer membranes. *Journal of Environmental Management, 151*, 353–360.

Chen, H. 2006. Recent advances in azo dye degrading enzyme research. *Current Protein & Peptide Science, 7*(2), 101–111.

Chen, R., Hob, H., and Sheu, Y.M. 2010. Development of swelling/floating gastroretentive drug delivery system based on a combination of hydroxyethyl cellulose and sodium carboxymethyl cellulose for Losartan and its clinical relevance in healthy volunteers with CYP2C9 polymorphism. *European Journal of Pharmaceutical Sciences, 39*, 82–89.

Chen, W., Meng, J., Han, X., Lan, Y., and Zhang, W. 2019. Past, present, and future of biochar. *Biochar, 1*(1), 75–87. https://doi.org/10.1007/s42773-019-00008-3

Cheng, M., Zeng, G., Huang, D., et al. 2018. High adsorption of methylene blue by salicylic acid–methanol modified steel converter slag and evaluation of its mechanism. *Journal of Colloid and Interface Science, 515*, 232–239.

Chintala, R., Schumacher, T.E., McDonald, L.M., et al. 2014. Phosphorus Sorption and availability from biochars and soil/biochar mixtures. *CLEAN – Soil, Air, Water, 42*(5), 626–634.

Dal'Acqua, N., Mattos, A.B.D., Krindges, I., et al. 2015. Characterization and application of nanostructured films containing Au and TiO$_2$ nanoparticles supported in bacterial cellulose. *The Journal of Physical Chemistry C, 119*(1), 340–349.

Deng, J., Lei, B., He, A., et al. 2013. Toward 3D graphene oxide gels based adsorbents for high-efficient water treatment via the promotion of biopolymers. *Journal Hazardous Materials, 263*, 467–478.

Dorathi, P.J., and Kandasamy, P. 2012. Dechlorination of chlorophenols by zero valent iron impregnated silica. *Journal of Environmental Sciences, 24*, 765–773.

Duarah, R., and Karak, N. (2019). Hyperbranched polyurethane/reduced carbon dot-zinc oxide nanocomposite-mediated solar-assisted photocatalytic degradation of organic contaminant: An approach towards environmental remediation. *Chemical Engineering Journal, 370*, 716–728.

Eisenhauer, N., Lanoue, A., Strecker, T., et al. 2017. Root biomass and exudates link plant diversity with soil bacterial and fungal biomass. *Scientific Reports, 7*(1), 1–8.

El Achaby, M., El Miri, N., Aboulkas, A., et al. 2017. Processing and properties of eco-friendly bio-nanocomposite films filled with cellulose nanocrystals from sugarcane bagasse. *International Journal of biological Macromolecules, 96*, 340–352.

Elanchezhiyan, S.S., and Meenakshi, S. 2016. Facile synthesis of metal incorporated chitin for the recovery of oil from oil-in-water emulsion using adsorptive method. *Journal of Cleaner Production, 139,* 1339–1350.

El Miri N., Abdelouahdi K., Barakat A., et al. 2015. Bio-nanocomposite films reinforced with cellulose nanocrystals: Rheology of film-forming solutions, transparency, water vapor barrier and tensile properties of film. *Carbohydrate Polymers, 129,* 156–167.

Elsawy, M.A., Kim, K., Park, J., and Deep, A. 2017. Hydrolytic degradation of polylactic acid (PLA) and its composites. *Renewable and Sustainable Energy Reviews, 79,* 1346–1352.

Erdem, B., Erdem, M., and Özcan, A.S. 2016. Adsorption of Reactive Black 5 onto quaternized 2-dimethylaminoethyl methacrylate based polymer/clay nanocomposites. *Adsorption, 22,* 767–776.

Faruk, O., Sain, M., Farnood, R., Pan, Y. and Xiao, H. 2014. Development of lignin and nanocellulose enhanced bio PU foams for automotive parts. *Journal of Polymers and the Environment, 22,* 279–288.

Fatoki, O.S., Ayanda, O.S., Adekola, F.A., and Ximba, B.J. 2013. Sorption of triphenyltin chloride to nFe_3O_4, fly ash and nFe_3O_4/fly ash composite material in seawater. *Clean – Soil Air Water, 42,* 472–479.

Ferraz, N., Carlsson, D.O., Hong, J.,et al. 2012. Hemocompatibility and ion exchange capability of nanocellulose polypyrrole membranes intended for blood purification. *Journal of the Royal Society Interface, 9,* 1943–1955.

Fischer, S., Thümmler, K., Volkert, B., Hettrich, K., Schmidt, I., and Fischer, K. 2008. Properties and applications of cellulose acetate. *Macromolecular Symposia, 262,* 89–96.

French, A.D., Pérez, S., Bulone, V., Rosenau, T., and Gray, D. 2018. Cellulose. *Encyclopedia of Polymer Science and Technology, 15,* 1–69. doi:10.1002/0471440264.pst042.pub2

Gai, X., Wang, H., Liu, J., et al. 2014. Effects of feedstock and pyrolysis temperature on biochar adsorption of ammonium and nitrate. *PLoS ONE, 9*(12), 1–19. https://doi.org/1 0.1371/journal.pone.0113888

García, N.L., Ribba, L., Dufresne, A., Aranguren, M.I., and Goyanes, S. 2009. Physico-mechanical properties of biodegradable starch nanocomposites. *Macromolecular Materials and Engineering, 294*(3), 169–177.

Garlotta, D. 2001. A literature review of poly(lactic) acids. *Journal of Polymers and the Environment, 9*(2), 63–84.

Giri, S., Das, R., van der Westhuyzen, C., and Maity, A. 2017. An efficient selective reduction of nitroarenes catalyzed by reusable silver-adsorbed waste nanocomposite. *Applied Catalysis B: Environmental, 209,* 669–678.

Gomes, R.F., de Azevedo, A.C.N., Pereira, A.G., et al. 2015. Fast dye removal from water by starch-based nanocomposites. *Journal of Colloid and Interface Science, 454,* 200–209.

Grishkewich, N., Mohammed, N., Tang, J., and Tam, K.C. 2017. Recent advances in the application of cellulose nanocrystals. *Current Opinion in Colloid and Interface Science, 29,* 32–45.

Guigo, N., Vincent, L., Mija, A., Naegele, H., and Sbirrazzuoli, N. 2009. Innovative green nanocomposites based on silicate clays/lignin/natural fibres. *Composites Science and Technology, 69*(11–12), 1979–1984.

Harmoudi, H.E., Gaini, L.E., Daoudi, E., and Rhazi, M. 2014. Removal of 2,4-D from aqueous solutions by adsorption processes using two biopolymers: Chitin and Chitosan and their optical properties. *Optical Materials, 36*(9), 1471–1477.

Heinze, T., Liebert, T., Heinze, U., and Schwikal, K. 2004. Starch derivatives of highdegree of functionalization 9: Carboxymethyl starches. *Cellulose, 11,* 239–245.

Huang, D., Wang, X., Zhang, C., et al. (2017). Sorptive removal of ionizable antibiotic sulfamethazine from aqueous solution by graphene oxide-coated biochar nanocomposites: Influencing factors and mechanism. *Chemosphere, 186,* 414–421.

Huang, Y., Zhu, C., Yang, J., Nie, Y., Chen, C., Sun, D. 2014. Recent advances in bacterial cellulose. *Cellulose*, *21*, 1–30.

Inyang, M., Gao, B., Zimmerman, A., Zhang, M., and Chen, H. 2014. Synthesis, characterization, and dye sorption ability of carbon nanotube–biochar nanocomposites. *Chemical Engineering Journal*, *236*, 39–46.

Islam, S., Rahman, M., Bhuiyan, A., and Islam, M.N. 2017. Chitin and chitosan: structure, properties and applications in biomedical engineering. *Journal of Polymers and the Environment*, *25*(3), 854–866.

Janaki, V., Vijayaraghavan, K., Oh, B.T., Ramasamy, A.K., and Kamala-Kannan, S. 2013. Synthesis, characterization and application of cellulose/polyaniline nanocomposite for the treatment of simulated textile effluent. *Cellulose*, *20*(3), 1153–1166.

Jiang, S., Li, Y., and Ladewig, B.P. 2017. A review of reverse osmosis membrane fouling and control strategies. *Science of the Total Environment*, *595*, 567–583.

Jin, L., Sun, Q., Xu, Q., and Xu, Y. 2015. Adsorptive removal of anionic dyes from aqueous solutions using microgel based on nanocellulose and polyvinylamine. *Bioresource Technology*, *197*, 348–355.

Jindo, K., Mizumoto, H., Sawada, Y., Sanchez-Monedero, M.A., and Sonoki, T. 2014. Physical and chemical characterization of biochars derived from different agricultural residues. *Biogeosciences*, *11*(23), 6613–6621.

Jogunola, O., Eta, V., Hedenström, M., Sundman, O., Salmi, T., and Mikkola, J.-P. 2016. Ionicliquid mediated technology for synthesis of cellulose acetates using different co-solvents. *Carbohydrate Polymers*, *135*, 341–348.

Jung, S., Park, Y.-K., and Kwon, E.E. 2019. Strategic use of biochar for CO_2 capture and sequestration. *Journal of CO_2 Utilization*, *32*, 128–139.

Kadam, A.A., and Lee, D.S. 2015. Glutaraldehyde cross-linked magnetic chitosan nanocomposites: Reduction precipitation synthesis, characterization, and application for removal of hazardous textile dyes. *Bioresource Technology*, *193*, 563–567.

Kanmani, P., Aravind, J., Kamaraj, M., Sureshbabu, P., and Karthikeyan, S. 2017. Environmental applications of chitosan and cellulosic biopolymers: A comprehensive outlook. *Bioresource Technology*, *242*, 295–303.

Khan, A., Badshah, S., and Airoldi, C. 2011. Dithiocarbamated chitosan as a potent biopolymer for toxic cation remediation. *Colloids and Surfaces B: Biointerfaces*, *87*, 88–95.

Khataee, A., Kayan, B., Gholami, P., Kalderis, D., and Akay, S. 2017. Sonocatalytic degradation of an anthraquinone dye using TiO2-biochar nanocomposite. *Ultrasonics Sonochemistry*, *39*, 120–128.

Khattak, A.K., Afzal, M., Saleem, M., Yasmeen, G., and Ahmad, R. 2000. Surface modification of alumina by metal doping. *Colloids and Surfaces A: Physicochemical and Engineering Aspects*, *162*, 99–106.

Kim, C.-W., Kim, D.-S., Kang, S.-Y., Marquez, M., and Joo, Y.L. 2006. Structural studies of electrospun cellulose nanofibers. *Polymer*, *47*, 5097–5107.

Kim, S. 2018. Competitive biological activities of chitosan and its derivatives: Antimicrobial, antioxidant, anticancer, and anti-inflammatory activities. *International Journal of Polymer Science*, *2018*, 13 pages, Article ID: 1708172. doi: 10.1155/2018/1708172

Kim, S.A., Kamala-Kannan, S., Lee, K.J., et al. 2013. Removal of Pb(II) from aqueous solution by a zeolite–nanoscale zero- valent iron composite. *Chemical Engineering Journal*, *217*, 54–60.

Kimura, M., Shinohara, Y., Takizawa, J., et al. 2015. Versatile molding process for tough cellulose hydrogel materials. *Scientific Reports*, *5*, 16266. https://doi.org/10.1038/srep1 6266

Kolodyńska, D., Gęca, M., Pylypchuk, I.V., and Hubicki, Z. 2016. Development of New Effective Sorbents Based on Nanomagnetite. *Nanoscale Research Letters*, *11*, 152–162.

Kumar, A., Kumar, A., Sharma, G., et al. 2017. Sustainable nano-hybrids of magnetic bio-char supported g-C_3N_4/FeVO$_4$ for solar powered degradation of noxious pollutants – Synergism of adsorption, photocatalysis and photo-ozonation. *Journal of Cleaner Production*, *165*, 431–451.

Kumar, M.N.R. 2000. A review of chitin and chitosan applications. *Reactive and Functional Polymers*, *46*(1), 1–27.

Kumar, S., Terashima, C., Fujishima, A., Krishnan, V., and Pitchaimuthu, S. 2019 Photocatalytic degradation of organic pollutants in water using graphene oxide composite. In M. Naushad (editor), *A New Generation Material Graphene: Applications in Water Technology*. Springer Nature, Cham, Switzerland. doi: 10.1007/978-3-319-75484-0_17

Kumari, K.G.I.D., Moldrup, P., Paradelo, M., and de Jonge, L.W. 2014. Phenanthrene sorption on biochar-amended soils: application rate, aging, and physicochemical properties of soil. *Water, Air, and Soil Pollution*, *225*(9), 2105. https://doi.org/10.1007/s11270-014-2105-8

Kumari, S., Chauhan, G.S., and Ahn, J.H. 2016. Novel cellulose nanowhiskers-based polyurethane foam for rapid and persistent removal of methylene blue from its aqueous solutions. *Chemical Engineering Journal*, *304*, 728–736.

Lawal, O.S., Storz, J., Storz, H., Lohmann, D., Lechner, D., and Kulicke, W.-D. 2009. Hydrogels based on carboxymethyl cassava starch cross-linked with di-or polyfunctional carboxylic acids: Synthesis, water absorbent behavior and rheological characterizations. *European Polymer Journal*, *45*(12), 3399–3408.

Lawrinenko, M., Wang, Z., Horton, R., et al. 2017. Macroporous carbon supported zer-ovalent iron for remediation of trichloroethylene. *ACS Sustainable Chemistry and Engineering*, *5*(2), 1586–1593.

Lehmann, J. 2019. Science-to-action through global and regional biochar networks. *Biochar*, *1*, 42773. https://doi.org/10.1007/s42773-019-00029-y

Li, F., Mascheroni, E., and Piergiovanni, L. 2015. The potential of nanocellulose in the packaging field: a review. *Packaging Technology and Science*, *28*, 475–508.

Li, P., Gao, B., Li, A., and Yang, H. 2018. Highly selective adsorption of dyes and arsenate from their aqueous mixtures using a silica-sand/cationized-starch composite. *Microporous and Mesoporous Materials*, *263*, 210–219.

Li, R., Liu, C., and Ma, J. 2011a. Studies on the properties of graphene oxide-reinforced starch biocomposites. *Carbohydrate Polymers*, *84*, 631–637.

Li, S., Wang, Z., Zhao, X., Yang, X., Liang, G., and Xie, X. 2019. Insight into enhanced car-bamazepine photodegradation over biochar-based magnetic photocatalyst Fe$_3$O$_4$/BiOBr/BC under visible LED light irradiation. *Chemical Engineering Journal*, *360*, 600–611.

Li, Y., Chen, C., Li, J., and Sun, X.S. 2011b. Synthesis and characterization of bionano-composites of poly (lactic acid) and TiO$_2$ nanowires by in situ polymerization. *Polymer* *52*(11), 2367–2375.

Li, Y., Xiao, H., Chen, M., Song, Z., and Zhao, Y. 2014. Absorbents based on maleic anhydride-modified cellulose fibers/diatomite for dye removal. *Journal of Materials Science*, *49*(19), 6696–6704.

Li, Y., Zhang, Z., van Leeuwen, H.P., Cohen, S., Martien, A., and Norde, W. 2011c. Uptake and release kinetics of lysozyme in and from an oxidized starch polymer microgel. *Soft Matter*, *7*(21), 10377–10385.

Li, Z., Sun, Y., Yang, Y., et al. 2020. Biochar-supported nanoscale zero-valent iron as an efficient catalyst for organic degradation in groundwater. *Journal of Hazardous Materials*, *383*, 121240. https://doi.org/10.1016/j.jhazmat.2019.121240

Lin, Y.H., Tseng, H.H., Wey, M.Y. and Lin, M.D. 2010. Characteristics of two types of stabilized nano zero-valent iron and transport in porous media. *Science of Total Environment*, *408*, 2260–2267.

Liu, T., Wang, Z.L. Yan, X. and Zhang, B. 2014. Removal of mercury (II) and chromium (VI) from wastewater using a new and effective composite: Pumice-supported nanoscale zero-valent iron. *Chemical Engineering Journal*, 245, 34–40.

Liu, X., Hu, Q., Fang, Z., Zhang, X., and Zhang, B. 2009. Magnetic chitosan nanocomposites: A useful recyclable tool for heavy metal ion removal. *Langmuir*, 25, 3–8.

Ma, X., Zheng, X., Yang, H., et al. (2016). A perspective on lignin effects on hemicelluloses dissolution for bamboo pretreatment. *Industrial Crops and Products*, 94, 117–121.

Mackenzie, K., Bleyl, S., Georgi, A., and Kopinke, F.D. 2012. Carbo-iron – An Fe/AC composite – As alternative to nano-iron for groundwater treatment. *Water Research*, 46(12), 3817–3826.

Mahfoudhi, N., and Boufi, S. 2017. Nanocellulose: A challenging nanomaterial towards environment remediation. In M. Jawaid, S. Boufi, and H.P.S. Abdul Khalil (editors), *Cellulose-reinforced Nanofibre Composites*, pp. 277–304. Woodhead Publishing, Duxford, United Kingdom. doi: 10.1016/B978-0-08-100957-4.00012-7

Malathi, S., Daniel, S.C.G.K., Vaishnavi, S., Sivakumar, M., and Balasubramanian, S. 2014. Chitosan-based polymer nanocomposites for heavy metal removal. In A.K. Mishra (editor), *Nanocomposites in Wastewater Treatment*, pp. 1–22. CRC Press, Boca Raton, United States.

Masheane, M.L., Nthunya, L.N., Maline, S.P., Nxumalo, E.N., and Mhlanga, S.D. 2016. Chitosan-based nanocomposites for de-nitrification of water. *Physics and Chemistry of the Earth*, 100, 212–224.

Masina, N., Choonara, Y.E., Kumar, P., et al. 2017. A review of the chemical modification techniques of starch. *Carbohydrate Polymers*, 157, 1226–1236.

Mbey, J.A., Hoppe, S., and Thomas, F. 2012. Cassava starch–kaolinite composite film. Effect of clay content and clay modification on film properties. *Carbohydrate Polymers*, 88(1), 213–222.

Meera, K.S., and Arunbabu, D. 2019. Magnetic cellulose green nanocomposite adsorbents for the removal of heavy metal ions in water/wastewater. In D. Gnanasekaran (editor), *Green Biopolymers and their Nanocomposites*, pp. 423–437. Springer, Singapore. doi: 10.1007/978-981-13-8063-1_18

Meng, B., Tao, J., Deng, J., Wu, Z., and Yang, M. 2011. Toughening of polylactide with higher loading of nano-titania particles coated by poly (e-caprolactone). *Materials Letters*, 65(4), 729–732.

Mierzwa-Hersztek, M., Gondek, K., Klimkowicz-Pawlas, A., Baran, A., and Bajda, T. 2018. Sewage sludge biochars management-Ecotoxicity, mobility of heavy metals, and soil microbial biomass. *Environmental Toxicology and Chemistry*, 37(4), 1197–1207.

Milwich, M., Speck, T., Speck, O., Stegmaier, T., and Planck, H. 2006. Biomimetics and technical textiles: Solving engineering problems with the help of nature's wisdom. *American Journal of Botany*, 93(10), 1455–1465.

Mohamed, M.A., Abd Mutalib, M., Mohd Hir, Z.A., et al. 2017. An overview on cellulose-based material in tailoring bio-hybrid nanostructured photocatalysts for water treatment and renewable energy applications. *International Journal of Biological Macromolecules*, 103, 1232–1256.

Mohamed, M.A., Salleh, W.N.W., Jaafar, J., Asri, S.E.A.M., and Ismail, A.F. 2015. Physicochemical properties of green nanocrystalline cellulose isolated from recycled newspaper, *RSC Advances*, 5, 29842–29849.

Mohammad, F., Arfin, T., and Al-Lohedan, H.A. 2017. Enhanced biological activity and biosorption performance of trimethyl chitosan-loaded cerium oxide particles. *Journal of Industrial and Engineering Chemistry*, 45, 33–43.

Momčilović, M., Purenović, M., Bojić, A., Zarubica, A., and Ranđelović, M. 2011. Removal of lead (II) ions from aqueous solutions by adsorption onto pine cone activated carbon. *Desalination*, 276(1-3), 53–59.

Mostafa, K.M. 1997. Synthesis of poly (acrylamide)-starch and hydrolyzed starch graft co-polymers as a size base material for cotton textiles. *Polymer Degradation and Stability*, *55*(2), 125–130.

Mu, B., Tang, J., Zhang, L., and Wang, A. 2017. Facile fabrication of superparamagnetic graphene/ polyaniline/Fe_3O_4 nanocomposites for fast magnetic separation and efficient removal of dye. *Scientific Reports*, *7*(1), 5347. https://doi.org/10.1038/s41598-017-05 755-6

Namazi, H., Hasani, M., and Yadollahi, M. 2019. Antibacterial oxidized starch/ZnO nanocomposite hydrogel: synthesis and evaluation of its swelling behaviours in various pHs and salt solutions. *International Journal of Biological Macromolecules*, *126*, 578–584.

Naseem, A., Tabasum, S., Zia, K.M., Zuber, M., Ali, M. and Noreen A. 2016. Lignin derivatives based polymers, blends and composites: A review. *International Journal of Biological Macromolecules*, *93*, 296–313.

Nogi, M., Kim, C., Sugahara, T., Inui, T., Takahashi, T., and Suganuma, K. 2013. High thermal stability of optical transparency in cellulose nanofiber paper. *Applied Physics Letters*, *102*, 181911. https://doi.org/10.1063/1.4804361

Okoya, A.A., Akinyele, A.B., Ofoezie, I.E., Amuda, O.S., Alayande, O.S. and Makinde, O.W. 2014. Adsorption of heavy metal ions onto chitosan grafted cocoa husk char. *African Journal of Pure and Applied Chemistry*, *8*(10), 147–16.

Olad, A., Azhar, F.F., Shargh, M., and Jharfi, S. 2014. Application of response surface methodology for modeling of reactive dye removal from solution using starch-montmorillonite/polyaniline nanocomposite. *Polymer Engineering and Science*, *54*(7), 1595–1607.

Orue, A., Corcuera, M.A., Pena, C., Eceiza, A., and Arbelaiz, A. 2014. Bionanocomposites based on thermoplastic starch and cellulose nanofibers. *Journal of Thermoplastic Composite Materials*, *29*, 817–832.

Oz, M., Lorke, D.E., Hasan, M., and Petroianu, G.A. 2011. Cellular and molecular actions of methylene blue in the nervous system. *Medicinal Research Reviews*, *31*(1), 93–117.

Park, B.K., and Kim, M.M. 2010. Applications of chitin and its derivatives in biological medicine. *International Journal of Molecular Sciences*, *11*(12), 5152–5164.

Pattnaik, S., and Busi, S. 2018. Fungal-derived chitosan-based nanocomposites: A sustainable approach for heavy metal biosorption and environmental management. In R. Prasad (editor), *Mycoremediation and Environmental Sustainability*, Vol. 2, pp. 325–350. Springer International Publishing, Cham, Switzerland. doi: 10.1007/ 978-3-319-77386-5_13

Paulos, G., Mrestani, Y., Heyroth, F., Gebre-Mariam, T., and Neubert, R.H. 2016. Fabrication of acetylated dioscorea starch nanoparticles: Optimization of formulation and process variables. *Journal of Drug Delivery Science and Technology*, *31*, 83–92.

Petersson, M., and Stading, M. 2005. Water vapour permeability and mechanical properties of mixed starch-monoglyceride films and effect of film forming conditions. *Food Hydrocolloids*, *19*(1), 123–132.

Qin, G., Gong, D., and Fan, M.Y. 2013. Bioremediation of petroleum-contaminated soil by biostimulation amended with biochar. *International Biodeterioration and Biodegradation*, *85*, 150–155.

Saber-Samandari, S., Saber-Samandari, S., Heydaripour, S., and Abdouss, M. 2016. Novel carboxymethyl cellulose based nanocomposite membrane: Synthesis, characterization and application in water treatment. *Journal of Environmental Management*, *166*, 457–465.

Sadeghi-Kiakhani, M., Arami, M., and Gharanjig, K. 2013. Preparation of chitosan-ethyl acrylate as a biopolymer adsorbent for basic dyes removal from colored solutions. *Journal of Environmental Chemical Engineering*, *1*(3), 406–415.

Sahithya, K., Das, D., and Das, N. 2016. Adsorptive removal of monocrotophos from aqueous solution using biopolymer modified montmorillonite–CuO composites: Equilibrium, kinetic and thermodynamic studies. *Process Safety and Environmental Protection, 99,* 43–54.

Sahithya, K., Das, D., and Das, N. 2015. Effective removal of dichlorvos from aqueous solution using biopolymer modified MMT–CuO composites: Equilibrium, kinetic and thermodynamic studies. *Journal of Molecular Liquids, 211,* 821–830.

Sajjadi, M., Nasrollahzadeh, M., and Sajadi, S.M. 2017. Green synthesis of Ag/Fe$_3$O$_4$ nanocomposite using *Euphorbia peplus* Linn leaf extract and evaluation of its catalytic activity. *Journal of Colloid and Interface Science, 497,* 1–13.

Sankar, M.U., Aigal, S., Maliyekkal, S.M., Chaudhary, A., Kumar, A.A., Chaudhari, K., and Pradeep, T. 2013. Biopomer-reinforced synthetic granular nanocomposite for affordable point-of-use water purification. *Proceedings of the National Academy of Sciences of the United States of America, 10*(21), 8459–8464. https://doi.org/10.1073/pnas.122 0222110

Shaghaleh, H., Xu, X., and Wang, S. 2018. Current progress in production of biopolymeric materials based on cellulose, cellulose nanofibers, and cellulose derivatives. *RSC Advances, 8*(2), 825–842.

Shaibu, S.E., Adekola, F.A., Adegoke, H.I., and Ayanda, O.S. 2014. A comparative study of the adsorption of methylene blue onto synthesized nanoscale zero-valent iron-bamboo and manganese-bamboo composites. *Materials, 7*(6), 4493–4507.

Sharif, A., Mondal, S., and Hoque, M.E. 2019. Polylactic acid (PLA)-based nanocomposites: Processing and properties. In M.L. Sanyang and M. Jawaid (editors), *Bio-based Polymers and Nanocomposites.* Springer Nature, Switzerland. doi: 10.1007/978-3-030-05825-8_11

Sharma, G., Bhogal, S., Gupta, V.K., et al. 2019. Algal biochar reinforced trimetallic nanocomposite as adsorptional/photocatalyst for remediation of malachite green from aqueous medium. *Journal of Molecular Liquids, 275,* 499–509.

Sharma, G., Naushad, M., Kumar, A., et al. 2017. Efficient removal of coomassie brilliant blue R-250 dye using starch/poly (alginic acid-cl-acrylamide) nanohydrogel. *Process Safety and Environmental Protection, 109,* 301–310.

Shen, X., Shamshina, J.L., Berton, P., Gurau, G., and Rogers, R.D. (2016). Hydrogels based oncellulose and chitin: Fabrication, properties, and applications. *Green Chemistry, 18,* 53–75.

Singh, J., Kaur, L., and McCarthy, O.J. 2007. Factors influencing thephysico-chemical, morphological, thermal and rheological properties of some chemically modified starches for food applications—A review. *Food Hydrocolloids, 21*(1), 1–22.

Singh, R., and Mahto, V. 2017. Synthesis, characterization and evaluation of polyacrylamide graft starch/clay nanocomposite hydrogel system for enhanced oil recovery. *Petroleum Science, 14*(4), 765–779.

Sizmur, T., Fresno, T., Akgül, G., Frost, H., and Moreno-Jiménez, E. 2017. Biochar modification to enhance sorption of inorganics from water. *Bioresource Technology, 246,* 34–47.

Soheilmoghaddam, M., Pasbakhsh, P., Wahit, M.U., et al. 2014. Regenerated cellulose nanocomposites reinforced with exfoliated graphite nanosheets using BMIMCL ionic liquid. *Polymer, 55,* 3130–3138.

Sophia A.C., and Lima, E.C. 2018. Removal of emerging contaminants from the environment by adsorption. *Ecotoxicology and Environmental Safety, 150,* 1–17.

Spagnol, C., Rodrigues, F.H., Pereira, A.G., Fajardo, A.R., Rubira, A.F., and Muniz, E.C. 2012. Superabsorbent hydrogel nanocomposites based on starch-g-poly (sodium acrylate) matrix filled with cellulose nanowhiskers. *Cellulose, 19*(4), 1225–1237.

Sreekumar, P., Al-Harthi, M., De, S.K. 2012 Reinforcement of starch/polyvinyl alcohol blend using nano-titanium dioxide. *Journal of Composite Materials*, *46*, 3181–3187.

Sui, Z., and BeMiller, J.N. 2013. Relationship of the channels of normal maize starch to the properties of its modified products. *Carbohydrate Polymers*, *92*(1), 894–904.

Suman, Kardam A., Gera, M., and Jain, V.K. 2015. A novel reusable nanocomposite for complete removal of dyes, heavy metals and microbial load from water based on nanocellulose and silver nano-embedded pebbles. *Environmental Technology*, *36*(6), 706–714.

Sun, X., Wu, Q., Lee, S., Qing, Y., and Wu, Y. 2016. Cellulose nanofibers as a modifier for rheology, curing and mechanical performance of oil well cement. *Scientific Reports*, *6*, 31654. https://doi.org/10.1038/srep31654

Tan, X., Liu, Y., Zeng, G., Wang, X., Hu, X., Gu, Y., and Yang, Z. 2015. Application of biochar for the removal of pollutants from aqueous solutions. *Chemosphere*, *125*, 70–85.

Tareq, R., Akter, N., and Azam, M.S. 2019. Biochars and biochar composites. In Y.S. Ok, D.C.W. Tsang, N. Bolan and J.M. Novak (editors), *Biochar from Biomass and Waste*, pp. 169–209. Elsevier, Amsterdam, The Netherlands. doi: 10.1016/B978-0-12-81172 9-3.00010-8

Teixeira, E. de Morais, Corrêa, A.C., Manzoli, A., et al. 2010. Cellulose nanofibers from white and naturally colored cotton fibers. *Cellulose*, *17*, 595–606.

Teow, Y.H., Nordin, N.I., and Mohammad, A.W. 2019. Green synthesis of palm oil mill effluent-based graphenic adsorbent for the treatment of dye-contaminated wastewater. *Environmental Science and Pollution Research*, *26*(33), 33747–33757.

Thomas, B., Raj, M.C., et al. 2018. Nanocellulose, a versatile green platform: From biosources to materials and their applications. *Chemical Reviews*, *118*(24), 11575–11625.

Thomas, M.S., Koshy, R.R., Mary, S.K., Thomas, S., and Pothan, L.A. 2019. *Starch, chitin and chitosan based composites and nanocomposites chitin and chitosan based composites and nanocomposites* (Biobased Polymers Series). Springer Nature, Cham, Switzerland. doi: 10.1007/978-3-030-03158-9_1

Tirtom, V.N., Dincer, A., Becerik, S., Aydemir, T., and Celik, A. 2012. Comparative adsorption of Ni(II) and Cd(II) ions on epichlorohydrin cross-linked chitosan–clay composite beads in aqueous solution. *Chemical Engineering Journal*, *197*, 379–386.

Tjong, S.C. 2006. Structural and mechanical properties of polymer nanocomposites. *Materials Science and Engineering: R: Reports*, *53*, 73–197.

Tran, V.S., Ngo, H.H., Guo, W., et al. 2015. Typical low cost biosorbents for adsorptive removal of specific organic pollutants from water. *Bioresource Technology*, *182*, 353–363.

Urbina, L., Guaresti, O., Requies, J., et al. 2018. Design of reusable novel membranes based on bacterial cellulose and chitosan for the filtration of copper in wastewaters. *Carbohydrate Polymers*, *193*, 362–372.

Verma, A.K., Dash, R.R., and Bhunia, P. 2012. A review on chemical coagulation/ flocculation technologies for removal of colour from textile wastewaters. *Journal of Environmental Management*, *93*(1), 154–168.

Vikrant, K., and Kim, K.H. 2019. Nanomaterials for the adsorptive treatment of Hg (II) ions from water. *Chemical Engineering Journal*, *358*, 264–282.

Volkova, N., Ibrahim, V., Hatti-Kaul, R., and Wadso, L. 2012. Water sorption isotherms of Kraft lignin and its composites. *Carbohydrate Polymers*, *87*, 1817–1821.

Wang, B., Gao, B., and Fang, J. 2017. Recent advances in engineered biochar productions and applications. *Critical Reviews in Environmental Science and Technology*, *47*(22), 2158–2207.

Wang, J., and Chen, C. 2014. Chitosan based biosorbents: Modification and application for biosorption of heavy metals and radionuclides. *Bioresource Technology*, *160*, 129–141.

Wang, R.Z., Huang, D.L., Liu, Y.G., et al. 2019. Recent advances in biochar-based catalysts: Properties, applications and mechanisms for pollution remediation. *Chemical Engineering Journal, 371,* 380–403.

Wang, S. Lu, A. and Zhang, L. 2016. Recent advances in regenerated cellulose materials. *Progress in Polymer Science, 53,* 169–206.

Wang, Y., Zhang, C., Zhao, L., Meng, G., Wu, J., and Liu, Z. 2017. Cellulose-based porous adsorbents with high capacity for methylene blue adsorption from aqueous solutions. *Fibers and Polymers, 18*(5), 891–899.

Wan Ngah, W.S., Teong, L.C., and Hanafiah, M.A.K.M. 2011. Adsorption of dyes and heavy metal ions by chitosan composites: A review. *Carbohydrate Polymers, 83,* 1446–1456.

Wu, H., Feng, Q., Yang, H., Lu, P., Gao, B., and Alansari, A. 2019. Enhanced phenanthrene removal in aqueous solution using modified biochar supported nano zero-valent iron. *Environmental Technology, 40*(23), 3114–3123.

Wu, S., He, H., Inthapanya, X., et al. 2017. Role of biochar on composting of organic wastes and remediation of contaminated soils—A review. *Environmental Science and Pollution Research, 24*(20), 16560–16577.

Xia, Y., Fang, J., Li, P. et al. 2017. Solution-processed highly superparamagnetic and conductive PEDOT: PSS/Fe$_3$O$_4$ nanocomposite films with high transparency and high mechanical flexibility. *ACS Applied Materials and Interfaces, 9*(22), 19001–19010.

Xiao, C. 2012. Current advances of chemical and physical starch-based hydrogels. *Starch, 65,* 82–88.

Xiao, X., Chen, B., Chen, Z., Zhu, L., and Schnoor, J.L. 2018. Insight into multiple and multi-level structures of biochars and their potential environmental applications: A critical review. *Environmental Science and Technology, 52*(9), 5027–5047.

Xie, T., Reddy, K.R., Wang, C., Yargicoglu, E., and Spokas, K. 2015. Characteristics and applications of biochar for environmental remediation: A review. *Critical Reviews in Environmental Science and Technology, 45*(9), 939–969.

Xiong, X., Yu, I.K.M., Cao, L., Tsang, D.C.W., Zhang, S., and Ok, Y.S. 2017. A review of biochar-based catalysts for chemical synthesis, biofuel production, and pollution control. *Bioresource Technology, 246,* 254–270.

Xu, R., Yong, L.C., Lim, Y.G., and Obbard, J.P. 2005. Use of slow-release fertilizer and biopolymers for stimulating hydrocarbon biodegradation in oil contaminated beach sediments. *Marine Pollution Bulletin, 51*(8), 1101–1110.

Yan, J., Han, L., Gao, W., Xue, S., and Chen, M. 2015. Biochar supported nanoscale zer-ovalent iron composite used as persulfate activator for removing trichloroethylene. *Bioresource Technology, 175,* 269–274.

Younes, I., and Rinaudo, M. 2015. Chitin and chitosan preparation from marine sources. Structure, properties and applications. *Marine Drugs, 13*(3), 1133–1174.

Yuan, H., Lu, T., Huang, H., Zhao, D., Kobayashi, N., and Chen, Y. 2015. Influence of pyrolysis temperature on physical and chemical properties of biochar made from sewage sludge. *Journal of Analytical and Applied Pyrolysis, 112,* 284–289.

Yusuf, M. 2019. Synthetic dyes: A threat to the environment and water ecosystem. In Shabbir, M. (editor), *Textiles and Clothing: Environmental Concerns and Solutions,* pp. 11–26. John Wiley and Sons, Salem, Massachusetts. doi: 10.1002/9781119526599

Zakaria, N.H., Muhammad, N., and Abdullah, M.M.A.B. 2017. Potential of starch nano-composites for biomedical applications. *IOP Conference Series: Materials Science and Engineering, 209*(1), 012087. doi: 10.1088/1757-899X/209/1/012087.

Zeng, Z., Ye, S., Wu, H., et al. 2019. Research on the sustainable efficacy of g-MoS$_2$ decorated biochar nanocomposites for removing tetracycline hydrochloride from antibiotic-polluted aqueous solution. *Science of the Total Environment, 648,* 206–217.

Zhang, L., Zeng, Y. and Cheng, Z. 2016. Removal of heavy metal ions using chitosan and modified chitosan: A review. *Journal of Molecular Liquids, 214,* 175–191.

Zhang, M., and Gao, B. 2013. Removal of arsenic, methylene blue, and phosphate by bio-char/AlOOH nanocomposite. *Chemical Engineering Journal, 226,* 286–292.

Zhang, M., Gao, B., Yao, Y., Xue, Y., and Inyang, M. 2012. Synthesis, characterization, and environmental implications of graphene-coated biochar. *Science of the Total Environment, 435–436,* 567–572.

Zhang, S., and Lu, X. 2018. Treatment of wastewater containing Reactive Brilliant Blue KN-R using TiO2/BC composite as heterogeneous photocatalyst and adsorbent. *Chemosphere, 206,* 777–783.

Zhang, X., Wang, H., He, L., et al. 2013. Using biochar for remediation of soils contaminated with heavy metals and organic pollutants. *Environmental Science and Pollution Research, 20*(12), 8472–8483.

Zhao, R., Torley, P., and Halley, P.J. 2008. Emerging biodegradable materials: Starch-and protein-based bio-nanocomposites. *Journal of Materials Science, 43*(9), 3058–3071.

Zhao, Y., Wang, Y., Xiao, G., and Su, H. 2019. Fabrication of biomaterial/TiO$_2$ composite photocatalysts for the selective removal of trace environmental pollutants. *Chinese Journal of Chemical Engineering, 27*(6), 1416–1428.

Zhijiang, C. Chengwei, H. and Guang, Y. 2012. Poly (3-hydroxubutyrate-co-4-hydroxubutyrate)/ bacterial cellulose composite porous scaffold: Preparation, characterization and bio-compatibility evaluation. *Carbohydrate Polymers, 87,* 1073–1080.

Zhou, C., Wu, Q., Lei, T., and Negulescu, I.I. 2014. Adsorption kinetic and equilibrium studies for methylene blue dye by partially hydrolyzed polyacrylamide/cellulose na-nocrystal nanocomposite hydrogels. *Chemical Engineering Journal, 251,* 17–24.

Zhou, Z.Y., Tian, N., Li, J.T., Broadwella, I., and Sun, S.G. 2011. Nanomaterials of high surface energy with exceptional properties in catalysis and energy storage. *Chemical Society Reviews, 40,* 4167–4185.

Zhu, Z., Fan, W., Liu, Z., et al. 2018. Fabrication of the metal-free biochar-based graphitic carbon nitride for improved 2-mercaptobenzothiazole degradation activity. *Journal of Photochemistry and Photobiology A: Chemistry, 358,* 284–293.

Zia, F., Sobhani, H., Mohammadi, M., et al. 2017. Alginate-based hybrid nanocomposite materials. In K.M. Zia, M. Zuber, and M. Ali (editors), *Algae Based Polymers, Blends, and Composites: Chemistry, Biotechnology and Material Sciences,* pp. 603–648, pp. 603–648. Elsevier, Amsterdam, The Netherlands. http://dx.doi.org/10.1016/B978-0-12-812360-7.00017-3

12 International Legislation for Containment of Persistent Organic Pollutants and Hazardous Chemicals

Mahiya Kulsoom[1], Vertika Shukla[2], and Narendra Kumar[1]

[1]Department of Environmental Science, School for Earth and Environmental Sciences, Babasaheb Bhimrao Ambedkar (Central) University, Lucknow 226025, India

[2]Department of Geology, School for Earth and Environmental Sciences, Babasaheb Bhimrao Ambedkar (Central) University, Lucknow 226025, India

12.1 INTRODUCTION

The environment consists of the sum total of our surroundings. Living and nonliving components together form an environment, which can sustain and replenish if given enough time. The mutual relationship between the environment, society, and law and order reflects the present scenario of human development. Human interference through unplanned industrialization and urbanization exerts more pressure than the threshold level, stressing the environment. Over the years, global growth and development has damaged the flora and fauna of the planet, posing a threat to human existence. The key to a healthy environment is the balance between demand and supply. An increase in demand results in continuous contamination of the environment by different pollutants, among which persistent organic pollutants (POPs) exhibit a specific blend of physical and chemical properties which make them very stable. Once released into the environment, they break down very slowly, remaining intact for an unusually long period of time. The risks and side effects of these chemicals regarding the earth are greater than than their benefits. POPs are priority pollutants, consisting of pesticides, industrial chemicals like polychlorinated biphenyls, polybrominated diphenyl ethers, and perfluorooctanesulfonate, and by-products of industrial processes like dioxins and furans. POPs are mostly highly lipid soluble and semivolatile, although some are water soluble, such as perfluorooctanesulfonate.

They can be transported over long distances in the atmosphere, resulting in wide-spread distribution across the globe, including in areas where they have never been used or manufactured (Buccini, 2003). POPs have the tendency of bioaccumulation in living organisms with slow metabolisms, and thus they exist for a long time in our bodies and in distant places. They are capable of long-range air transport on aerosols or dust particles and accumulate in abiotic matrices as well (Kaupp 2000). The greater the number of functional groups like chlorine, the greater the chemical's resistance to degradation by biological, photolytic, or other chemical processes. The carbon chlorine bond is very stable against hydrolysis, thus providing greater resistance (Wong et al., 2005, Chu et al., 2006). Partial treatment or improper disposal of a waste containing or contaminated with POPs can lead to release of those POPs into the environment. Some disposal practices can also initiate unintentional production and emission of POPs. Persistent pollutants bioaccumulate in the food web and present a threat of adverse effects to human and environmental health.

The eco-toxic impacts of POPs have prompted concern and thorough research to control or totally ban their use through international agreements. POPs are very stable, and thus even after all new sources are eliminated, they remain in the environment for extended periods of time. They settle down in an area for a long period of time because they do not break down very easily; then they move around, starting from air and water into soil, with subsequent absorption by plants and easy transfer to animals and humans through food chains. Their high persistence and lack of biological degradation make them concentrate more in marine environments. Transportation takes place at low concentrations by movement of fresh and marine waters (Buccini, 2003; Csizer, 2002; Sweetman et al., 2005). These contaminants cause problems such as cancer, birth defects, learning disabilities, and immunological, behavioral, neurological, and reproductive dysfunction in humans and other animal species (Sweetman et al., 2005). POPs contaminate food and water and accumulate in the food chain, finding their way to species such as eagles, polar bears, orcas, and humans. There is evidence that many people worldwide may now carry enough POPs in their body fat (where POPs accumulate) to cause serious health effects, including illness and death.

Since 1972, several important international agreements have been negotiated between developed and developing countries to protect the environment. The United Nations Conference on the Human Environment, 1972, marked the beginning of cross-border efforts to protect, preserve, and improve the environment. Environmental treaties are needed to bring focus to emerging environmental issues and make this planet safe and healthy for all living creatures. In this chapter, we provide an overview of international agreements working toward environmental wellness. This overview can be used for further study and research purposes. It is important to find gaps between regulations and their implementation. Public awareness and participation is one key factor necessary for achieving results; change is possible only if it starts from the base. Big actions cannot reach their goals without implementation on an everyday basis (OAG, 2004; American University School of International Services, 2020).

12.2 INTERNATIONAL AGREEMENTS AND CONVENTIONS ON PERSISTENT ORGANIC POLLUTANTS AND HAZARDOUS CHEMICALS

The destruction caused by World War II created awareness of transboundary issues like human rights, the environment, and so on. Environmental issues such as ozone depletion, air pollution, climate change, ocean pollution, and so on, are global in nature; thus, there is an urgent need for increased awareness of these issues which greatly affect human health and the planet. International environmental agreements enable countries to work together toward the better health of the planet. Domestic actions are often insufficient to protect the environment, resources, and public health. Vital environmental issues have a global impact; thus international agreements related to these issues have become a common platform, with sets of rules and regulations by which participating members are expected to abide. The chemical industry is a sensitive and crucial sector for environmental regulation, as chemicals and their by-products released into the environment cause deterioration of human and ecological health (Menezes and de Souza, 2005).

International environmental agreements have been signed to reduce the impacts of industrialization and development. These conventions are categorized for conservation and protection of nature, energy production, conflicts including nuclear weapons, pollution and climate change, regulation of habitats, and maintaining ecosystems including terrestrial life and freshwater and marine water. The United Nations Environment Program (2001) reported that more than 500 binding and nonbinding environmental agreements to date. Nearly 60% of these treaties were framed around or after 1972 (OAG, 2004). The conventions on ozone-layer depletion, POPs, heavy metals, climate change, and desertification are major achievements for the planet. There are six agreements with the highest number of member countries: the Convention on International Trade in Endangered Species of Wild Fauna and Flora, the Convention on Biological Diversity, the Kyoto Protocol, the Montreal Protocol on Substances That Deplete the Ozone Layer, the Paris Agreement, and the World Heritage Convention (American University School of International Service, 2020). Action plans like the Basel Convention (on the control of transboundary movements of hazardous wastes and their disposal; 1989), the Rotterdam Convention on the Prior Informed Consent Procedure for Certain Hazardous Chemicals and Pesticides in International Trade, and the Stockholm Convention are multilateral agreements protecting humans and the environment from hazardous chemicals and waste. To serve a similar objective, another agreement was launched: the Aarhus Protocol on Persistent Organic Pollutants, under the 1979 Geneva Convention on Long-Range Transboundary Air Pollution (UNECE, 1998). The goal of the Aarhus Protocol is to eliminate the discharge and emission of POPs into the environment. At present, the other relevant international agreement is the Stockholm Convention on Persistent Organic Pollutants, which lists persistent substances and has been ratified by 17 countries from the United Nations Economic Commission for Europe region. The Stockholm Convention, signed in May 2001, focuses on reducing and eliminating the release of 12 POPs known as the Dirty Dozen. Its objective is to protect human and environmental health from POPs.

The Stockholm Convention is global in range and focuses on three categories of chemicals: pesticides, industrial chemicals, and secondary substances or by-products (GEF, 2001). The regulatory framework on emissions and controls of hazardous chemicals discussed in this chapter is presented in Table 12.1.

12.2.1 LONDON CONVENTION AND PROTOCOL, 1972

The Convention on the Prevention of Marine Pollution by Dumping of Waste and Other Matter (1972) is among the first international conventions for protecting the marine environment from human activities. The convention, which came into force in 1975, was amended in 1996 to state that all dumping of waste material is pro-hibited. The objective of this convention is to control all sources of marine pollution either by preventing waste dumping or protecting marine life. There are 87 mem-bers to this convention (IMO, 2019a, IMO, 2019b).

Scheduled substances are listed on the black, gray, and reverse lists. Dumping of items on the black list (Annex I) is prohibited. For the gray list (Annex II), strict precautions and special care should be taken in disposal. And for the reverse list (Annex III), disposal is allowed, considered as trace contaminants or harmless to the environment. Organohalogen compounds, heavy metals, and other persistent pol-lutants like petroleum products, crude oil, radioactive waste, industrial waste, fishing nets, and geological materials which can cause direct harm chemically or physically are listed in Annex I to avoid any permanent harm to marine life. Materials which are nontoxic but can harm the marine ecosystem due to their bulky nature, like containers, scrap metal, and so on, need special permission for their dumping; and sludge, sediment, and other general waste requires a general permit but is allowable for disposal (IMO, 2019b).

In the 1996 amendment, all dumping was prohibited except for wastes on the reverse list. The modernization of the convention eventually replaced it as the Protocol that came into force in 2006; currently there are 53 parties to the London Protocol. After 40 years of the London Convention, strong success for the marine ecosystem and humankind was noticed. Unregulated dumping of incinerated waste, which was at its peak in the 1960s and 1970s, came to halt. The amend-ment, which came into action one year after its adoption, implemented a total ban on the dumping of radioactive waste into the sea, and within two years (by 1995), industrial waste dumping was also phased out, as was dumping of incinerated industrial waste and sewage sludge (IMO, 2019a).

12.2.2 CONVENTION ON LONG-RANGE TRANSBOUNDARY AIR POLLUTION, 1979

The Convention on Long-Range Transboundary Air Pollution (LRTAP) is a structured convention adopted in 1979 which came into force in 1983. It focuses on reducing and preventing air pollution—the main cause of acid rain—as much as possible. The convention is based on scientific assessments made so that parties can take coordinated actions to improve human health and ecosystems. It also helps

TABLE 12.1

Various International Agreements for the Control of Hazardous Chemicals, Including Persistent Organic Pollutants

S. No	Agreement	Leading Organization	Adoption	Entry in Force	Objective	Reference
1	London Convention and Protocol	United Nations International Maritime Organisation	1972	1975	To effectively control all sources of marine pollution	IMO, 2019a
2	Convention on Long-Range Transboundary Air Pollution	United Nations Economic Commission for Europe (UNECE)	1979	1983	To limit, reduce, and gradually prevent air pollution, including long-range transboundary pollution	World Economic Forum, 2020
3	Vienna Convention	United Nations Environmental Program (UNEP)	1985	1988	To protect the ozone layer	UNEP, 2020b
4	Montreal Protocol	UNEP	1987	1989	To limit or ban the use of ozone-depleting substances	UNEP, 2020a
5	Basel Convention	UNEP	1989	1989	To protect human and environmental health against hazardous waste	UNEP, 2011
6	Waigani Convention	UNEP	1995	2001	To ban imports of hazardous waste	SPREP, 2012
7	Aarhus Protocol	UNECE	1998	2003	To eliminate any production, use, or discharge of POPs	EC, 2020
8	Rotterdam Convention on the Prior Informed Consent Procedure for	UNEP	1998	2004	To protect human health and environment health by	UNEP, 2010c

(Continued)

TABLE 12.1 (Continued)

S. No	Agreement	Leading Organization	Adoption	Entry in Force	Objective	Reference
	Certain Hazardous Chemicals and Pesticides in International Trade				sharing responsibilities of hazardous chemicals	
9	Stockholm Convention on Persistent Organic Pollutants	UNEP	2001	2004	To protect human health and environment health from persistent organic pollutants	UNEP, 2019b
10	Strategic Approach to International Chemicals Management	UNEP	2002	2005	To achieve safe and sound management of chemicals	UNEP, 2007
11	4th session of the UN Environment Assembly	UNEP	2012	2012	To find innovative solutions for environmental challenges and sustainable consuption and production	UNEA, 2012
12	Minamata Convention	UNEP	2013	2017	To protect human health and environment from adverse effects of mercury	UNEP, 2020a
13	Paris Agreement 2015	United Nations Framework Convention on Climate Change	2015	2016	To fight climate change and focus efforts toward actions needed for low carbon emissions	UNFCC, 2020
14	2030 Agenda for Sustainable Ddevelopment 2015	United Nations Development Program (UNDP)	2015	2015	To set new goals and targets to stimulate action for sustainable development	UNDP, 2020a
15	New Urban Agenda	UNDP	2016	2016	To achieve housing and sustainable urban development	UN Habitat, 2020

with coordinating research, information exchange, and consultation between the parties. To date, more than 51 countries have joined, and eight agreements have been added to address the specific environmental concerns of ground-level ozone, heavy metals, POPs, sulfur and nitrogen oxides, volatile organic compounds, and monitoring and evaluation of air pollution across boundaries. LRTAP set tight emission limits for each source (combustion, electricity plants, thermal plants, plastic and other production, and manufacturing units). The LRTAP POPS Protocol was opened for signature at the United Nations Economic Commission for Europe meeting in Aarhus in June 1998. It is one of the eight protocols—or focused parts of a large global agreement—aimed specifically at persistent organic pollutants (UNEP, 2019a; UNECE, 2020).

The eight protocols identify specific air pollutants and preventive or curative measures to be taken by each party to cut their emission. The convention creates access to emission and measurement data, modeling, and effects of pollutants on ecosystems, health, agriculture, and materials. The first protocol, with 26 parties, set an emission limit by 2010 for sulfur oxides, nitrogen oxides, volatile organic compounds, and ammonia. The second protocol, with 30 parties, is for POPs. The third protocol, with 30 parties, is on heavy-metal contamination. The fourth protocol, which has 29 parties, deals with reduction of sulfur emissions. The fifth protocol, with 24 parties, set limits for emissions of volatile organic pollutants. The sixth protocol, with 34 parties, handles nitrogen oxides and their transboundary flux. The seventh protocol, with 25 parties, requires a minimum 30% reduction of Sulfur oxide and their transboundary flux. And the eighth protocol, with 43 parties, deals with long-term financing of the cooperative program for monitoring and evaluating long-range transmission of air pollutants in Europe.

The LRTAP convention has produced some concrete results. Emissions of sulfates and particulate matter have dropped by 40% in North America and 30%–80% in Europe. Nitrogen oxides have been reduced by half, and lead pollution by almost 80%, between 1990 and 2012 in member countries in the United Nations Economic Commission for Europe (World Economic Forum, 2020; UNEP, 2019a; UNECE, 2020).

12.2.3 Vienna Convention, 1985

The Vienna Convention for the Protection of the Ozone Layer was framed in 1985 and came into effect in 1988 and ratified in the year 2009. The world had noticed a change in the ozone layer due to rapid industrialization. Countries came forward to work together to safeguard the ozone layer and prevent the harmful effects to human health and the environment that would result from a depleted ozone layer. This was the first convention of its kind, signed by 197 states (including all UN member states). It was expected to make countries responsible for their own actions to combat ozone depletion. The Vienna Convention established a global monitoring and reporting system for the ozone layer and its depletion (UNEP, 2020b; InforMEA, 2019).

This convention promoted cooperation among nations and invited international agencies to assess climate change and exchange information about the ozone layer and causes of its deterioration, like climate, atmospheric changes, and human activities.

It also suggested the creation of a panel to study atmospheric changes and ozone depletion and produce a report for the Conference of Parties analyzing the data and suggesting new policies to limit the production and emission of chlorofluorocarbons. The Secretariat works together with the countries for exchange of information about ozone, such as the prevention and protection of environmentally sensitive areas through Green Initiative programs. The Vienna Convention was outlined for the protection of the ozone layer; its Montreal Protocol is specially dedicated to substances that deplete the ozone layer. This agreement is an agenda laying down principles agreed upon by the parties to protect and prevent further harm to the ozone layer, but it does not require countries to control actions to protect the ozone layer (UNEP, 2020a; InforMEA, 2019).

Parties to the Vienna Convention meet every three years to discuss important issues including finance, administration, research, and systemic observation. The convention has enabled a reduction of over 97% in global consumption of ozone-depleting substances (UNEP, 2020a).

12.2.4 Montreal Protocol, 1987

The Montreal Protocol under the Vienna Convention was agreed upon in 1987. The convention and protocol are the first of their kind to achieve global consent. Under the Montreal Protocol, parties agree to phase out consumption and further production of chemicals that deplete the ozone layer. It is a multilateral agreement to regulate consumption, further production, and restricted use of almost 100 chemicals that are categorized as ozone-depleting substances (ODSs). After being released into the atmosphere, these chemicals damage the stratospheric ozone layer—the Earth's only protective shield against harmful ultraviolet radiation—creating a hole in it. The phaseout is expected to reach its specific deadlines, rapidly reversing ozone depletion (UNEP, 2020c; MJIL, 2020).

ODSs are divided into groups according to the level of destruction they cause. According to the treaty, production of each substance must be eliminated by the given deadline. The phaseout of these pollutants is a stepwise process that is different for different countries. A 10-year deadline is set for developing countries to phase out ODSs in stepwise manner (as mentioned in Article 5 of the treaty). Developing and developed members have different roles and responsibilities, but each is bound with time-targeted commitments. Commitments include trading and reporting, annual reporting of emission, import and export with licensing, and more. ODSs include several halogenated hydrocarbons; compounds with chlorine or bromine are particularly harmful to the ozone layer, such as chlorofluorocarbons, halons, carbon tetrachloride, methyl chloroform, and hydrobromofluorocarbons, whereas compounds with fluorine do not deplete the ozone layer. Some ODSs, like nitrous oxide, are not covered under the Montreal Protocol (UNEP, 2020c; MJIL, 2020).

Twenty-five years after signing, members of this protocol celebrated significant milestones achieved. Significantly, 98% of 100 hazardous ODSs had been phased out. Every country is in agreement with strict responsibilities, and the Montreal Protocol achieved the status of the first global protocol with universal ratification when South Sudan ratified it in 2013. It is expected that 98% of ODSs will be phased out by the Montreal Protocol, and the ozone layer is estimated to return to its pre-1980 condition by 2050–2075 (UNEP, 2020c; MJIL, 2020).

12.2.5 BASEL CONVENTION, 1989

The Basel Convention, on the control of transboundary movements of hazardous wastes and their disposal, was adopted in 1989 and came into force in 1992. It is the one of the most widespread agreements on hazardous and other associated wastes: with 185 parties, it has approximately universal membership. Environmental awareness and strict environmental laws increased resistance to hazardous waste and its cross-border disposal. Some countries often looked for cheap disposal options in developing countries. To combat this toxic trade, the Basel Convention was formulated (UNEP, 2011).

It was framed to protect humans and the environment from the adverse impacts of mismanaging hazardous wastes worldwide. It is a complete treaty, focused on hazardous waste materials around the world and governing the complete life cycle, from production to transport to ultimate disposal. It includes a cradle-to-grave management system for hazardous wastes. Annex 1 of the convention lists hazardous wastes, which include infectious biomedical waste, flammable substances, and toxic, poisonous, explosive, or eco-toxic chemicals. The Basel Convention imposes strict regulations on the movement of wastes, and trade between a party and a nonparty country is not permitted (according to Article 4.5). It requires each member to minimize waste generation and dispose of its own waste in its own territory. Communication of information on hazardous waste is required by each of the members legally bound under the convention. The convention suggests environmentally sound management of waste, and (in Article 14) provides for technical assistance and technology exchange between countries for better waste management (Basel convention, 2020: UNEP, 2011).

12.2.6 WAIGANI CONVENTION, 1995

The Waigani Convention was framed to ban the import of hazardous waste into island nations (extending to the economically excluded zone, 200 nautical miles offshore). Pacific island countries are bound to follow it. It assists in transboundary management and movement of waste, including radioactive waste, and disposal techniques within the Pacific region. It was opened for signature in Waigani, Papua New Guinea, in 1995 and came into force in 2001. It was framed to restrict, minimize, or eliminate the cross-border movement of hazardous radioactive waste specifically in the Pacific region. If dumping is necessary, it follow a complete environmental stepwise procedure and should occur as close as possible to the resource. The convention also encourages limiting the production or use of waste in that region. The countries which ratified it are Australia, the Cook Islands, Fiji, Kiribati, the Federated States of Micronesia, New Zealand, Niue, Papua New Guinea, Samoa, the Solomon Islands, Tonga, Tuvalu, and Vanuatu (SDG, 2020; SPREP, 2012).

This convention provided an effective mechanism to the protect South Pacific from becoming an international dumping area of waste traders. Before it was formed, this region was used as a highway for ships which carried hazardous waste for dumping. The convention was expected to initiate a process of cleaning up waste in the region. A major benefit of the convention was the prevention of dumping any radioactive or hazardous waste in the region, thus reducing any possible risk of a nuclear or hazardous waste disaster. Parties to the convention feel safer and more secure due to this reduced risk (SDG, 2020; SPREP, 2012).

The Waigani Convention caused reduced production of toxic waste, and what is produced is disposed of in an environmentally sound manner. The implementation strategy adopted by the convention included sharing of information between countries and to the secretariat: Export notifications, written consent for approval or disapproval of import and export, documentation of waste movements, information about the management and disposal of waste, and notification about accidents (SPREP, 2012).

12.2.7 AARHUS PROTOCOL, 1998

The Aarhus Protocol on Persistent Organic Pollutants was adopted in June 1998 and amended in 2009. It primarily address 16 chemical substances on the basis of their risk factor: 11 pesticides, two industrial chemicals, and three by-products. Its final objective is to restrict any emission or release of POPs. The protocol includes mechanisms for managing the wastes of banned products; it completely bans the production and use of aldrin, chlordane, chlordecone, dieldrin, endrin, hexabromobiphenyl, mirex, and toxaphene, whereas some other POPs are scheduled for elimination at a future stage, like DDT, heptachlor, polychlorinated biphenyls, and hexaclorobenzene. Emissions of polycyclic aromatic hydrocarbons, dioxins, hexachlorobenzene, and furans should be below their 1990 levels. The protocol also specifies limit values of wastes generated by incineration of municipal, hazardous, and medical waste (EC, 2020).

The Aarhus Protocol focuses on the interaction between the public and authorities. Members of the convention are required to make necessary provision for the public and their participation (at national, local, and community levels) to make the protocol effective. There are three main rights provided to the public in regard to the environment: access to environmental information (any information which is demanded by the public should be available to them as soon as possible), public participation in environmental decision making (the public has the power to decide whether the decision will make a significant impact on the environment and society or not), and access to justice. The right to justice is the last step, and is accountable for the other two, giving authority to the public for justice. If the right to information has not been granted, then national law has not been respected. Environmental information means information on the present state of the environment, policies or measures taken, and the present state of human health and safety which can be affected by the environment. Public participation in decision making enables environmentalists and nongovernmental organizations to comment and intervene, so that ground-level research can help in better planning.

Nongovernmental organizations often look for the best alternative for the environment and people who will be affected by any development project which will have a significant impact on the environment. It also involves public administration, which will elaborate laws and regulations. Dccess to justice means that right to review proceedings that challenge decisions made without keeping in view the general environmental law and public demands. All steps taken under the protocol should be fair, equitable, less expensive, eco-friendly, timely completed, and effective. Parties to this protocol should establish mechanisms to reduce or remove any barrier to public participation, such as financial, scientific, or cultural (EC, 2020).

12.2.8 ROTTERDAM CONVENTION, 1998

Numerous issues have been resolved with regard to transboundary movement of chemicals and their management. In 1992, the United Nations Conference on Environment and Development framed the Rotterdam Convention on the Prior Informed Consent Procedure for Certain Hazardous Chemicals and Pesticides in International Trade. The convention was adopted in 1998 and came into force in 2004. Its objective was to protect the ecosystem and humans from hazardous chemicals and their potential harms. It also states guidelines for using hazardous chemicals in an environmentally sound manner, adopting a nationalized process for the import and export of waste, and sharing information among parties. In July 2007, the Rotterdam Convention had 73 signatories and 181 parties (UNEP, 2010b).

The convention mandates formal generation and circulation of information so that decisions can be made by importing countries about future consignments of chemicals. Importing countries should agree with the decisions of exporting countries. The convention promotes sharing of responsibility between importing and exporting countries. Information exchange often protects from potentially hazardous chemicals. The convention provides technical assistance to develop countries' infrastructures (UNEP, 2010b; IISD, 2010).

The Rotterdam Convention either bans or severely restricts chemicals and pesticides that have severe impacts on humans and the environment. The Chemical Review Committee is a subordinate body of the convention established to review chemicals and pesticide formulations according to the criteria set out in Annexes II and IV, respectively, and make recommendations to the Conference of the Parties for listing any such chemical in Annex III. The parties can nominate chemicals for inclusion in the Prior Informed Consent procedure. Once a chemical is included in Annex III, a "decision guidance document" is framed which contains all the information about the chemical, its life cycle, its effects on human health and the environment, and regulatory decisions about banning or restricting its use. This document is circulated to all parties, who have nine months to respond, which can involve allowing or forbidding import, with or without specific conditions. Import decisions are circulated, and exporting-country parties are obligated to take appropriate measures. In transboundary trade, various parties are provided with a line of defense against hazardous chemicals. The convention encourages international efforts to protect the health of living beings, and enables countries to decide whether or not to import the hazardous chemicals and pesticides it lists (UNEP, 2010a).

12.2.9 STOCKHOLM CONVENTION, 2001

The 2001 Stockholm Convention on Persistent Organic Pollutants, under the auspices of the United Nations Environment Program (UNEP), is a multilateral environmental agreement among 131 nations to abolish the world's most persistent, toxic, and bioaccumulative semivolatile substances, which have high mobility and long residence times in the environment. On top of the Aarhus Protocol, the Stockholm Convention raised the profile of POPs to the global level. Table 12.2 includes all the POPs listed in the Stockholm Convention. The convention specifically tracks POPs over entire life cycle, and suggests proper and safe environmentally friendly systems for their management and disposal. Article 4.4 of the convention suggests that members eliminate the use and production of listed chemicals (pesticides or industrial chemicals). It also suggests that members screen out the listed chemicals. The Stockholm Convention is focused on eliminating the

---

TABLE 12.2

Persistent Organic Pollutants Listed in Amendments to the Stockholm Convention (Adapted from Xu et al., 2013)

Chemical	Chemicals	Type
2001 amendment		
1	Aldrin	Pesticide
2	Dieldrin	
3	Endrin	
4	Chlordane	
5	Heptachlor	
6	Hexachlorobenzene	
7	Mirex	
8	Toxaphene	
9	Dichlorodiphenyltrichloroethane(DDT)	
10	Polychlorinated biphenyl	Industrial chemical and by-product
11 and 12	Polychlorinated dibenzodioxins	By-product
2009 amendment		
13	Chlordecone (Kepone)	Pesticide
14	Lindane	
15	α-Hexachlorocyclohexane	Pesticide and by-product
16	β-Hexachlorocyclohexane	
17	Hexabromobiphenyl	Industrial chemical

(Continued)

TABLE 12.2 (Continued)

Chemical	Chemicals	Type
18	Tetradecarbomodiphenyl ether and pentadecarbomodiphenyl ether	
19	Hexadecarbomodiphenyl ether and heptadecarbomodiphenyl ether	
20	Perfluorooctanesulfonic acid and its salts	
21	Pentachlorobenzene Pesticide	Industrial chemical and by-product
2011 amendment		
22	Endosulfan	Pesticide
2013 amendment		
23	Hexabromocyclododecane	Flame-retardant additive
2015 amendment		
24	Hexachlorobutadiene	By-product
25	Pentachlorophenol and its salts	Pesticide
26	Polychlorinated naphthalenes	Industrial chemical
2017 amendment		
27	Decabromodiphenyl ether	Industrial chemical
28	Hexachlorobutadiene	By-product
29	Short-chain chlorinated paraffins	Industrial chemical
2019 amendment		
30	Dicofol	Pesticide
31	Perfluorooctanoic acid and its salts	Industrial chemical

release of POPs from international production and use and from unintentional production via industry and as by-products, and on reducing stockpiles. Best available technologies and best environmental practices have been elaborated to guide member countries in the best protection and implementation of the convention (http://chm.pops.int/; UNEP, 2019c).

The Stockholm Convention provides (in Article 12) for regional centers for proper training and technical support and information exchange for proper handling of POPs. The convention was an important milestone in international law and practice, environmental protections, and the business community. It was designed to focus on a range of actions to be taken toward the depletion and ultimately elimination of POPs. It advises members to develop strategies for identifying point and nonpoint sources to manage POPs. POP waste is expected to be destroyed or irreversibly transformed.

Due to its dynamism, the Stockholm Convention is often considered a living document: it permits the addition of new groups of POPs in any of the annexes over time. They are scheduled for either restriction or banning of their production, and with release from miscellaneous unintentional processes limited. These organic compounds can occur naturally from volcanic activity and vegetation fires, or anthropogenically like some well-known pesticides, industrial chemicals, and by-products (Buccini, 2003; Wong et al., 2005).

12.2.10   STRATEGIC APPROACH TO INTERNATIONAL CHEMICALS MANAGEMENT, 2002

The Strategic Approach to International Chemicals Management was a landmark initiative in international collaboration to protect human health and the environment. The idea was formulated in Johannesburg in 2002 and New York in 2005, and then adopted in 2006. It provided a framework for achieving the implementation goals of the Johannesburg plan by 2020, through safe and sound management of chemical substances throughout their life cycle. It states that chemicals should be produced and used in such a way as to minimize any significant negative impact on the environment and humans. It also acknowledges that the use of chemicals is essential for modern society and economy, but the world must be aware of the potential threat these chemicals pose to sustainable development. To reach sustainable development goals, sound and safe use of chemicals is mandatory. The global plan of action has fixed activities to achieve the goal (UNEP, 2007; UNantITAR 2020).

This strategy minimizes health risks to workers who are in close contact with chemicals throughout their life cycle. Protection of vulnerable parts of the ecosystem and human communities which are exposed to chemicals should be taken into account during decision-making processes. Decisions are expected to be implemented in a transparent, comprehensive, and efficient manner based on applicable scientific understanding. Human health, environmental effects, economic and social analysis, and risk studies involving reduction or elimination of chemicals should be involved in safety information, to prevent any unnecessary unsafe exposure. It was expected that by 2020, chemicals that pose unreasonable and unmanageable risks would no longer be produced. Costs and benefits should be considered, as well as environmentally friendly substitutes. The unnecessary risk posed by unintended release of by-products or chemicals is generally unmanageable, and thus poses a risk to our ecosystem that should be minimized, including through environmentally sound methods for recycling and recovering lethal chemicals and waste. The United Nations Institute for Training and Research provided technical assistance during the implementation of the Strategic Approach, including developing national profiles and implementation plans, designing national pollutant release registers, and undertaking elementary activities to implement a global harmonized system of lableling and classifying greenhouse gases (UNEP, 2007; UNITAR, 2020).

12.2.11   FOURTH SESSION OF THE UN ENVIRONMENT ASSEMBLY, 2012

The United Nations Environment Assembly was created in 2012 by the Rio+20 Conference and the UN General Assembly. It is the world's highest decision-making body, with universal membership of 193 states, and the governing body of the United Nations Environment Program, which executive director Achim Steiner has called "the world's parliament on the environment." The next meeting will take place in 2021. This assembly meets biennially to agree on priorities for global environmental policies and establish strict international environmental laws. It also provides leadership, geopolitical action on the environment, and contributions for better implementation of the UN 2030 Agenda for Sustainable Development. The theme for the fourth session UNEA was "Innovative solutions for environmental challenges and sustainable consumption and production." The decisions made at that meeting involve all environmental challenges related to poverty and resource management, including sustainable food security and biodiversity, as well as resource efficiency, chemical and energy management, and new, innovative, and sustainable business development. The meeting adopted a ministerial declaration, 23 declarations, and three decisions (IISD, 2019).

12.2.12 MINAMATA CONVENTION ON MERCURY, 2013

The Minamata Convention is a global treaty to protect human health and the environment from the harmful effects of mercury. It was proposed in 2013 in Geneva and came into force in 2017. It emphasizes the chemical and physical properties of mercury, including its natural occurrence, use in everyday life, and release into the air, water, and soil. The Minamata Convention has 128 signatories (UNEP, 2020a).

The objective of the convention is to control the anthropogenic release of mercury during its life cycle. It proposes a ban on any new mercury mines, and a phasing-out of existing ones. The use of mercury in consumable products and processes is restricted or banned, thus reducing demand. Strict control measures are proposed to restrict emissions into air and release into water and land, thus reducing the danger from contamination. Small-scale artists and their gold mining should also be regulated, as mercury is used to extract gold from ore and then released into the environment. The convention sets guidelines for the interim storage of mercury, mercury compounds, and mercury-supplemented products, as well disposal according to proper safe and sound technical practices. Mercury is capable of contaminating sites and causing serious health and environmental problems whose long-term effects are often observed in various trophic levels. The Minamata Convention proposes the use of best environmental practices (UNEP, 2020a). Members should promote and facilitate public awareness programs on the adverse effects of mercury and its compounds and on alternatives available for its use, and share developments and technologies related to mercury pollution and control. Members are expected to promote mercury-free products and use the best environmental friendly technologies to reduce emission (UNEP, 2020a).

Each party should perform an initial assessment of its domestic demand and follow regional plans to facilitate implementation of guidelines framed by this convention. Every party to this convention has to report measures and challenges during the implementation period. The convention takes responsibility to help member countries by guiding them through shortcomings.

12.2.13 PARIS AGREEMENT, 2015

The 2015 United Nations Climate Change Conference, held in Paris, reached a landmark decision to fight climate change and focus global efforts toward actions needed for low carbon emissions. The Paris Agreement was opened for signature on Earth Day (April 22) at the UN headquarters in New York and came into force on November 4, 2016, 30 days after it had been approved or accepted by parties contributing a total of at least 55% of global greenhouse gas emissions. It marked a historic turning point by connecting leaders across the globe—195 nations—for the first time in a common cause to fight climate change, including a climate fund and raising proper understanding and awareness. The agreement aims to strengthen the global response to climate change and the climate crisis by developing a framework for transparent monitoring, reporting, and progressive change of greenhouse gases through national and individual efforts (Natural Resources Defense Council, 2020; UNFCC, 2020).

Financial and technical help is provided to countries, especially underdeveloped and developing ones, to reach their respective goals. The Paris Agreement increases awareness of climate change and provides a to-do list to combat its effects and future consequences, especially in developing countries. The aim is to keep the global temperature increase in this century below 2°C above preindustrial levels; with current efforts, that increase should not exceed 1.5°C. The agreement started a new chapter in the global fight against climate change. The strategic policy targeted regarding climate change and energy is known as 20/20/20: reduction of carbon dioxide emission by 20%, increased use or renewable energy by 20%, and a 20% increase in energy efficiency. The agreement helps countries prepare for the impacts of climate change, follow a climate-resilient path, and adopt laws faciliating low greenhouse gas emissions. Some mitigation steps include conserving and marking old and new greenhouse gas sinks, adopting the latest technologies to avoid pollution, conserving and enhancing forests, switching to renewable energy, and—most importantly—spreading awareness and involving locals in curbing climate change (Natural Resources Defense Council, 2020; UNFCC, 2020).

Under the Paris Agreement, economically rich countries commit to spend money each year to help poorer countries. Kenya uses an app called AfriScout to find the best grassland nearby using satellite data. India has grown a 550-hectare forest on a sandbar in the Brahmaputra River. Many Westerners have switched to a vegan diet. Opting for a plant-based diet and lifestyle has resulted in reduced emission of greenhouse gases. Switching to green agricultural practices like organic farming, crop rotation, and restricted or no stubble burning also helps in reducing carbon emissions (UNFCC, 2020).

12.2.14 2030 AGENDA FOR SUSTAINABLE DEVELOPMENT, 2015

The 17 sustainable development goals (see Chapter 13) were adopted by all UN members in 2015 as a universal pledge to protect the planet, end poverty, and ensure peace and prosperity for all. They are often known as global goals, because action taken in one part of the world affects other parts; thus, it is important that collaborative actions be taken to reach the targets of environmental, social, and economic balance. The sustainable development goals have an interlinked nature, focusing on every aspect of humanity, from poverty, the environment, health, and discrimination to hunger and development. The 2030 Agenda is a action plan to achieve the sustainable development goals and 169 associated objectives for a healthy planet and its people. All goals are considered global challenges, and all members and stakeholders work in collaboration to achieve them (UNDP, 2020b).

12.2.15 New Urban Agenda, 2016

In 2016, the New Urban Agenda was adopted at the United Nations Conference on Housing and Sustainable Urban Development to serve as a new image for cities and municipalities for the next 20 years. The United Nations Development Program (UNDP) extended its full support for the implementation of the New Urban Agenda with the launch of its Sustainable Urbanization Strategy. This implementation will contribute toward localization of the 2030 Agenda to achieve sustainable development goals. It focuses on goal 11 especially, to make cities and human settlements safe, resilient, and sustainable. A year later, the UNDP launched its strategic plan for 2018–2021, covering policy and planning, which aimed for countries to end extreme poverty and inequality so that they can achieve the 2030 Agenda for.

Cities contribute 70% of the worlds greenhouse gas emissions and consume about 75% of the world's energy. They play a major role not only in contributing to greenhouse gas but also as a victim of changing climatic conditions across the globe. Rapid urbanization, climate change, and pollution have exposed cities to negative and harmful effects. This is a global challenge which can be solved with mitigation measures. Cities have the capacity to provide potential solutions and innovative research (Habitat III 2020; UNDP, 2020b).

The UNDP has adopted a strategy plan with six signature solutions for sustainable urbanization. Four of the solutions focus on sustainable urbanization. Solution 1 is to improve urban and rural cities in terms of poverty, equality, livelihoods, and social protection. Solution 2 strengthens governments at municipal and subnational levels. Solution 3 is to enhance the national recovery capacity of resilient societies, which will help countries avoid crisis situations and return to stable development if they should occur. Particularly for urban settlements, Solution 5 focuses on clean and renewable energy and enhancing energy efficiency to reduce pollution in urban areas (Habitat III 2020; UNDP 2020b).

The UNDP is further evolving and adopting innovative and efficient patterns. It responds to a development pattern more efficiently according to the emerging needs of the urbanized world and to serve the half of the global population that resides in cities. This plan also calls for new ways to help poor sectors work toward better sustainable development, preventing crises and providing faster recovery (Habitat III 2020; UNDP 2020a).

12.3   CONCLUSION

Environmental issues such as ozone-layer depletion, air pollution, climate change, and ocean pollution are global in nature, and thus there is an urgent need for increased awareness of these issues that affect human health and the planet. International environmental agreements enable countries to work toward the better health of the planet. Domestic action is often insufficient to protect the environment, resources, and public health, so agreements and conventions take place across borders to address the wide range of pollutants, their sources, and mitigation measures. International agreements focus on governmental policies, actions, and enforcement for important environmental issues. This enable countries to work together to address the vital issues. These global summits are held regularly to address and regulate various emerging environmental crises.

These treaties, being legally binding, provide a kind of insurance to limit and check environmental hazards. Since they are dynamic in nature, they can be modified according to the need of the hour to accommodate the concerns of the signing parties. Monetary or temporal relaxations have been extended to parties. However, the status of nations availing themselves of such benefits is regularly assessed and shuffled, considering the demand and performance of the beneficiary nations. The best part of these agreements is that they are open to all, and nations can join them without any procedural complexities (UN habitat 2020).

Each signatory body is expected to elevate its performance by involving community groups and building a sense of social responsibility among citizens as well as their representatives. Further, to maintain zeal and enthusiasm, these treaties are kept inclusive in nature. Different environmental responsibilities and duties are assigned to various nations for wider reach. In the spirit of good laws, countries are expected to strive for their best possible performance (UN habitat 2020).

REFERENCES

American University School of International Services. 2020. Service. https://ironline.american.edu/blog/beginners-guide-environmental-agreements/

Buccini, J. 2003. The development of a global treaty on persistent organic pollutants (POPs). *Persistent Organic Pollutants* (pp. 13–30). Springer, Berlin, Heidelberg.

Chu, W.K., M.H. Wong, and J. Zhang. 2006. Accumulation, distribution and transformation of DDT and PCBs by *Phragmites australis* and *Oryza sativa* L.: II. Enzyme study. *Environmental Geochemistry and Health*, 28(1–2), 169–181.

Csizer Z. 2002. *UNIDO Programmes on Persistent Organic Pollutants (POPs)*. UNIDO, Bratislava.

EC. 2020. European Commission, Aarhus protocol. https://ec.europa.eu/environment/aarhus/index.htm

GEF. 2001. The UNDP-GEF POPs Resource Kit, United Nations Development Programme.

Habitat III. 2020. New Urban Agenda. http://habitat3.org/the-new-urban-agenda/

IISD. 2010. https://enb.iisd.org/process/chemical_management-picintro.html

IISD. 2019. https://sdg.iisd.org/commentary/policy-briefs/what-did-unea-4-do-for-the-environment/

IMO. 2019a. https://www.imo.org/en/About/Conventions/Pages/Convention-on-the-Prevention-of-Marine-Pollution-by-Dumping-of-Wastes-and-Other-Matter.aspx

IMO. 2019b. https://www.imo.org/en/OurWork/Environment/Pages/London-Convention-Protocol.aspx

InforMEA. 2019. https://www.informea.org/en/treaties/vienna-convention

Kaupp, H., and M.S. McLachlan. 2000. Distribution of polychlorinated dibenzo-P-dioxins and dibenzofurans (PCDD/Fs) and polycyclic aromatic hydrocarbons (PAHs) within the full size range of atmospheric particles. *Atmospheric Environment, 34*(1), 73–83.

Menezes, R.P.B., and A. de Souza. 2005. Using the WTO/TBT enquiry point to monitor tendencies in the regulation of environment, health, and safety issues affecting the chemical industry. *Environment International, 31*(3), 407–416.

MJIL. 2020. http://www.mjilonline.org/analysis-of-the-success-of-the-vienna-convention-for-the-protection-of-the-ozone-layer-and-the-montreal-protocol/#:~:text=36%20Associate%20Editor-,The%20Vienna%20Convention%20for%20the%20Protection%20of%20the%20Ozone%20Layer,treaties%20in%20United%20Nations%20history

Natural Resources Defense Council. 2020. https://www.nrdc.org/stories/paris-climate-agreement-everything-you-need-know

OAG. 2004. OAG report. https://www.oagbvg.gc.ca/internet/English/parl_cesd_200410_01_e_14914.html

SDG. 2020. https://sustainabledevelopment.un.org/partnership/?p=7456

SPREP. 2012. http://macbio-pacific.info/wp-content/uploads/2017/08/Waigani_Convention-1.pdf

Sweetman, A.J., M. Dalla Valle, K. Prevedouros and K.C. Jones. 2005. The role of soil organic carbon in the global cycling of persistent organic pollutants (POPs): Interpreting and modelling field data. *Chemosphere, 60*(7):959–972.

UNDP. 2020a. 2030 agenda for sustainable development 2015. https://www.undp.org/content/undp/en/home/2030-agenda-for-sustainable-development.html

UNDP. 2020b. https://www.undp.org/content/undp/en/home/blog/2018/cities-2030--implementing-the-new-urban-agenda.html

UNEA. 2012. 4th session of UN environment assembly, 2012, IISD Fourth Session of the UN Environment Assembly (UNEA-4). https://sdg.iisd.org/events/fourth-session-of-the-un-environment-assembly-unea-4/#:~:text=The%20fourth%20session%20of%20the,2).&text=The%20President%20of%20UNEA%2D4%20will%20be%20Estonia

UNECE. 1998. The 1998 Aarhus Protocol on Persistent Organic Pollutants (POPs), United Nations Economic Commission for Europe, On line at: SPREP Waigani, Convention Handbook.

UNECE. 2020. Protocol on persistent organic pollutants (POPs). http://www.unece.org/fileadmin//DAM/env/lrtap/status/lrtap_s.htm

UNEP. 2019a. http://chm.pops.int/Partners/MEAs/LRTAP/tabid/4148/Default.aspx

UNEP. 2019b. http://chm.pops.int/TheConvention/Overview/tabid/3351/Default.aspx

UNEP. 2011. http://www.basel.int/TheConvention/Overview/TextoftheConvention/tabid/1275/Default.aspx

UNEP. 2020a. Minamata convention. http://mercuryconvention.org/Home/tabid/3360/Default.aspx

UNEP. 2020b. Ozonaction. https://www.unenvironment.org/ozonaction/who-we-are/about-montreal-protocol

UNEP. 2010a. Rotterdam convention. http://www.pic.int/TheConvention/Overview

UNEP. 2010b. Rotterdam convention. http://www.pic.int/TheConvention/Overview/Howitworks/tabid/1046/language/en-US/Default.aspx

UNEP. 2010c. Rotterdam convention. http://www.pic.int/TheConvention/Overview/Textofthe Convention/tabid/1048/language/en-US/Default.aspx

UNEP. 2019c. Stockholm convention. http://www.pops.int/TheConvention/Overview/History/Overview/tabid/3549/Default.aspx

UNEP. 2007. Strategic approach to international chemicals management, 2002. https://sustainabledevelopment.un.org/content/documents/SAICM_publication_ENG.pdf

UNEP. 2020c. Vienna convention. https://ozone.unep.org/treaties/vienna-convention

UNFCC. 2020. https://unfccc.int/process-and-meetings/the-paris-agreement/what-is-the-paris-agreement

UN habitat. 2020. https://unhabitat.org/about-us (assessed on 15 October 2020).

UNITAR. 2020. https://unitar.org/sustainable-development-goals/planet/our-portfolio/strategic-approach-international-chemicals-management

Wong, M.H., Leung, A.O.W., Chan, J.K.Y., and Choi, M.P.K. 2005. A review on the usage of POP pesticides in China, with emphasis on DDT loadings in human milk. *Chemosphere*, *60*(6), 740–752.

World Economic Forum. 2020. https://www.weforum.org/agenda/2020/03/air-pollution-treaty-climate-change-lrtap/

Xu, W., Wang, X., and Z., Cai. 2013. Analytical chemistry of the persistent organic pollutants identified in the Stockholm Convention: A review. *Analytica Chimica Acta*, *790*, 1–13. https://www.undp.org/content/undp/en/home/2030-agenda-for-sustainable-development.html

13 United Nations Sustainable Development Goals: A Future Free from Persistent Organic Pollutants and Other Toxic Chemicals for All

Anupam Khajuria[1] and Prabhat Verma[2]
[1]United Nations Centre for Regional Development, Nagoya, Japan
[2]Osaka University, Osaka, Japan

13.1 INTRODUCTION

Persistent organic pollutants (POPs) are toxic chemicals that have harmful effects on human health and on the environment. Today they are found virtually everywhere on the planet, which raises alarm about the sustainability of our environment. This concern is even more serious because POPs can evidently accumulate, disseminate in the environment via transport by air and water, and spread among various species through food chains. They can persist in the environment because they have the potential to biomagnify through the food chain, bioaccumulate in ecosystems, and travel long distances. POPs are human-made, and thus need our careful attention and efforts to minimize their adverse effects on the environment we live in. The production and use of a variety of chemicals have grown exponentially in the past three decades in a number of consumable products, including food. Many of the synthetic chemicals that are added to improve product characteristics have been proven beneficial for industry, for agricultural crop production, and in pest and disease control, which has encouraged their incorporation into our regular needs without consideration of the long-term risk of their negative effects. Among the estimated 100,000 chemical substances that are commonly used in consumable products, many end up as pollutants and contamination, both in food and in the environment. In fact, POPs may exist in many products that we use in our daily lives without our even realizing it, and they may ultimately remain in various environmental media for a prolonged time (UNSD, 1992). Consequently, a certain amount may also remain in human bodies, having unforeseen negative effects on human health as well as the environment. In the recent past, awareness of the negative effects of these harmful chemicals on our well-being has gradually grown, and as a result, a considerable effort to address the issue has been seen on various platforms. POPs are diverse and complex, and therefore necessitate cross-sectoral cooperation to tackle the integrated societal and environmental challenges they pose.

The movement of POPs is complex, and their compounds can exist in different phases. They can stay in the environment in the form of gas, or be adsorbed to airborne particles. As they travel across the environment, they can be exchanged amid various environmental media through air, water, and soil. Some POPs can be carried for long distances, travel many miles, and evaporate from water into the air or become attached to airborne particles. POPs can also travel across the planet through oceans and rivers, as well as via animal carriers, such as migratory species, though to a lesser extent (Shahare, 2017). Most of the POPs in the atmosphere could return to earth in the form of snow, mist, or rain but remain intact in the ecosystem and harm humans, animals, and the environment. Therefore, among several possible actions to minimize harm from POPs, some important steps are restricting their transboundary spread and safely disposing of them in a secure way.

Ever since we started to recognize the possible threat to human health and the environment posed by the increased use of chemicals in various aspects of life, there have been continuous efforts to address it, including restricting the movement of hazardous chemical and disposing of them safely. Several international conventions and conferences have been dedicated to this concern. Most notably, the Basel Convention on the control of transboundary movements of hazardous wastes and their disposal was adopted as early as 1989 to recognize the future threats of hazardous chemicals in use (Basel Convention, 1989). This convention seeks to protect human health and the environment against the harmful effects of various types of wastes defined as hazardous, and suggests proper disposals of them based on their sources and their characteristics. Another important recognition was in 1992, when the United Nations Conference on Environment and Development addressed these concerns by outlining six priority program areas for action to safeguard environmentally nourishing management of harmful chemicals (UNCED, 1992).

Although discarding POPs altogether is not a feasible option, it is certainly possible to use them wisely in a cost-effective manner while still ensuring a high degree of safety. In this regard, chapter 19 of the UN Conference on Environment and Development's Agenda 21 outlines a framework of environmentally healthy management of toxic chemicals (UNSD, 1992). By setting its 2030 Agenda for Sustainable Development (in 2015), the United Nations established a set of goals to end poverty, protect the planet, and guarantee prosperity for all (United Nations, 2015). This agenda interlinked many aspects of well-being and contentment that were also related to the use and management of toxic chemicals. The global indicator framework of each goal of the agenda is reflected in various targets and indicators. Each of these 17 Sustainable Development Goals (SDGs) includes specific targets to be achieved by 2030. The linkage of socioeconomics and chemicals is an initiative to explore and realize the potential of toxic chemicals and to find a way to grasp their influence and innovate toward the SDGs. However, it is still necessary to ensure environmentally promising and appropriate management of toxic chemicals, which lies within the principles of the 2030 Agenda.

The major concerns about the negative effects of POPs can be addressed by ensuring their safe use and finding ways to optimize their production, minimize their unwanted movement, decrease the possibility of their incorporation into the environment, and intelligently recycle, reuse, and properly dispose of them. The 2030 Agenda considers all these important steps to curtailing the negative effects of toxic chemicals in our lives and the environment. This chapter addresses POPs and other toxic chemicals in a number of the 2030 Agenda's SDGs (United Nations, 2015). We consider recent United Nations declarations, conventions, and summits related to toxic chemicals such as POPs, and discuss how to facilitate and coordinate international actions and partnerships to achieve a nontoxic environment and meet the SDGs. This chapter further discusses the relevance of 3R (reduce, reuse, and recycle) practices, in addition to the 4R paradigm (replace, reduce, reuse, and recycle), the connectivity of toxic chemicals, and circular economy within sustainable development. A circular economy carries significant importance in environmental implications, institutional roles, and actions toward recycling products in tune with the global agenda of achieving a nontoxic environment.

13.2   TOXIC CHEMICALS IN THE UNITED NATIONS SDGS

The exposure of humans and the environment to harmful chemicals is a major concern in developing countries and a major challenge in relation to the circular economy (discussed later). The Stockholm Convention on Persistent Organic Pollutants—organized under the umbrella of the United Nations Environmental Program, signed in 2001, and effective from 2004—is the first global environmental treaty that aims to protect human health and the environment from toxic chemicals that remain in the environment for long periods by eliminating or restricting their production and use (Stockholm Convention, 2001). The Basel and Stockholm Conventions have significant potential roles to play, and indeed, the conventions and their parties have clear agendas to consider several specific actions in meeting their objectives.

In the Johannesburg Plan of Implementation, which was adopted in 2002 at the World Summit on Sustainable Development (WSSD, 2002), governments identified the goal "chemicals [be] used and produced in ways that do not lead to significant adverse effects on human health and the environment," with a target date of 2020. The outcome document of the 2012 United Nations Conference on Sustainable Development, called "The Future We Want" (United Nations, 2012), reaffirmed the goal of achiving, by 2020, environmentally sound management of toxic chemicals during their entire life cycle and management of hazardous wastes in ways that minimize significant adverse effects on human health and the environment.

Since 1989, various conventions and revisions, including the Basel Convention (Basel Convention, 1989), the Rotterdam Convention (Rotterdam Convention, 1998), the Stockholm Convention (Stockholm Convention, 2001), the Minamata Convention on Mercury (Minamata Convention on Mercury, 2013), the London Convention (London Convention, 1972), the Montreal Protocol (Montreal Protocol, 1987), the Waigani Convention (Waigani Convention 2001), and the United Nations 2030 Agenda for Sustainable Development (United Nations, 2015), have directly or indirectly provided measures to control transboundary movement, eliminate or reduce the release of hazardous chemicals into the environment, and protect human health and the environment. Several agreements and conventions have coordinated efforts to ensure effective and proper chemical management, and integrated it into relevant SDGs and their associated targets. The Stockholm Convention emphasizes (in Article 6) that once POPs become waste, parties to the convention are obliged to dispose of them in such a way that the POP content is either completely destroyed or irreversibly transformed (Stockholm Convention, 2001). It forbids any kind of recovery or reclamation of the POPs, including re-cycling, direct reuse, or alternative use. These measures have been suggested to be significant contributors to poverty alleviation, as there is a strong linkage between poverty and increased risks of exposure to POPs and toxic wastes.

The 17 SDGs and 169 associated targets demonstrate the scale and ambition of this universal agenda (Agenda for Sustainable Development 2015). The 2030 Agenda and the targets are integrated and indivisible, and show balance in three aspects—economic, social, and environmental—on the basic principle that "no one is left behind." While chemicals and wastes are somewhat emphatically reflected in several goals and targets, including Goal 6 (clean water and sanitation), Goal 11 (sustainable cities and communities), Goal 12 (responsible consumption and pro-duction), and Goal 13 (climate change), the sound and sustainable management of chemicals and wastes are less acknowledged in a few other goals and targets. Some cases that show reference to hazardous chemicals in the targets and indicators of several SDGs.

The 2030 Agenda reiterates the goal to "reduce the negative impacts of urban activities and of chemicals which are hazardous for human health and the en-vironment, including through the environmentally sound management and safe use of chemicals, the reduction and recycling of wastes and the more efficient use of water and energy." SDG 3, "Ensure healthy lives and promote wellbeing for all at all ages," includes target 3.9, which aims to "substantially reduce the number of deaths and illnesses from hazardous chemicals and air, water and soil pollution and contamination" by 2030. And SDG 6, "Ensure availability and sustainable man-agement of water and sanitation for all," seeks in 6.3 to "improve water quality by reducing pollution, eliminating dumping and minimizing release of hazardous chemicals and materials, halving the proportion of untreated wastewater and sub-stantially increasing recycling and safe reuse globally."

In SDG 9, "Build resilient infrastructure, promote inclusive and sustainable in-dustrialization and foster innovation," target 9.4 assigns members to "upgrade infrastructure and retrofit industries to make them sustainable, with increased resource-use efficiency and greater adoption of clean and environmentally sound technologies and industrial processes, with all countries taking action in accordance with their respective capabilities." Similarly, in SDG 12, "Ensure sustainable consumption and production patterns," target 12.4 is to "achieve the environmentally sound management of chemicals and all wastes throughout their life cycle, in accordance with agreed international frameworks, and significantly reduce their release to air, water and soil in order to minimize their adverse impacts on human health and the environment" by 2020. The two main indicators of target 12.4 show the direct linkage between chemicals and wastes: indicator 12.4.1 says the number of parties to international multilateral environmental agreements on hazardous and other chemicals and wastes that meet their commitments and obligations in transmitting information as required by each relevant agreement; and indicator 12.4.2 focuses on the treatment, generation, and management of hazardous wastes.

As is apparent, various targets and indicators of the SDGs are linked with hazardous wastes and define the importance of sound management of chemicals and wastes (SMCW) for humans and the environment. Prioritization of management of toxic chemicals and wastes is a fundamental challenge that is also key to achieving progress toward some related SDGs. The 2030 Agenda has a wider scope of targets linked with hazardous chemicals and wastes than the outcome document of the Rio +20 Conference in 2012 (United Nations, 2012). The SDGs address access to inclusive institutions and partnerships, which helps to create an enabling environment and could support minimization of the negative effects of toxic chemicals.

The sound management of POPs and other toxic chemicals plays a significant role in achieving sustainable, inclusive, and resilient human and social development, and helps contribute toward meeting SDGs. Indeed, the objectives of all 17 SDGs can be directly linked with SMCW. Some of the key factors of SMCW for achieving the SDGs are summarized in Table 13.1. Integrating SMCW and the SDGs creates new implementation methods, which show up in multilateral environmental agreements—notably the Basel Convention, Rotterdam Convention, Stockholm Convention, Montreal Protocol, and Minamata Convention—and in other relevant international commitments, synergies, and policy frameworks. Recently, the fourth session of the UN Environment Assembly addressed clusters of themes such as sustainable consumption and production, resource efficiency, and chemicals and wastes (UNEA, 2019). The combination of scientific research and policy frameworks on toxic chemicals can significantly advance the work of prioritizing efforts toward meeting the 2020 global goal on sound and effective management of chemicals. There is a need for urgent and resolute action at all levels to implement the 2030 Agenda, including through an improved enabling framework for SMCW in the long term.

13.3   IMPACT OF POPS ON ISSUES RELATED TO CLIMATE CHANGE

Anthropogenic emissions of toxic chemicals from the preindustrial era to the present may still persist for centuries and cause long-term changes in the environment

TABLE 13.1

Key Factors of Sound Management of Chemicals and Wastes (SMCW) in Achieving Sustainable Development Goals

Sustainable Development Goal	Connection to SMCW
1 (No poverty)	Chemicals are part of almost all human activities, including those which may require extra costs, such as water purification, high-end medicines, and agricultural pesticides. If chemicals are not well managed, the poorest communities may face the highest health risks.
2 (Zero hunger)	Poorly managed fertilizers and pesticides may contain hazardous chemicals and could pose significant risks to human health, causing pollution and land degradation and leading to food insecurity.
3 (Good health and well-being)	Exposure to chemicals occurs in everyday life through multiple ingestions. The production of chemicals continues to increase, which also increases the potential for chemical exposure leading to ambient air pollution. This poses a challenge to good health and well-being for all.
4 (Quality education)	Exposure to toxic chemicals could cause noncommunicable diseases or reduce students' abilities by physical impairment that may impede a quality education.
5 (Gender equality)	Chemicals affect men and women in different ways via sociocultural and physiological conditions, and could lead to gender-dependent imbalances.
6 (Clean water and sanitation)	Water resources may become polluted by chemicals originating from both human wastes and industrial effluent wastes, which leads to chemical pollutants in water reservoirs.
7 (Affordable and clean energy)	The global chemical industry affects every sector of the economy. During manufacturing, more than 95% of goods come in contact with chemicals. Therefore, the manufacturing processes and research capabilities of the chemical industry can help conserve energy by delivering energy efficiently. They can also help develop renewable resources and reduce greenhouse gas emissions.
8 (Decent work and economic growth)	In economic activities where chemical exposure is significant, it is of high concern that the safety of people be ensured and, at the same time, employment opportunities not be compromised.
9 (Industry, innovation and infrastructure)	Innovation in SMCW through eco-friendly design and product life-cycle management will reduce the chances of toxic chemicals slipping into the environment.
10 (Reduced inequalities)	Poor and marginalized communities have higher levels of exposure of toxic chemicals, and might not have enough resources to protect themselves.

(Continued)

TABLE 13.1 (Continued)

Sustainable Development Goal	Connection to SMCW
11 (Sustainable cities and communities)	Sustainable cities and communities adopt reduced use of toxic chemicals.
12 (Responsible consumption and production)	Chemical innovation and safer chemical alternatives could contribute to eco-friendly design and support responsible and sustainable patterns of consumption and production.
13 (Climate action)	Chemical contamination in the environment can severely affect climate, whereas SMCW can help to mitigate climate change.
14 (Life below water)	Toxic pollutants effectively discharge into oceans, which could increase levels of toxic chemicals and lead to harmful marine ecosystems.
15 (Life on land)	Toxic chemicals and wastes could cause environmental degradation and disrupt the land.
16 (Peace and justice/strong institutions)	An institutional framework and strong coordination among stakeholders for SMCW would help reduce toxic chemicals.
17 (Partnerships for the Goals)	SMCW could contribute to enhancing policy coherence among different stakeholders for sustainable development through public–private partnerships.

and climate systems. The environmental fate and transport of POPs are influenced directly and indirectly by factors that affect the environment, such as precipitation, temperature, wind speed, and solar radiation (Teran et al., 2012). Climate warming can therefore influence the environmental behavior of POPs by boosting their volatilization and affecting their partitioning among air, water, soil, and sediment. The growing concern over climate change led to the establishment of the Intergovernmental Panel on Climate Change, which deals with the reduction of environmental exposure to POPs (IPCC, https://www.ipcc.ch/). One of the most concerning environmental issues is transboundary air pollution; several efforts have been made to help eliminate these emissions through the adoption of international conventions and agreements. Most notably, the Strategic Approach to International Chemicals Management goals are closely related to chemical management, the environment, and sustainable development (SAICM, 2015). They include a set of 11 basic elements that recognize the attainment of SMCW at national and regional levels (Table 13.2).

If climate change increases exposure to POPs, it will increase the risks related to their harmful effects on human health and wildlife, and increase species vulnerability. However, the proposals and suggestions about the linkages between SDGs and climate action still differ from action on the ground level, mostly because of the lack of quality data, the capabilities to analyze these data, and the lack of leadership to take cross-sectoral decisions. Integration among various international organizations and initiatives toward eliminating and managing POPs would help to define the reference framework for POPs, delineate the complex relationship between climate change and POP abatement, and take into

TABLE 13.2

Basic Elements to Achieve Sound Management of Chemicals and Wastes (SAICM, 2015)

Number	Basic Elements
1	Legal frameworks that address the life cycle of chemicals and wastes
2	Relevant enforcement and compliance mechanisms
3	Implementation of chemical- and waste-related multilateral environmental agreements, as well as health, labor, and other relevant conventions and voluntary mechanisms
4	Strong institutional frameworks and coordination mechanisms among relevant stakeholders
5	Collection, and systems for the transparent sharing, of relevant data and information among all relevant stakeholders using a life-cycle approach, such as the implementation of the Globally Harmonized System of Classification and Labeling of Chemicals
6	Industry participation and defined responsibilities across the life cycle, including cost-recovery policies and systems as well as the incorporation of sound chemical management into corporate policies and practices
7	Inclusion of the sound management of chemicals and wastes in national health, labor, social, environmental, and economic budgeting processes and development plans
8	Chemical risk assessment and risk reduction through the use of best practices
9	Strengthened capacity to deal with chemical accidents, including institutional strengthening for poison centers
10	Monitoring and assessment of the impacts of chemicals on health and the environment
11	Development and promotion of environmentally sound and safer alternatives

consideration the negative impact of climate change. In this regard, the Fifth Assessment Report of the Intergovernmental Panel on Climate Change recognized that human activities may disrupt the climate, and addressed the risks of stark, prevailing, and irreversible impacts for humans and ecosystems, and long-lasting changes in all components of the climate system (Climate Change, 2014).

Climate change carries a growing threat to equitable and sustainable development. In 2015, 195 countries signed the first-ever global climate deal, known as the Paris Agreement, to adapt to and build resilience to climate change and limit global warming to well below 2 °C (Paris Agreement, 2015). The United Nations SDGs provided an established background for assessing the linkage between global warming of 1.5 °C or 2 °C and the behavior of toxic chemicals (United Nations, 2015). Temperature is one of the key climate drivers, determining the global distribution of POPs through increased volatility and rapid degradation. Climate change can actually alter almost any characteristic related to POPs' environmental fate, including their transport from origin to environment. Climate change thus has the potential to directly affect present and future management of POPs, and an increased climate temperature is likely to enhance exposure to POPs. Moreover, the risks of global warming in the context of SDGs imply a system transition that can be enabled by an increase in policy interventions and technological innovation to manage POP emission, suggesting a strong linkage between the two.

Further integration of energy aspects and carbon dioxide emissions into resource efficiency will allow more linking of the 3Rs, resource efficiency, and circular economic policies into the climate-change debate. Persistent strategies and actions could promote climate-resilient avenues for sustainable development and at the same time help improve livelihoods, social and economic well-being, and sound and efficient environmental management.

13.4 RELEVANCE OF 3R PRACTICES AND CONNECTIVITY OF TOXIC CHEMICALS

The 3R practices (reduce, reuse, and recycle) are a fundamental hierarchy strategy for waste management. They follow the sequence of first identifying reduction opportunities, which refers to reducing the amount of waste by increasing resource efficiency and extending product lifetimes; then reuse opportunities, which refers to reusing parts of used items after giving them proper treatment; and then recycling opportunities, which refers to recycling resources as raw materials. This strategy is also relevant for reducing toxic wastes. The first step, reducing waste generation, is the most environmentally sustainable solution for the reduction of toxic wastes. It may also include a policy to substitute less-hazardous components, implement more efficient processs, and practice on-site neutralization. The second step, reusing waste, is effectively a method to close the loop, rerouting wastes from disposal for reuse in either the same product or another without any reconditioning or energy investment toward reclaiming valuables. The reuse of toxic waste must be carefully handled, and may include reverse chemical distribution fuel blending and waste-to-energy technology. The final step, recycling, implies putting toxic wastes through a process in which POPs are reclaimed as a resource that can be used for the same product or a different one. Some examples of toxic-waste recycling include universal waste management of batteries and light bulbs, electronic-waste recycling, and oil recovery. Advanced recycling technology may require additional energy and costs to recover valuables.

The 3Rs can be applied to the entire life cycle of products, from the extraction of raw materials to manufacture or use, reuse, recycling, disposal, and resource metabolism with the driving forces/pressure/state/impact/response framework. Applying this framework helps to assess the decoupling between economic growth and environmental threats by the environmental Kuznets curve (Khajuria, 2010). It also helps evaluate the cause-and-effect relationship as an essential step forward in the analysis of environmental problems, and identify the role of each element in reducing negative global impacts.

UN SDG 12 includes many targets related to sustainable materials management, as well as proper waste management within the 3Rs. It includes "achieving environmentally sound management of chemicals and all wastes throughout their life cycle" and "substantially reducing wastes generation through prevention, reduction, recycling and reuse." Toxic chemicals have a noticeable focus in international collaboration to develop 3R policies and programs that help decouple environmental issues through innovation, design, and transition to resource-intensive products and a circular economy approach (Khajuria, 2017a).

SMCW within the framework of the 3Rs is indispensable to evading the risks of POPs to human health and ecosystems, and in reducing their substantial costs to national economies. Likewise, it is essential to exploiting the potential benefits of their contribution to human well-being and social development (United Nations, 2019). The safe management of toxic chemical and wastes identifies ways to detoxify air, water, and soil, promote the use of safe chemicals and alternatives, minimize the use of toxic substances, and prevent or reduce the generation of hazardous wastes.

Most countries are progressively working toward the application of an integrated approach and practicing 3R strategies. Although some countries are lacking in data or facing inconsistency in data analysis, there is a need to reduce the amount of resources extracted and discharged as waste throughout chemical-product life cycles in order to achieve a sound material-cycle society. Proper gathering of information and analysis of 3R performance are useful in institutional agreement, infrastructure coordination, and 3R recycled products and technologies.

The problem of POPs and toxic chemicals may be overcome through effective 3R policies, plans, programs, and underscoring the multiple benefits of pursuing a circular economy development approach. The 3R initiatives for chemical products aim to reduce the use of chemical waste and increase recycling practices, which leads to reduced environmental impacts throughout product life cycles.

Efforts to develop 3R policies would be a useful step in promoting resource-efficient, green, and sustainable products and recycled materials. In addition, establishing robust strategies, enabling alternative paradigms, and embracing the 3R approach inevitably improve toxicity and human well-being. POPs are usually included in a special group of substances of high concern because they are unmanageable, except through specific attention and measures to close material loops in a circular fashion. The "Stop the POPs" approach takes steps to add a new R—replace—which in the chemical sector leads to green procurement policies toward a resource-efficient and pollution-free environment. With the inclusion of this new R, the 4R paradigm is well suited to POPs.

13.5 INSIGHTS OF CIRCULAR ECONOMY ON TOXIC CHEMICALS AND POPS

The traditional linear economy model is based on the principle of "take–make–consume–dispose," which uses resources once and then disposes of them. However, there is a tremendous opportunity to rethink the way we handle resources and wastes, and redesign products so that they can be "made to be made again." This can be done by bringing wastes partly back into the production stream and keeping resources in use as long as possible: the model of circular economy. It would allow us to extract the maximum value from resources in use, then recover and regenerate products and materials at the end of each service life. Looking beyond the current extractive industrial model of linear economy, a circular economy model redefines growth by circulating resources and gradually decoupling economic activity from the consumption of limited resources. This results in positive societal benefits by moving toward renewable energy sources. Circular economy is built on three basic principles—designing out wastes and pollution, keeping products and materials in use, and regenerating natural systems (NUA, 2017). The concept recognizes the necessity that the economy work effectively for all organizations and individuals, both globally and locally. It helps to reduce resource dependency and hence restrains production costs. A transition from linear to circular economy not only will reduce the adverse impacts of the linear economy but is expected to represent a systemic transition that would build long-term resilience, generate business and economic opportunities, and provide environmental and societal benefits. It would not only reduce wastes but drive greater resource productivity, deliver a more competitive economy, and help reduce the environmental impacts of production and consumption globally. Circular economy has strong promise for reducing pressure on the environment, enhancing security of raw materials, and delivering innovative technologies and new jobs. Figure 13.1 illustrates the basic but critical difference between linear and circular economy models.

The model of circular economy, when adopted by the chemical industry, is particularly important with POPs, because it helps not only with efficient production but also with a drastic reduction of toxic waste, because a large portion of waste can be reused in the production cycle. The potential of circular economy to reduce the hazards posed by POPs has already been well recognized. The European Commission adopted the Circular Economy Package in 2015 (Werner et al. 2018), which includes a European Union action plan that puts concrete measures in place to target various phases of product life cycles, such as production, consumption, and waste management. It also sets an explicit timeline for when these actions are to be accomplished. In Quito, Ecuador, in 2016, the New Urban Agenda was adopted at the international level with a universal objective for governments to strive to move toward a circular economy in the next two decades (European Commission, 2015).

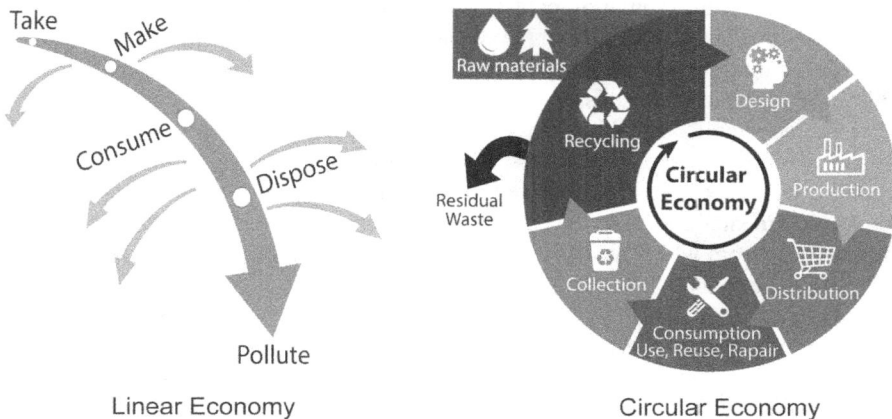

FIGURE 13.1 Linear and circular economies.

However, circular economy in the context of POPs and toxic chemicals could potentially face some challenges in recycling and reuse, along with having risk from exposure to products. Therefore, the general safety of both workers and the environment is of high concern and priority. In addition, it could pose challenges in terms of financing, economic skills, and other business models. A circular economy includes two major enabling factors: material is recycled in a secure way, ensuring that it does not lose its value; and a comprehensive and dedicated approach is taken to managing chemicals and wastes in which cost-related problems are avoided from the start. Indeed, the waste hierarchy in circular economy establishes a range of measures for waste prevention, minimization, reuse, recycling, resource conservation, safety, and energy recovery in terms of sustainability criteria.

13.6 GREEN INDUSTRY VERSUS CIRCULAR ECONOMY FOR POPS

Chemicals play a vital role in facilitating the circular economy by developing new green products and promoting eco-efficient use of materials and resources. The principle of green industry is to design chemical products that are less hazardous to human health and the environment. Green chemistry has the potential to become a central approach to circular economy for guaranteeing safer alternative products, including nonchemical alternatives and cleaner production processes. However, recycling extremely hazardous and high-risk chemicals, in line with circular economy, can potentially circulate toxic chemicals in that loop, challenging the principles of green industry. Therefore, a trade-off between circular economy and green industry would be needed. In the circular economy action plan, the briefing report for the European Commission in 2017 published a road map on the "analysis of the interface between chemicals, products and waste legislation and identification of policy options" (Bourguignon, 2017). When pentaBDE and octaBDE, which are constituents of materials such as foam and plastics, were listed in the Stockholm Convention, the parties agreed to an exemption permitting recycling of these materials until 2030. However, since this exemption contradicts Article 6 of the treaty, which prohibits the recycling of POPs (Stockholm Convention, 2001), the governments questioned the expert committee of the treaty to provide an opinion. The response included the following: "The objective is to eliminate brominated diphenyl ethers from the recycling streams as swiftly as possible. To meet this objective, the principal recommendation is to separate articles containing brominated diphenyl ethers before recycling as soon as possible. Failure to do so will inevitably result in wider human and environmental contamination and the dispersal of brominated diphenyl ethers into matrices from which recovery is not technically or economically feasible and in the loss of the long-term credibility of recycling" (POPRC, 2010).

A sustainable society is based on dynamic balances between production and consumption, the ecosystem and economics, and growth and conservation (Khajuria et al., 2009). "Chemicals 4.0," the fourth industrial revolution, describes how substances are transformed in all stages of the value chain to integrate and optimize digital, physical, and biological cycles (Honkonen and Khan, 2017). Recycling materials that contain toxic chemicals can potentially contaminate the subsequent products and continue the legacy of hazardous discharges and exposures. Therefore, recycling of toxic-chemicals containing POPs could be damaging to the principle of green industry, because of their persistent toxicity, which can contaminate food chains. However, it can support the circular economy approach. It enhances resource efficiency while avoiding toxin release from poor recycling practices or the use of specific thermal recycling processes. It includes promotion of the preventive 4R paradigm—that is, segregation of POPs-containing materials from waste streams—and the application of operations in line with the waste management hierarchy, including treatment before disposal. It focuses on the promotion of environmentally sound and effective technologies, processes, services, and business models with the involvement of private sector including industry. In order to obtain the best benefits of both green industry and circular economy and at the same time maintain a balance between them, we must differentiate hazardous POPs of high concern from POPs with low hazardous threats. While the latter can be processed following the principles of circular economy, the former may be stopped from entering the recycling process.

13.7 THE WAY FORWARD AND INSIGHTS ON THE 2030 AGENDA

The circular economy is an integral and integrated approach to sustainable development. It provides a significant input of key elements on the proper control of chemical use, reuse, and recycling. In contrast, certain products contain hazardous chemicals of high concern, which must be prevented from reentering the circular economy for sustainable and safe products. In developing countries, policies and legislation to promote the 3Rs have gained much attention since 2009 (Khajuria, 2017b). Furthermore, countries are progressively working toward an integrated approach to waste-management practicing reduction, reuse, and recycling strategies. It is essential to initiate practical governmental efforts to improve 3R goals with a set of policy and performance indicators. It would be a useful step in promoting a resource-efficient sustainable society, as well as a step forward toward the goals and targets of the 2030 Agenda.

A resource-intensive approach could be cost-effective by strengthening national, international, and public–private partnerships, making efforts toward better use of available resources. Promoting research activity could improve various methods for assessing chemicals that can stimulate and support multidisciplinary approaches to chemical safety issues. Review and exchange of assessment reports on chemicals with other countries would be helpful for meeting national chemical assessment plans and programs. Various updates of National Implementation Plans and forward steps would help to support countries in reducing and eliminating POPs. In addition, some issues that need to be taken care of are developing a comprehensive legal and institutional regulatory framework, creating an integrated approach between development plans, industry involvement, and financing, and accelerating innovation in safe materials.

Since sustainable management of chemicals and wastes was included in the 2030 Agenda, it has received renewed momentum in the mainstream, with SMCW

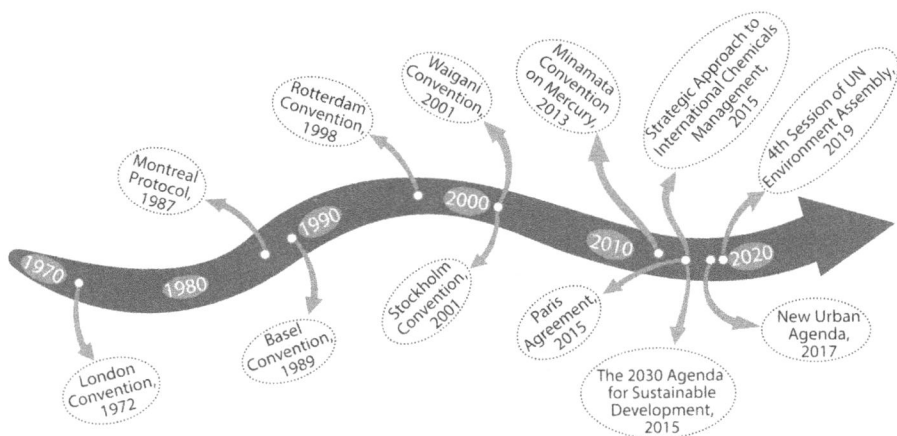

FIGURE 13.2 Timeline of protocols and declarations on the sound management of chemicals and wastes.

prioritized at the national level and international chemical and waste agreements implemented, including the Strategic Approach to International Chemicals Management (SAICM, 2015). One can find concerns related to the importance of chemical waste management as far back as the London Convention of 1972 (London Convention, 1972); several norms, protocols, and declarations related to effective and sound management systems for chemical wastes can be found along the timeline (Figure 13.2), which shows a sudden boost in 2015 Figure 13.2.

Sustainable and green chemistry refers to the substitution of hazardous or harmful chemicals with sustainable substances as alternatives. It contributes to the protection of natural resources, the safety of human health and the environment, and the realization of sustainable development. Sustainable chemistry is a holistic approach that goes beyond the production of safe chemicals to create social, economic, and sustainability benefits in line with the SDGs. It has received growing attention and can be well described as a potential game changer with regard to the design, production, and use of chemicals (UNEP, 2015). Green industry underlines the potential greening of each product (Khajuria, 2015). Sustainable green chemistry is inclusive and could make an essential contribution toward SMCW as well as toward achieving all the SDGs and going beyond the benefits for human health and the environment. In addition, following recent trends in international environmental laws, a legal binding agreement would be another option for sustainable and sound management of chemicals aligned with the 2030 Agenda.

13.8 CONCLUDING REMARKS

This chapter has discussed the escalating concern about human health and the environment due to the increased use of toxic and hazardous chemicals, such as POPs. These chemicals quickly seep into the atmosphere, biomagnify, live a long time in the environment, travel long distances, and pass from one species to other through food chains, which all makes them materials of high safety concern. Several forums and conventions have taken this concern seriously, resulting in some useful declarations and protocols. The chapter has reviewed the chronological progress in international forums and particularly considered toxic chemicals as they relate to a number of goals and targets of the United Nations 2030 Agenda for Sustainable Development. There are several key factors that may help reduce the possible adverse effects of POPs. For example, the ongoing concern of climate change is directly related to the transboundary spread of POPs, because the transport potential of toxic chemicals increases with climate change. Similarly, the implementation of green chemistry can play an important role in safe production and in the use of alternative nontoxic materials. Policy actions should implement enhanced restrictions in managing the safe production and commercial use of toxic chemicals, including POPs. The circular economy, which encourages channeling a part of waste back into the resource pipeline for reprocessing goods and materials, helps not only to reduce demand for raw chemical resources but also to generate jobs and save energy while reducing resource consumption and waste. More research on toxic chemicals is needed to ensure safe and green chemistry businesses, opportunities, and government policies and plans where circular economy is feasible. Various goals, targets, and indicators in different forums have considered these possibilities in the recent past, and new possibilities, technologies, and methodologies are becoming real with time.

REFERENCES

Agenda for Sustainable World. 2015. Transforming Our World: The 2030 Agenda for Sustainable Development, Resolution adopted by General Assembly on 25 September 2015. https://www.un.org/ga/search/view_doc.asp?symbol=A/RES/70/1&Lang=E

Basel Convention. 1989. http://www.basel.int/TheConvention/Overview/tabid/1271/Default.aspx

Bourguignon, D. 2017. Chemicals and the Circular Economy – Dealing with Substances of Concern', Briefing for European Parliament, Oct 2017. PE 608.725. https://www.europarl.europa.eu/RegData/etudes/BRIE/2017/608725/EPRS_BRI(2017)608725_EN.pdf

Climate Change. 2014. Fifth Assessment Report (AR5) Synthesis Report. https://www.ipcc.ch/site/assets/uploads/2018/02/SYR_AR5_FINAL_full.pdf

European Commission. 2015. Communication from the Commission to the European Parliament, The Council, The European Economic and Social Committee and the Committee of the regions – Closing the loop – An EU Action Plan for the Circular Economy. COM/2015/0614 final. https://eur-lex.europa.eu/legal-content/EN/TXT/?uri=CELEX%3A52015DC0614

Honkonen T. and S. Khan. 2017. Chemicals and Waste Governance Beyond 2020 – Exploring Pathways for a Coherent Global Regime. https://norden.diva-portal.org/smash/get/diva2:1061911/FULLTEXT01.pdf

IPCC. https://www.ipcc.ch/

Khajuria, A. 2017a. Contribution of 3R and Resource Efficiency in Achieving SDGs Through the Linkage of DPSIR Framework. Proceeding of the 28th Annual Conference of Japan Society of Material Cycles and Waste Management, 12–14 September 2017, 497–498. https://www.jstage.jst.go.jp/article/jsmcwm/28/0/28_497/_pdf/-char/ja

Khajuria, A. 2010. *PhD thesis 'Application of the DPSIR Framework for Municipal Solid Waste Management in South Asian Developing Countries', October 2010*, Osaka University, Japan. https://www.ir.library.osaka-u.ac.jp/repo/ouka/all/593/24206_%E8%AB%96%E6%96%87.pdf

Khajuria, A. 2015. Reduce-Reuse-Recycle: Technology and Policy as Driving Force for Economic Development in Waste Management System. Proceeding of the 26th Annual Conference of Japan Society of Material Cycles and Waste Management, 570–571, doi: 10.14912/jsmcwm.26.0_570

Khajuria, A. 2017b. 3Rs Solutions for a Resource Efficient Society ~ Experience from the Regional 3R Forum in Asia and the Pacific. Proceeding of the 4th International Conference on Final Sinks, 24–27 October 2017, Kyoto, Japan, 99–100.

Khajuria, A., T. Matsui, T. Machimura, and T. Morioka. 2009. Promoting Sustainability with Ecological, Economic and Social dimensions in developing countries. *Chinese Journal of Population, Resources and Environment*, 7 (4):15–18, DOI: 10.1080/10042857.2009.10684947

London Convention. 1972. http://www.imo.org/en/OurWork/Environment/LCLP/TC/Documents/London%20Protocol%20Why%20it%20is%20needed%2020%20years.pdf

Minamata Convention on Mercury. 2013. http://www.mercuryconvention.org/Convention/Text/tabid/3426/language/en-US/Default.aspx

Montreal Protocol. 1987. https://www.unenvironment.org/ozonaction/who-we-are/about-montreal-protocol

NUA. 2017. New Urban Agenda, http://habitat3.org/wp-content/uploads/NUA-English-With-Index-1.pdf

Paris Agreement, 2015. https://unfccc.int/sites/default/files/english_paris_agreement.pdf

POPRC. 2010. Persistent Organic Pollutants Review Committee. Report on work programmes on new persistent organic pollutants. UNEP/POPS/POPRC.6/13 POPRC-6/2, http://chm.pops.int/Default.aspx?tabid=1312

Rotterdam Convention. 1998. http://www.pic.int/TheConvention/Overview/tabid/1044/language/en-US/Default.aspx

SAICM. 2015. Strategic Approach to International Chemicals Management Overall orientation and guidance for achieving the 2020 goal of sound management of chemicals, 29 June 2015, endorsed at ICCM4 in October 2015. http://www.saicm.org/Portals/12/Documents/OOG%20document%20English.pdf

Shahare V. 2017. *Techniques for Measurement and Removal of Dioxins and Furans*. CRC Press, ISBN 9781498771498. LC record available at: https://lccn.loc.gov/2017030553

Stockholm Convention. 2001: http://chm.pops.int/TheConvention/Overview/tabid/3351/Default.aspx

Teran T., L. Lamon, and A. Marcomini. 2012. Climate change effects on POPs' environmental behaviour: a scientific perspective for future regulatory actions. *Atmospheric Pollution Research*, 3, 466–476. DOI: 10.5094/APR.2012.054. https://reader.elsevier.com/reader/sd/pii/S1309104215304220?token=8B1161F9F7ED5085B9423CF653C1B9AD2BA00B66ACB5E1D7B9089457C3104AC35EF6CECE5689FF7077336277DA186F13

UNCED. 1992. United Nations Conference on Environment and Development Conference Report. https://www.un.org/ga/search/view_doc.asp?symbol=A/CONF.151/26/Rev.1%20(Vol.%20I)&Lang=E

UNEA. 2019. United Nations Environment Assembly Fourth Session, *UNEA* 4: http://enb.iisd.org/download/pdf/enb16153e.pdf

UNEP. 2015. United Nations Environment Assembly (UNEA) of the United Nations Environment Programme, Second session. Implementation of resolutions adopted by the United Nations Environment Assembly at its first session. Addendum. Resolution

1/5: chemicals and waste. UNEP/EA.2/6/Add. https://undocs.org/pdf?symbol=en/ UNEP/EA.2/6/Add.3

United Nations. 2019. Report on the activities of the Basel and Stockholm conventions regional centres. Conference of the Parties to the Basel Convention on the Control of Transboundary Movements of Hazardous Wastes and Their Disposal Fourteenth meeting. UNEP/CHW.14/INF/29 and Conference of the Parties to the Stockholm Convention on Persistent Organic Pollutants Ninth meeting UNEP/POPS/COP.9/INF/28. http://www.pops.int/TheConvention/ConferenceoftheParties/Meetings/COP9/tabid/7521/ctl/Download/mid/20311/Default.aspx?id=53&ObjID=26611

United Nations. 2012. Sixty-sixth session Agenda item 19, Resolution adopted by the General Assembly on 27 July 2012, 66/288. The future we want. https://www.un.org/ga/search/view_doc.asp?symbol=A/RES/66/288&Lang=E

United Nations. 2015. Transforming Our World: The 2030 Agenda for Sustainable Development. https://www.un.org/ga/search/view_doc.asp?symbol=A/RES/70/1&Lang=E

UNSD. 1992. United Nations Sustainable Development Agenda 21 – Chapter 19, Environmentally Sound Management of Toxic Chemicals, including prevention of illegal international traffic in toxic and dangerous products. https://sustainabledevelopment.un.org/content/documents/Agenda21.pdf

Waigani Convention. 2001. https://www.sprep.org/convention-secretariat/waigani-convention

Werner, M., R. Bass, P. Premchandran, K. Brandt and D. Sturges. 2018. The role of safe chemistry and healthy materials in unlocking the circular economy, published by Google and Ellen MacArthur Foundation. https://www.ellenmacarthurfoundation.org/assets/downloads/The-Role-of-Safe-Chemistry-and-Healthy-Materials-in-Unlocking-the-Circular-Economy.pdf

WSSD. 2002. World Summit on Sustainable Development. Paragraph 23 of the Johannesburg Plan of Implementation: Report of the World Summit on Sustainable Development, Johannesburg, South Africa, 26 August–4 September 2002 (United Nations publication, Sales No. E. 03. II. A. 1 and corrigendum), chap. I, resolution 2, annex. https://www.un.org/ga/search/view_doc.asp?symbol=A/CONF.199/L.1&Lang=E

Index

1,2-bis(2,4,6-tribromophenoxy) ethane (BTBPE), 60, 61, 63, 64, 65, 68, 69, 72
2-ethyl-hexyl tetrabromobenzoate (EH-TBB), 60, 66, 72
3 R (reduce, recycle and reuse), 341, 347
4 R (replace, reduce, reuse, and recycle), 341
Aarhus Protocol, 321
accelerated solvent extraction (ASE), 253
Agenda for Sustainable Development, 333, 334, 340, 342, 353
ammonium polyphosphate (APP), 240
antimony-flame retardants, 238

bacterial cleanup, 284
Basel Convention, 321, 342
bioaccumulation, 2, 118
bioattenuation, 281
bioaugmentation, 281
bioavailability, 8
biobased nanometrials, 290
biocompatibility, 291
biomagnifiaction, 10, 118
bionanocomposites, 290
biopolymers, 291
bioremediation, 21, 192, 276
biosparging, 195, 281
bio-transformers, 10
biotransport, 140
brominated flame retardants (BFRs), 59, 245
bromodiphenyl ether (BDE), 60, 248

carbon nanotubes, 44
cellulose-based nanocomposites, 294
Chemicals 4.0, 350
chlorinated paraffins (CPs), 59
circular economy, 341, 348–351
Codex Committee on Contaminants in Food, 166
cold condensation, 109
Convention on Biological Diversity, 321
Convention on International Trade in Endangered Species, 321

daily intake, 98
dechlorane plus (DP), 59, 64
decision guidance document, 329
dehydration, 173
dietary accumulation, 10
Dirty Dozens, 32, 283
drying, 168

electrical and electronic equipment (EEE), 58
emerging POPs, 34, 181

flame retardants (FRs), 57, 237
fluidized-bed combustion, 90
food contamination, 165
food preservation, 168
food processing, 168
food web, 2
frying, 168
The Future We Want, 342

Galaxolide, 183
grasshopper effect, 110, 183
green chemistry, 350

halogenated flame retardants (HFRs), 60
Hazardous Wastes (Management and Handling) Rules, 19
health risk, 344
hexabromobiphenyl (HBB), 58
hexabromocyclododecane (HBCD), 58
hexachlorobutadiene (HCBD), 71
high impact polystyrene (HIPS)
human exposure, 57
hydrophobicity, 10

incineration, 87
India's Environment (Protection) Act, 186
indoor residual spraying (IRS), 203
intumescent flame retardant (IFRs), 243
intumescent flame retardant, 238

Johannesburg plan, 332

latitudinal transport, 114
legacy contamination, 63
lifestyle compounds, 183
linear economy, 348
London Convention, 342
Long Range Transboundary Air Pollution
    (LTRAP), 323

magnetic activated carbon, 44
mechanochemical degradation
melamine polyphosphate (MPP), 240
micro pollutants, 189
microbial adaptation, 9
Minamata Convention on Mercury, 333, 342
mineral oxide flame retardant, 238
montmorillonite, 244
Montreal Protocol, 321, 342

nanocomposite materials, 238, 244
nanotechnology, 41
New Urban Agenda, 335, 349
nitrogenated flame retardants, 241
novel brominated flame retardant, 238
novel flame retardants (NFRs), 238

octabromodiphenyl ether (octaBDE), 113, 248
organochlorine pesticides (OCPs), 112
ozone depleting substances (ODS), 326
ozone depletion, 321

Parabens, 188
Paris Agreement, 334
partition coefficient, 1
pasteurization, 168
Paul Müller, 203
personal care products, 183
phaseout, 55

photocatalysis, 42
phytoremediation, 21, 43
plasticizer additives, 58, 64
polybrominated diphenyl ethers (PBDEs), 59
polydimethylsiloxane (PDMS), 242
polyethylene (PE)

QuECHERS (quick, easy, cheap, effective,
    rugged, and safe), 214

renewability, 291
risk assessment, 98, 190, 346
Rotterdam Convention, 342

short-chain chlorinated paraffins (SCCPs), 55
silicon-based flame retardants, 241
soil organic matter, 7
sound management of chemicals and wastes
    (SMCW), 343
steaming, 173
Stockholm Convention, 32, 341
Strategic Approach to International Chemicals
    Management (SAICM), 332, 346
Sustainable Development Goals (SDGs), 341

thermal treatment, 168, 172
transboundary, 1
triclosan, 183, 188
tunability, 291

unintentional occurrence, 57
United Nations Conference on the Human
    Environment, 320

Vienna Convention, 325

Waigani Convention, 327, 342

For Product Safety Concerns and Information please contact our EU
representative GPSR@taylorandfrancis.com
Taylor & Francis Verlag GmbH, Kaufingerstraße 24, 80331 München, Germany